Named in remembrance of

the onetime *Antioch Review* editor

and longtime Bay Area resident,

the Lawrence Grauman, Jr. Fund

supports books that address

a wide range of human rights,

free speech, and social justice issues.

The publisher and the University of California Press Foundation gratefully acknowledge the generous support of the Lawrence Grauman, Jr. Fund.

How Ten Global Cities Take On Homelessness

How Ten Global Cities Take On Homelessness

INNOVATIONS THAT WORK

Linda Gibbs, Jay Bainbridge,
Muzzy Rosenblatt, and
Tamiru Mammo

UNIVERSITY OF CALIFORNIA PRESS

University of California Press
Oakland, California

© 2021 by Linda Gibbs, Jay Bainbridge, Muzzy Rosenblatt, and
Tamiru Mammo

Library of Congress Cataloging-in-Publication Data

Names: Gibbs, Linda, author. | Bainbridge, Jay, author. | Rosenblatt,
  Muzzy, author. | Mammo, Tamiru, author.
Title: How ten global cities take on homelessness : innovations that
  work / Linda Gibbs, Jay Bainbridge, Muzzy Rosenblatt, Tamiru
  Mammo.
Description: Oakland, California : University of California Press, [2021] |
  Includes bibliographical references and index.
Identifiers: LCCN 2020039066 (print) | LCCN 2020039067 (ebook) |
  ISBN 9780520344662 (hardback) | ISBN 9780520344679 (paperback) |
  ISBN 9780520975613 (ebook)
Subjects: LCSH: Homelessness.
Classification: LCC HV4493 .G43 2021 (print) | LCC HV4493 (ebook) |
  DDC 362.5/92—dc23
LC record available at https://lccn.loc.gov/2020039066
LC ebook record available at https://lccn.loc.gov/2020039067

Manufactured in the United States of America

25 24 23 22 21
10 9 8 7 6 5 4 3 2 1

Contents

Preface

This book is as much a beginning as a culmination, drawing from decades of experience that we, the authors, bring to the field of homelessness. We see possibilities of achieving goals that could not have been imagined even a decade ago. Our perspective has been amplified in recent years by engagements in cities on three continents of vastly different urban experiences. Patterns of urban migration, local economic conditions, and the rigor of social safety net services vary significantly. It is surprising, therefore, how strikingly similar the global challenges are of addressing the condition of street homelessness.

In the following pages, we set out a call to action. Urban streets littered with encampments of people sleeping rough has become something city dwellers everywhere simply accept. We have witnessed effective ways to coax these people off the streets and give them a chance for a better life. Despite frustrations, lack of resources, and a near impossibility of convincing some people who are sleeping rough to come inside, we have seen remarkable and lifesaving actions across many cities. The dedicated staff who work in outreach, shelter, and housing have inspired us with their unrelenting commitment to innovate and persevere until workable solutions are found for their clients. We believe these proven strategies can, and should, be replicated.

Even though we face difficulties and challenges, we still have hope. Each of us in our work has realized a piece of this hope.

Linda Gibbs served as the commissioner overseeing homelessness in New York City from 2002 through 2005, where she created the city's plan to reduce homelessness. She then served as New York City's deputy mayor for health and human services from 2006 to 2013 before becoming principal for social services at Bloomberg Associates, a philanthropic, pro bono consultancy serving mayors in achieving their vision in meeting unique municipal challenges. Jay Bainbridge, an associate professor of public administration in the School of Management at Marist College, worked at the New York City Department of Homeless Services, where he helped develop the city's first homeless street count, and he continues to consult on homeless services policy and planning for national and international cities. Muzzy Rosenblatt is chief executive officer and president of Bowery Residents' Committee (BRC), a nonprofit organization committed to bringing stability and dignity to nearly ten thousand homeless and at-risk individuals each year in New York City. Tamiru Mammo, after more than a decade working for New York City in the mayor's office and as chief of staff at the largest municipal hospital system in the country, joined Bloomberg Associates as a manager of social services. In that role he has led comprehensive homeless reform efforts in Bogotá, Mexico City, and Athens and has supported homeless program development in Paris, Nashville, and Baltimore.

When former New York City mayor Michael Bloomberg established Bloomberg Associates after he left City Hall in 2013, each of us was invited to join, in a full-time or consulting capacity. The idea was simple—leverage the knowledge of a group of leaders from the New York City government to help mayors of other cities nationally and internationally to tackle their complex issues. Doing this work pro bono, we provide hands-on guidance to help mayors focus on their challenges. In this way we closely witness the dynamics in cities as diverse as Paris and Baltimore, Bogotá and Nashville. By far the most frequently requested strategic advice has to do with overcoming street homelessness. While the municipal leaders, nonprofits, advocates, communities, and resources involved are as varied as the people who are on the streets, the challenge is the same: persuading outreach, shelter, behavioral health services, and housing providers to coordinate their services in a way that reaches each person on the street, assesses their individual needs, and offers them safe shelter and stable housing that works for them.

The ten cities we discuss in this book differ greatly in the size and severity of their homeless populations—from Athens, with a total population of close to 700,000 and just 350 people on the streets, 200 in temporary social housing, and 200 in night shelters, to our hometown of New York City, with a population of 8 million and over 70,000 in shelters but just over 3,500 on the streets. The other cities—Baltimore, Bogotá, Edmonton, Houston, Los Angeles, Mexico City, Nashville, and Paris—vary in the scope of challenges they face and the level of their work's sophistication. Some, like Athens, have no coordinated system and their work is driven largely by nonprofits. Edmonton approaches the homeless with coordinated entities that include public and private partners; while, in New York City, the municipality has to be reminded to make a space at the table for less powerful voices. Every city, however, uniformly brings talent, energy, and resources to pursuing its efforts with determination to withstand the setbacks and maintain momentum in a field that has few quick wins.

In August 2018 the four authors gathered with practitioners from the ten global cities in a weeklong peer-learning forum in the Rockefeller Foundation's retreat space in the Italian town of Bellagio. Our goal was to plumb the group's collective knowledge. With so much experience shared, participants could both contribute and work through thorny issues plaguing their efforts. We workshopped our individual initiatives, refining theories of change and developing implementation strategies. Some ideas were dropped completely when they didn't survive the harsh questioning from battle-tough peers, while other new concepts spread by week's end to colleague cities' agendas. We also spent long hours over meals and late-night discussions, sharing our observations and frustrations about the overall environment. What makes one city so effective at keeping momentum going while other cities risk losing all progress when leadership changes or a crisis hits? The greatest successes were found where a combination was present of effective management, sufficient resources

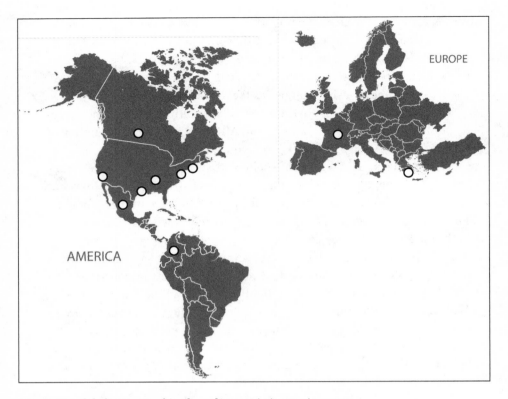

Map 1. Ten global cities attacking homelessness in innovative ways.

invested in evidence-based practices, and skilled leadership that rallied the troops through triumphs and failures.

It is at these intersections that this book evolved. This is not a guidebook. Every city faces a unique set of circumstances that influences where opportunities can be found and barriers tackled or minimized. Our hope is that in sharing our reflections on the common themes of successful strategies, we convey insights to help strengthen and sustain work going on in cities across the world.

We present in the following pages a broad range of lessons to draw on in shaping interventions that work, some of which may not fit every city, and others of which may initially work only to be followed by backsliding and unintended consequences. New iterations tailored to local needs may undermine effectiveness or generate unexpected impact. Our message: follow the evidence of what works, implement and iterate, monitor data in real time, and pivot when signals indicate something is amiss.

But don't do this alone, from the sole perspective of those who seek to get people off the streets. Make sure all your partners gather at the table, because nothing as complicated as homelessness can be solved in isolation. It takes creative and committed people working on the front lines in social welfare, criminal justice, housing, health care, and family services. Find these warriors of reform and combine forces. Create a culture of collaboration marked by trust, accountability, and a driving passion to bring more people inside to a place where they can find safety, dignity, and joy.

Acknowledgments

This book is a global project with input from across the world.

We are particularly thankful to Kristin Misner-Gutierrez for her substantial contributions to the content, especially for the bulk of the chapters on housing, as well as her excellent research skills and the graphic and editorial oversight she provided.

Susan Kellam provided expert editing, writing, and advice, challenging us to clarify our language and ideas and leading us to unify our voices across chapters and authors.

Many global city partners inspired us and made this work possible, as they helped us workshop ideas, provided stories and facts about their cities, and gave us invaluable feedback on the book as a whole, especially Théodora Papadimitriou from Athens; Terry Hickey from Baltimore; Yurani Miledis Martinez Diaz from Bogotá; Susan McGee from Edmonton; Marc Eichenbaum from Houston; Chris Ko, Ben Winter, and Jayanthi Daniel from Los Angeles; Almudena Ocejo Rojo from Mexico City; Anne Havard and Judith Tackett from Nashville; and Sylvian Lemoine, Vanessa Benoit, and Christophe Vitu from Paris.

We are grateful to the Rockefeller Foundation Bellagio Center for hosting us for a week as we fleshed out the outline of our book, and to

Bloomberg Associates for funding the original initiatives that laid the groundwork for the shared work. We thank Mayor Michael Bloomberg, who many years ago inspired us all to do more and go farther and reject hopelessness, and has afforded us the opportunity to now share what we've learned.

We also remain humbled and inspired by the people we've met—whether they were sleeping rough, were living in shelters, or had successfully transitioned to their own homes—for their resiliency and determination to overcome the challenge of homelessness.

Finally, and most importantly, we thank our families. We are blessed to have them as mentors, supporters, and friends.

All proceeds from sales of this book will be donated to the Bowery Residents' Committee.

Introduction

Finding ways to help struggling people in the face of flawed social service systems and inadequate affordable housing is a global quest. Cities around the world have much to learn from one another's successes, and failures, in grappling with the visible challenge of homelessness. Despite cultural, political, and economic differences, the universal conditions of sleeping rough are strikingly similar.

Some observers believe that homelessness is the fault of the individual who refuses to comply with social norms around work and lifestyle, making homelessness a problem the individual created. Economic analyses of the disparity of income distribution, however, lead housing policy experts to conclude that the growth in homelessness is associated with this inequality and the lack of rental support strategies to help the most vulnerable as the affordable-housing market shrinks. Social policy experts find fault in the weak service-delivery systems responsible for mental health, recovery from drug addiction, child welfare, and domestic violence prevention, among other services. To some degree, all of these causal statements are true.

Despite the complexity and the challenges of homelessness, cities are making tremendous strides toward solving what is often considered unsolvable. Each dedicated city worker, nonprofit staffer, and advocate brings talent, energy, and resources to the task, approaching their efforts with determination to withstand the setbacks and maintain momentum in a field with tough odds. What keeps these tireless workers at their task? Despite the images of street encampments and individuals without homes that form a common tableau in most cities, evidence and strategies are being compiled that build a strong case for being able to tackle homelessness.

TEN CITIES, TEN DIFFERENT CHALLENGES

Street homelessness in Athens emerged as a citywide problem in 2014 at the height of two crises: the financial crisis resulting from a deep austerity program imposed by the European Union; and a humanitarian crisis brought on by the continued refugee flight from Syria and the Middle East. Thousands of individuals and families landed on the shores of Greek islands and were evacuated to Athens. It was no coincidence that the largest encampment of refugees formed in Victoria Square, a short walk from the Athens Solidarity Center, the city's main multiservice center for the poor and street homeless. The nearby Athens railway station is a common magnet for rough sleepers seeking opportunities for food, panhandling for change, and, once the station is deserted at night, bedding down in quiet abandoned corners. The refugee crisis complicated Athens's efforts to address another mounting challenge—the growth in youth drug use that strained families and lowered the age of the city's homeless population as many young users were no longer welcome at home.

Responsibility for care of refugees rests largely with the European Union. Social services, including shelter and substance abuse services, are the responsibility of the national government. But the city of Athens could not wait while European and national programs were being developed. Immediate action was needed. Officials there went to work.

The once-thriving industrial city of Baltimore suffered a devastating economic blow as steelmaking operations faltered in the late twentieth century and especially after Bethlehem Steel at Sparrows Point closed permanently in 2012. By the twenty-first century, Baltimore had shifted to a largely service-oriented economy with a colorfully redeveloped Inner

Harbor and the world-famous Johns Hopkins Hospital; however, many displaced steelworkers have faced difficulties fitting into the new economy. A city of under 600,000, Baltimore has also been plagued by recent leadership changes and has struggled to garner the support needed to implement a cogent vision for homelessness. As part of the process to update Baltimore's homeless plan in 2017, the Mayoral Workgroup on Homelessness under then mayor Catherine Pugh issued a set of recommendations highlighting the critical importance of city leadership.[1]

The Baltimore Continuum of Care, a local body mandated by federal funding, began coordinating a three-year homeless action plan that focused on affordable housing, homelessness prevention, temporary shelter with exit strategies, increased economic opportunity, and racial equity.[2] Less than two years later, however, Mayor Pugh left office under a cloud and city council president Bernard Young ascended to the position. Mayor Young turned the homeless services function over to a new, independent agency, the Mayor's Office of Homeless Services.[3] The director was charged with implementing a strategy employing committed partners whose efforts had yet to be coordinated. Mayor Young lost his seat in the 2020 Democratic primary and will be replaced by yet another new mayor after the general election. Despite these challenges, the number of homeless in Baltimore is moving in the right direction, down from 2,669 in 2017 to 2,294 in 2019.[4]

Bogotá, Colombia, is a vast metropolis of close to 8 million people located on a plateau over 8,500 feet in elevation in the vast Andean mountain range. The city covers more than twice the area of New York City's five boroughs. Although some of its poorest areas are informal settlements on the outskirts of the city, the densest concentrations of people living unsheltered are located in or near the city center. The municipal government is largely left to provide shelter with little assistance from the national government or the nonprofit sector.

Most of the homeless on the streets were men who peddled recyclables to serve their addictions, and illegal drug activity was concentrated in the notorious slum El Bronx, controlled by drug dealers and impervious to police intervention. Frustrated by the long-standing acceptance of this situation, the mayor, Enrique Peñalosa, cleared El Bronx of encampments and drug activity in 2016. The city's social service agencies had dozens of staff on hand during the clear-out to triage and offer persons living on the street emergency accommodation and support services.

Shortly thereafter, the mayor launched interventions in four areas in addition to El Bronx. There were 2,863 rough sleepers found in all five areas combined in 2016, but only half took the city up on its offer of shelter. City officials realized they needed a better path off the streets for these vulnerable individuals, and a significant new investment was made, increasing the annual city budget for social services by 80 percent to expand the shelter system and make facilities and services more attractive to homeless people and diversified to meet varied needs.

Edmonton, with nearly 1 million residents, is the capital of the Canadian province of Alberta and is located in the oil-rich region of the Canadian Rockies. The city has become a recognized international leader in systems-level collaboration between agencies to address homelessness across sectors and over multiple administrations. Ahead of most other global cities, Edmonton implemented a street homeless count in 1999. After seeing the number of street homeless increase from 836 to 3,079 between 1999 and 2008, the city came together to develop a comprehensive ten-year plan, released in 2009 and updated in 2017.[5] Homeward Trust of Edmonton is the designated community entity responsible for coordinating and advancing the city's plan to prevent and end homelessness, with the city government as partner and collaborator.

Homeward Trust provides guidance to other Canadian cities struggling to end homelessness. Soon after the release of the 2017 plan, however, Edmonton municipal leaders realized their own homelessness reductions did not meet their targets. As constant iterators, the Edmonton partners used this setback as an opportunity to enhance the strength of their approach. In that same year, Prime Minister Justin Trudeau committed $40 billion to expand social housing and permanent supportive housing, allowing the city to deepen its housing-focused homeless strategy.

Houston, Texas is widely known as the US capital of oil wealth, as home to the National Aeronautics and Space Administration (NASA), and for having spawned an extensive system of world-class health care and research institutions. This city of 2.3 million, the fourth most populous in the United States, is one of the most ethnically diverse in the country.[6] Although the city has become more liberal leaning in recent years, strict tax-and-spend limits imposed by state laws and local ordinance narrow the available range of public benefits.

Strong mayoral leadership under Annise Parker zeroed in on the homelessness problem in 2011. Despite making remarkable progress toward reducing street homelessness through the Housing First approach, city officials faced increasing public and business demands to curb an emergence of new encampments that seemed to pop up overnight. Mayor Sylvester Turner, who succeeded Annise Parker in 2015, agreed to intervene with programs that could permanently keep people safe and off the streets.

The city of Los Angeles sits within the larger county of Los Angeles, which is home to 54,000 rough sleepers who move across the borders of its eighty-eight separate cities toward large commercial centers. For years, local officials bandied accountability among themselves without any one leader taking hold of the challenge to break the action logjam. A regional quasi-governmental planning body, the Los Angeles Homeless Services Authority (LAHSA), administers federal homeless resources, but has struggled over the years with only mixed success. LAHSA directors found forging a successful partnership difficult to sustain.

Around 2010, a powerful alliance of civil society partners began to erode this persistent barrier. This collaboration was kindled by a philanthropic-nonprofit-business partnership managed under the umbrella of the local United Way. Led without a dominating ego, all responsible partners come together around a neutral table to work collectively to finally tackle the magnitude of the homelessness challenge within their midst. For this reason, a new hope pervades the conversation.

With almost 9 million inhabitants, the national capital Mexico City (sometimes referred to using the shorthand CDMX—Ciudad de Mexico) has ample safe and affordable housing. Over the past several decades, people moved into the capital region from other states, settling the city's outskirts in makeshift housing, often without running water and electricity, and only gradually being incorporated into neighborhoods with city services. Those living on the street, though relatively few, included preteens (among other runaway youth) and families with young children, which prompted considerable citywide efforts toward prevention.

At the same time, scarce shelter resources have been tied up in facilities that function essentially as permanent nursing homes for the elderly. In a vibrant and thriving metropolis, these dynamics revealed flaws in the city's approach to serving youth and seniors. The mayor oversaw the CDMX Secretariat for Inclusion and Benefits, the primary agency providing adult homeless services, and the Secretariat for Comprehensive Family Development, which is in charge of preventing homelessness, particularly that of families. As the city received no assistance from the federal government, was underresourced, had little data on the problem, and lacked interagency coordination, Mayor Miguel Ángel Mancera convened an interagency workgroup in 2013 to develop a strategic plan for how to help homeless persons move off the street and to better articulate the city's vision and values. The mayor invested US$35 million annually to fund the strategy that evolved from this planning.

The booming city of Nashville, Tennessee, has managed to reduce its street homeless population even as construction cranes on every corner bring in more hotels, shops, and downtown residences. Displacement brought on by development and the resurgence of downtown residential life has focused public attention on the challenge of keeping people housed or in shelters. However, fractured responsibility among city agencies impeded progress. The local housing authority—the Metropolitan Development and Housing Agency (MDHA)—had control over much of the regional funding and served as the lead agency and collaborative applicant for federal continuum of care dollars, and as sponsor of the community advisory board. But MDHA itself provided no direct service. The separate Homeless Commission provided community input to the municipal homeless agency, but with no influence over the MDHA or the continuum of care. Only after frustrations abounded and progress was stifled were these planning bodies consolidated to ensure a single unified strategy that would represent the full range of government players. The new Homelessness Planning Council, which serves as the continuum of care's governance board, has adopted a three-year strategic plan. With that, the city has moved from a bifurcated to a unified governance structure on homelessness.

Yet mayoral leadership is still key and, on that score, Nashville has stumbled. Rapid changes in city leadership have left the homeless agency staff to lead from behind in hopes of maintaining the goodwill of nonprofit providers and advocates and motivating them to stay the course and act as a collaborative.

The most costly homeless services system in the world is installed in New York City. Driven by class action litigation from the 1970s that established the right to shelter for any person seeking it, New York City now shelters more than 70,000 people a night. Thousands of workers address the challenge with an array of prevention, shelter, and housing solutions with annual expenditures in excess of $3 billion.[7]

The City's homeless system was designed haphazardly through a series of court orders and consent decrees stemming from the 1970s litigation. For more than two decades, judges, not mayors, had final say on what the city could and should do. The result was a system based on compliance rather than impact and innovation. Yet the magnitude of the effort, combined with a commitment in recent years to research and evaluation, has generated an evidence base for what works. These concerted efforts successfully ended the class-action litigation governing the family services system and has allowed the Department of Homeless Services to move forward independently for the past decade. The numbers on the street are modest for a metropolitan area of the city's size, yet solving homelessness remains elusive.

While the national government in France has the responsibility of meeting the needs of the homeless across the country, the problem, escalating in Paris, became a priority issue raised in the 2014 campaign of Anne Hidalgo for mayor. When refugees began arriving in 2015 from Africa, Afghanistan, and the Middle East, Mayor Hidalgo led Paris in implementing a 106-point plan to tackle homelessness. Thousands gathered at Paris's northern borders, living on the streets or in government-provided tents by canals while sorting out their immigration or refugee situation. Addressing this mass humanitarian crisis while not losing sight of those who had long suffered on Paris streets became a defining moment for city officials and citizens as they urgently sought to understand these new dynamics and prioritize actions.

HOW CULTURE PLAYS A ROLE

A factor that distinguishes cities discussed in this book is the language used when addressing homelessness and the underlying cultural frameworks from which the words emanate. In Europe, the conversation is often rooted in the conceptual *right to housing*. In New York City, the *right to shelter* is legally enforceable, but not elsewhere in the United States; in other cities, homeless advocacy is rarely premised on any legal right to housing.

Latin American countries often refer to providing shelter and housing as tending to *individual human rights*. Embedded in these discussions about rights of the homeless are important cultural norms and practices. Unsanctioned settlement of land on the outskirts of Latin American cities has been common, with makeshift structures and an absence of such basics as running water and power. Over time, as these communities mature, municipal services are brought in and the land is de facto "ceded" to the prevailing group. This is viewed as the restoration of rights that the individuals lost when they moved to the city, rights that took time to regain. Included in this notion is a strong norm of homeownership and being grounded in one's community. Rental housing is relatively rare. In the Latin American context, solutions to homelessness are framed as restoring human rights to dignity and a sense of community.

While European states generally embrace the "right to housing," the words take on unique meaning across national boundaries. In Greece, rights and responsibilities reign heavily in family obligation. Housing is not only a local issue but a filial one, with family defined in broad terms. The tight structure of Greek support systems perhaps partially explains how migrants are not defined as homeless, even if they sleep on Greek streets, because these newcomers are not seen as part of Greek "family." France rallies around the ideas of *la patrie, égalité et fraternité* (homeland, equality, and fraternity): the state will take care of its own. Although some contention surrounds who "its own" are, French values bar any distinguishing demographic characteristics from defining what is French. On the survey of street homelessness, for example, it was not permissible to ask about country of origin or race. Yet migrants faced significant challenges and discrimination, and constituted a good third of the wave of rough sleepers in Paris at the time of the city's pilot street count in 2018.

In the United States the right to housing has never been a fundamental principle. US rights are viewed, instead, through the lens of freedom and opportunity. Americans' rights are not attached to any specific outcome. In fact, the business of homeownership in rental markets rests mainly in the capital rights to own, manage, and sell property. A diminishment of residents' rights to occupancy in recent years has been poignantly documented in the book *Evicted: Poverty and Profit in the American City*, by Matthew Desmond.[8]

Of course, these characterizations of rights across countries do not explain all the differences in levels or responses to homelessness. Rights are granted unevenly, and the face of homelessness bears evidence of broader patterns of bias and discrimination.

Cultural differences do lead to country-specific adaptations of solutions to homelessness and what it means to "bring people home." An even more tangible factor working in these modern cities is that they face similar national and global problems, which creates bonds that feed a sense of unity and common purpose among leaders and practitioners addressing homelessness and, at the same time, confronting the disparities in outcomes suffered by people subject to discrimination and racial injustice.

HOMELESSNESS, RACE, AND SYSTEMIC BIAS

The legacy of colonialism, slavery, land usurpation through western expansion, and the forced migration and assimilation of Indigenous peoples has left enduring scars on nations around the world, none more so than the United States. Across the ten cities highlighted in this book, these legacies remain glaring across the entire social spectrum. People of color and Indigenous people suffer discrimination from the time they are born, from poorer-quality health care and inferior schools to higher barriers to good jobs in the workplace and to accumulating such critical assets as housing. It should be no surprise, then, that the homeless population in many cities is weighted toward these social groups.

Although there is no biological basis for race, biases based on race persist, inequalities endure, and race categories continue to be used in public policy discourse. The conversation is shifting, however, and people are shining light on these disparities and acting to eradicate them. In the United States and Canada, explicit data are collected on a homeless person's self-identification based on race or ethnicity. By contrast, in Greece, Mexico, and Colombia, there is less explicit acknowledgement of these

Table 1   Select Racial Inequities among People Experiencing Homelessness, by City
(IDENTIFIED RACE AS A PERCENT OF HOMELESS POPULATION VERSUS
GENERAL POPULATION)

City	Year	Identified race	Race of homeless population (%)	Race of general population (%)
Baltimore[a]	2019	Black	70	63
Edmonton[b]	2018	Indigenous	57	6
Houston[c]	2019	Black	55	20
Los Angeles[d]	2018	Black	40	9
Nashville[e]	2019	Black	45	28
New York[f]	2019	Black	74	24

[a] "Baltimore City Continuum of Care 2019 Point in Time Count Report," *The Journey Home*, accessed June 30, 2020, https://homeless.baltimorecity.gov/sites/default/files/PIT%20 Report%20Draft%202019_Update%208.30.19_Update.pdf.
[b] Homeward Trust, "Community Update," November 28, 2018, 3, http://homewardtrust.ca/wp-content/uploads/2018/12/2018-Community-Update-Booklet.pdf.
[c] US Housing and Urban Development, "HUD 2019 Continuum of Care Homeless Assistance Programs Homeless Populations and Subpopulations: TX-700 Houston, Pasadena, Conroe /Harris, Fort Bend, Montgomery Counties CoC," January 21, 2019, https://files.hudexchange .info/reports/published/CoC_PopSub_CoC_TX-700-2019_TX_2019.pdf.
[d] Los Angeles Homeless Services Authority, *Report and Recommendations of the Ad Hoc Committee on Black People Experiencing Homelessness* (December 2018), 5, https://www.lahsa.org/item .ashx?id=2823-report-and-recommendations-of-the-ad-hoc-committee-on-black-people-experi-encing-homelessness.pdf&dl=true.
[e] US Housing and Urban Development, "HUD 2019 Continuum of Care Homeless Assistance Programs Homeless Populations and Subpopulations: TN-504 Nashville-Davidson County CoC," January 22, 2019, https://files.hudexchange.info/reports/published/CoC_PopSub_CoC_ TN-504-2019_TN_2019.pdf.
[f] US Housing and Urban Development, "HUD 2019 Continuum of Care Homeless Assistance Programs Homeless Populations and Subpopulations: NY-600 New York City CoC," January 22, 2019, https://files.hudexchange.info/reports/published/CoC_PopSub_CoC_NY-600-2019_ NY_2019.pdf.

biases; and, in the case of France, officials reject such categories to resist reinforcing them. In these latter places, policy discussions do sometimes revolve around individuals' nationality or affiliation as Indigenous people.

Despite the elimination of most explicitly discriminatory race-based laws, thinly veiled racially biased discrimination continues. This has been apparent in the resurgence of voting restrictions enacted in states across the United States since the nullification in 2013 of the protections in the

Voting Rights Act of 1965.[9] Beyond intentional acts, the deep and abiding reinforcement of racial stereotypes through all avenues of society influences everyone. Like the air we breathe, these stereotypes play out through the implicit biases of even those fair-and-just people who believe themselves to be race neutral. These biases, in turn, manifest as institutional or structural discrimination.[10]

So it should come as no surprise that people of color and Indigenous people from a disproportionate number of recipients of services for the poor—including homeless services.

In the United States and Canada, surveys to count the number of persons in shelters or sleeping rough demonstrate this phenomenon. In the United States, 40 percent of people experiencing homelessness were Black in 2019, 22 percent were Hispanic/Latinx, and 3.2 percent were Native American, even though these races constituted approximately 14 percent, 18 percent, and 2 percent of the general population, respectively.[11] In Canada, 30 percent of people experiencing homelessness across the country identified as Indigenous in 2018, while people who identify as Indigenous constitute only 5 percent of the country's total population.[12]

Racial minorities are also overrepresented among the poor in the homeless system. In New York City, for example, Black people represent 24 percent of the population living at or below the poverty level and make up 74 percent of the homeless population, while they are just 24 percent of the total city population.[13] Institutional bias systemically deprives people of color the opportunities that might alleviate poverty by discriminating among the poor in a way that pushes people of color and Indigenous people further to the margins of society.

New research in the field of structural racism and implicit bias is shedding light on strategies that can help unearth these unconscious biases, advance conversations that can reverse negative trends, and infuse institutions with actions that may help overcome subtle discriminations that perpetuate disparities.

Edmonton has sought to mitigate the overrepresentation of Indigenous people experiencing homelessness by working closely with these communities to turn around the country's colonial legacy through reconciliation and a demonstrated commitment to Indigenous cultures. Homeward Trust, the nongovernmental organization leading Edmonton's efforts on homelessness, has ensured a major role for Indigenous people by giving them a voice in planning and implementation through membership in its Participant Advisory Committee, the Youth Advisory Group, and the Indigenous Advisory Council. The Trust is also working to create culturally appropriate solutions to such problems as mental health, addiction, and trauma. There is also a push to include Indigenous healing traditions in wellness practices.

The Los Angeles Homeless Services Authority works with stakeholders to produce a comprehensive report through its Ad Hoc Committee on Black People Experiencing Homelessness. This first-of-its-kind study identifies institutional racism as a main driver of Black homelessness in Los Angeles. The first "Report and Recommendations of the Ad Hoc Committee on Black People Experiencing Homelessness" was released in late February 2019.[14] The committee examined institutional barriers facing Black people in various upstream and mainstream systems—including housing and labor markets, the criminal justice system, and the child welfare system—and explored how these barriers lead to overrepresentation in the population experiencing homelessness. In Los Angeles County, Black people constituted 40 percent of the homelessness population in 2017, 19 percent of the population in poverty, but only 9 percent of the general population.[15] The committee concluded that ending homelessness will require a collective commitment to dismantling racism and addressing racial disparities. Among the actions Los Angeles has committed to undertake are the following:

- Developing and launching an initiative at LAHSA to advance racial equity within its workforce and within the homeless crisis response system
- Reviewing coordinated entry system and assessment for potential biases
- Analyzing client experiences with Permanent Housing and Retention to understand why Blacks are less likely to retain housing placement

The report includes a process roadmap and toolkit for municipal officials elsewhere who are following a similar approach to studying the patterns of this phenomenon in their city.

Raising these conversations with firm clarity across homeless-serving systems can shed light on how disparities are perpetuated and create a path for overcoming them with concrete actions and a *true* commitment to equity for all.

AN URBANIZING WORLD AND THE CRISIS OF AFFORDABILITY

Concerted efforts on a global scale have resulted in improved well-being for hundreds of millions of residents across continents and cultures. Deep poverty reduction across the globe has been driven by progress in the poorest regions among those living on less than $1.25 a day. The United Nations' Millennium development target of cutting this rate of poverty by half was achieved five years ahead of the 2015 target.[16]

However, an extreme disparity in income distribution is growing.[17] Wealth increasingly concentrated in the hands of a global elite has created a dangerous situation where wages at the bottom, and in the middle, are not keeping pace with the rapidly growing costs of housing. The world is also rapidly urbanizing as people and jobs concentrate in cities. From Los Angeles to Athens, the ascendance of cities' fortunes has marked a defining trend in the global migration of people in the past several decades.

Despite these triumphs, or perhaps because of them, street homelessness persists.

Over the past 30 years, Cities around the globe are experiencing a dangerous rise in housing prices relative to income, with double, triple, or quadruple increases in some cities.[18] Too often, underutilized urban properties are being purchased for development to meet upscale housing demand. But not everyone can find a place to live in this new housing. As a result, low-income residents, often ethnic or racial minorities, are being pushed out of urban centers without cover of tenant protections or resources to compete with rising housing demand in increasingly posh neighborhoods.

Globally, housing assistance for low- and moderate-income households has been a task of national governments, which have largely not kept up with rapid urban and economic transformation. Traditional housing assistance programs reach fewer families. In sum, more affordable housing options are disappearing at the same time that help to absorb higher housing costs is shrinking.[19]

In response to local housing pressures, some residents can move; others, however, will double up with family or friends and eke out a life in more crowded housing. The harshest results clearly fall on those with the fewest options. Some individuals may have burned bridges long ago with anyone they had previously turned to for help, and others may be barred from sharing housing for such reasons as a criminal record prohibiting them from living in certain places. For young parents with growing families, there is often simply no room. The most vulnerable—in any city, in any country—can too easily become homeless, with no place to turn.

SOCIAL SERVICE SYSTEMS AND THE MOST VULNERABLE

Simply stated, the failure of social service systems designed to help those most at risk creates homelessness. The health care delivery system in nearly every nation is a patchwork of specialized providers, each constrained by siloed regulatory controls. As consumers, clients are required to navigate systems that base care on health insurance reimbursement or out-of-pocket payment. Public health insurance for the poor is often locally managed, meaning gaps in coverage resulting from moves exacerbate challenges in finding new physicians in new neighborhoods. Variation in the quality of health care systems amplifies this difficulty when those neighborhoods have historically been poorly served. Undiagnosed and untreated mental illness, sometimes accompanied by drug addiction, can compromise one's ability to manage life's responsibilities, from keeping a job to paying rent. Disruptions in rent payment and erratic behavior do not make for acceptable tenants, and such people, if unassisted, disappear from the housing market.

This cycle is made more vicious by the lack of integration among basic health services. Primary care, mental health, and substance abuse often fall under separate and distinct service systems, each with different rules, providers, and financing. Each system thus engages the client in isolation from their other ailments. Navigating among health services is a challenge, even for the healthy. Delving deeper, one finds that entire unders-

WORKING WITHIN THE SYSTEM

Linda Gibbs

Leading the Department of Homeless Services in New York City was a daunting and exhilarating challenge. When I started in 2002, the agency was wrapped in controversy, stretched thin by divided camps and loyalties, and responding inadequately to need. A friend warned me that taking the job would be a career ender.

From the start, I was alarmed to discover that the shelter providers had joined a class action lawsuit against the city, claiming inadequacy of the shelter application and placement process. The very people I was charged with supervising were asking a judge to tell me how to run the operation. How to get past this conundrum? If I couldn't bring together public agencies, nonprofit providers, housing services, and advocacy and support organizations, the dysfunction of the current system would persist.

Service provision was run as an assembly line. Because the assembly line involved multiple agencies and organizations, things tended to get messy. Out-boxes and in-boxes. Missed calls and turf conflicts. Who calls the shots and who follows? Inefficiencies and irrationality abounded.

Moving from managing clients in crisis to offering avenues into permanent homes was the goal, but the budget office was tired of feeding money to meet needs, only to see needs expand. They dismissed the possibility of prevention and insisted that housing assistance would only incentivize homelessness.

And our bureaucratic demands often made the client serve the worker—chasing down documentation, proving facts known to other public agencies—thereby putting further stress on families needing compassion and relief.

Ultimately, we were able to turn this situation around by building trust and collaboration, grounding our work in data and accountability, making investments backed up by evidence of success, and wresting control back from the courts.

To create a long-term vision, we merged the warring groups of people who felt forced to be together in a room into a collaborative team of problem

(continued)

solvers. Not everyone stayed; some who stayed were only looking out for their own self-interest. By tapping into the core shared value of overcoming homelessness as the driving force behind the plan, partners were allowed to see what bound them together rather than what divided them.

Then came the hard work of implementation. Government agencies were choosing not to collaborate to ensure ease for nonprofit providers, and those providers chose not to ensure that the most vulnerable people's needs were met. Case in point, management of supportive housing was caught in the crossfire of ego-driven agencies that couldn't get past infighting to improve outcomes. Three things proved necessary to jump-start efficiency. People had to agree, first, to clearly identify their unique roles and strengths; second, to come clean about their resources; third, on what to relinquish and what to control. Only after broad agreement could the process move more quickly and effectively, with resources rationally allocated across a large multiplayer system.

Like most public services, we were drowning in data but little was used to inform practice. Isolating and sharing key metrics of performance in regular accountability reviews was the bedrock of daily management. The adoption of a homeless street count estimate gave us a solid baseline for measuring progress. Investing in careful service program design and committing to evaluation broke the resistance of cynical budget officials. We structured a random-control assignment to rigorously evaluate a promising new HomeBase prevention program. The advocates sued to stop us, arguing that it was callous and coldhearted to randomly assign people to either a test group receiving services or a control group without services. After much time, cost, and delay, the evaluation was allowed to proceed. The results demonstrated definitively that prevention, if structured thoughtfully and implemented with care, can prevent homelessness. Based on the evidence, the program achieved the goal of being expanded citywide, preventing thousands of homelessness incidents annually.

And we put the client at the center. I will always hold close the memory of Jason-Eric Wilson, who entered the shelter intake process in 2002 with his father and younger sister. They had to do what every family was required to do on the application—fill out the detailed background questionnaire on need, living situation, employment, education, medical history, and so forth. Further, there were additional checks on men as head of household to demonstrate legal custody. Jason, at only sixteen and suffering from mental illness, spent three days with his family shuttling around to government offices collecting the documentation. The stress of the situation proved too much for Jason, who ended his life in a shelter in Harlem before the family's application was complete. That tragedy inspired me to put the system for integrated and shared case records across the finish line. HHS Connect now integrates select demographic detail, household data, service interactions, and case file documents from multiple city agencies. Rather than being sent out to find these, families are now assisted by intake workers in composing their histories and telling their stories.

We failed in many ways. Iterations of rental assistance schemes initially succeeded only to later implode. We were often outmaneuvered in court, with disastrous consequences for program effectiveness. Our successful interventions were not enough to stem the overall tide of need. Yet progress was clear and sustained. A trusting group of partners transformed the experience into a compassionate, client-centered service delivery network that has improved the lives of our most vulnerable residents.

erved neighborhoods suffer from inequalities in the availability of social services. A striking lack of critical assistance in neighborhoods of concentrated poverty, often populated disproportionately by people who have suffered discrimination and deprivation since birth, means that for many people dealing with behavioral health problems, their condition goes undiagnosed and untreated. People requiring help have nowhere to turn in their high-need but low-service communities. Problems start in the school system when youth are disciplined for acting out. Their risk level, as a consequence, continues to escalate. When a personal crisis hits, such as losing housing or a trusted companion, and problematic behavior occurs, public safety officials are often asked to intervene. Sometimes, this results in arrest and incarceration. Each of these unequal and punitive layers dangerously complicates the lives of vulnerable people.

WHAT IS STREET HOMELESSNESS?

There is no international definition of homelessness. Every country, and every city within some countries, defines it differently. (The appendix to this book lists the formal definitions in use in each of the ten cities discussed in the following chapters.) Yet most cities tend to divide the population into three categories: precariously housed or at risk of homelessness, sheltered homeless, and street homeless.

The *precariously housed or at-risk* category consists of people living in insecure or inadequate housing who thus face a heightened risk that they will lose or fail to secure housing. A family served an eviction notice is at risk because they may lose their current home, while a person being discharged from prison is at risk because they may not have a family home where they can return. Some countries categorize certain subgroups of the precariously housed as officially homeless.

Sheltered homeless are those who do not have a home but receive temporary shelter on a routine basis. The street homeless population consists of those without a home and who routinely sleep on the street. Some refer to the latter as rooflessness; others call it rough sleeping. (There are many ambiguities in these definitions. Is a person who is not guaranteed a nightly bed a sheltered person? Are a parent and child sleeping in a car sleeping rough? Different jurisdictions treat these ambiguities differently.)

The category *street homeless* receives primary attention in this book because the visible presence of vulnerable people poses the public challenge that most confounds mayors in the ten cities. Taking into account the variations in definition city by city, table 2 presents the cities' most recent estimates (2020) of the number of people believed to be on the streets of their communities. The table shows both the total estimate (not including those in shelter) and the ratio of the street homeless population to total population. The ratio is useful in normalizing the size of the street population across jurisdictions. As shown, the range is significant, with a low of one homeless person for every 3,616 people in Houston to a high of one for every 445 in Los Angeles.

Some caution should be taken with these estimates. The point-in-time street counts, explained further in chapter 10, are imprecise processes that vary by locality. In addition to definitional differences, the estimation

Table 2   Number of Street Homeless by City
(ABSOLUTE AND RELATIVE TO TOTAL POPULATION)

	Reference street count (year)[a]	Most recent street count (year)	Ratio of unsheltered to general population[b]
Athens, Greece	—	353 (2018)	1 in 1,881
Baltimore, Maryland	629 (2007)	380 (2019)	1 in 1,562
Bogotá, Colombia	4,515[c] (1997)	4,597 (2017)	1 in 1,612
Edmonton, Alberta	650 (2000)	392 (2018)	1 in 2,379
Houston, Texas[d]	4,418 (2011)	1,528 (2019)	1 in 3,616
Los Angeles, California	15,770 (2009)	27,221 (2019)	1 in 445
Mexico City, Mexico[e]	3,739 (2015)	4,354 (2017)	1 in 2,074
Nashville–Davidson County, Tennessee	390 (2007)	585 (2019)	1 in 1,147
New York City	4,395 (2005)	3,588 (2019)	1 in 2,324
Paris, France	3,035 (2018)	3,522 (2020)	1 in 657

[a] First year of reliable data.
[b] US city population data based on 2019 census. International data based on 2011 Greece census, 2018 Colombia census, 2016 Canada census, 2019 Mexico estimate, 2020 France estimate.
[c] Includes both sheltered and unsheltered.
[d] Street count numbers include the greater Houston area, including Harris County and Fort Bend County. General population numbers include 2019 Harris County and Fort Bend County population numbers.
[e] New methodology in 2017.

methodologies vary, with some cities covering every block while others relying on sampling or even focusing only on certain subregions. Nonetheless, the estimates are useful measures for comparing cities and serve as benchmarks that allow cities to track their own progress over time.

TACKLING THE CHALLENGE AT HOME

Local officials from the ten cities often speak with compassion for people rough sleeping and express frustration at their inability to assist this too often overlooked population. In Athens and Paris, the deputy mayors for social development have expressed anger over inadequate national actions; in Los Angeles and Houston, disagreement over whose problem it was to solve the migration of rough sleepers from broad regions outside city boundaries caused a stalemate. Mayors, often reluctant to spend limited city resources on problems that emanate from far beyond their borders, also fear that offering services will draw even more homeless into their cities. Waiting for a broader regional, state, or national partner to act, however, can result in ignoring urgent human need.

As a matter of law and policy, accountability for addressing homelessness is not clearly assigned at any level of government. In many countries, no clear charge to address homelessness has ever been granted the national government. Even where there is a national directive, the government responds too slowly or inadequately to the challenge. Mayors, however, cannot ignore the daily reality on their streets and at their doorstep. Although the community may not blame the mayor for creating homelessness, people expect their top elected municipal figure to fix the problem.

Public sentiment regarding street homelessness is complex, even contradictory. It can generate demands for action and cries to secure some dignity for exposed and downtrodden lives. The homeless become wrapped up in the city's values about what is humane and what is not. And in many places, people on the streets manifest deep social scars from bias and discrimination: the homeless population in US cities is disproportionately Black; in Canada, homeless are mostly Indigenous; and in Europe, they tend to be descendants of formerly colonized people. There is also the quality-of-life issue for people who don't want the streets of their city lined with encampments of those who claim the sidewalks as home. At the same time, there can be strong resistance to shelters in a community that fears the homeless as posing risks. The community can be a powerful ally and a powerful opponent in efforts to solve homelessness. The challenge is to enlist these public strengths in successful efforts.

EVIDENCE ON WHAT WORKS

Evidence is only slowly building on homeless programs that work and on the best strategies for employing these successes at a scale sufficient to have the broadest impact. The vast majority of public funds devoted to homeless services internationally are spent without any evidence of impact. Many programs are managed with compassion, but without the rigor of documenting outcomes generated by the interventions. The United Kingdom–based Centre for Homelessness Impact surveyed homelessness prevention practices across the globe and found them significantly lacking in evidence as to impact.[20] The authors urged a greater commitment to building a stronger field of results.

Evidence must be gathered on both well-functioning *programs* and well-functioning *systems*. Work done in the United States during the Obama administration on ending veterans' homelessness is proof that street homelessness can be tackled and with solid documentable results. Through the highly structured, systematic collaborations set up to deploy proven housing solutions in city after city, the number of homeless veterans on the streets was reduced to functional zero—the level at which no veteran is routinely sleeping on the street, though some may spend a few days on the streets before getting safely housed.

The building blocks for this success emerged over time. Street counts had earlier revealed many veterans on the street, despite efforts at the Veterans Administration to improve access to services, basic health care in particular. Work to end veterans' homelessness started at the federal level with President Barack Obama's 2009 call to achieve this goal by directing federal agencies to collaborate by sharing resources, streamlining access, and advancing evidence-based strategies. The initiative was fleshed out in "Opening Doors," the 2010 strategic plan of the United States Interagency Council on Homelessness that focused technical assistance and resources on the goal.[21] Significant new federal investment strengthened case management, increased enrollment in benefit programs, and expanded access to housing vouchers. Once ending homelessness among this population was made a priority and partners committed to the hard work of engaging veterans, connecting them to services, and employing proven strategies for quickly and safely housing them, things changed.

Local collaboratives stepped up to this challenge, applying for and receiving the federal resources necessary to make significant progress. Cities such as Houston brought together local partners to leverage the heightened federal push by connecting veterans on the streets to case management and giving them priority access to shelter and housing.

A SYSTEMS-LEVEL APPROACH

But solving homelessness only for veterans is not enough. Approaching this problem in its totality, as chapter 7 explains, requires a systems-level approach whereby each partner in a municipal collaboration understands and embraces the commitment to overcoming homelessness as core to its mission and as a marker of its success. Any single crucial component that falters may derail the effort. In a systems-level approach, all stakeholders agree to a shared goal, negotiate and commit to their contributions toward that goal, and work collectively to make the solutions work. As more players are brought to the table to coordinate solutions, opportunities emerge to address the challenge more comprehensively. Homelessness cannot be solved from the confines of a shelter system. Well-meaning and hardworking homeless-service providers by themselves do not have leverage over the tools and resources required to fix the problem.

Whether by choice or by default, leaders of cities are the first and last line of defense in the battle, balancing the need to ensure safe and humane solutions for people without shelter with the need to maintain their city's quality of life for all inhabitants. While many aspects of the challenge, such as access to affordable housing and effective mental health services, may be the responsibility of other agencies, organizations, and levels of government, if those fail, it is the mayors who are held accountable, and communities must respond. Those at the helm are left with the hard task of convening the many parties and hammering out solutions. An effective solution demands that local actions among multiple agencies, government and nongovernmental, be coordinated—something mayors are uniquely positioned to do.

In each of the ten cities discussed in this book, mayors stepped forward to define the problem and craft the solution. Athens took on a street count to shine a more accurate light on the challenge. Houston brought partners together to develop a regional approach to solving a problem bigger than the city itself. Bogotá brought the community into the solution by engaging local residents to spot problems early, when prevention could still work.

Some mayors, however, refuse, or prove inadequate to, the task. In Los Angeles, local providers and advocates helped shape a regional network for action that formed a strong foundation for later accelerating a new mayor's commitment to the issue. Political transitions may leave collaborative boards marooned and adrift. The community needs to rally at that point and find a sustaining approach. In Nashville, the churn of three mayors in three years opened a leadership gap filled by a streamlined collaboration among public agency and nonprofit partners working behind the scenes. A neutral convener who has the respect and legitimacy to provide the setting for collaborative decision making can effect systemic reforms if given sufficient authority. Edmonton's Homeward Trust offers a strong example of a nongovernmental entity that provides continuity over time and through political transitions. Successfully engaging government partners to leverage their resources and exercise their authority can be tricky but is necessary.

During transitions in political leadership, the community is also critical to keeping the issue high on the agenda for new leaders coming in. What can be challenging to community-led efforts is ceding authority when a strong public-sector leader arrives on the scene. A wise leader will respect and leverage existing collaborations, just as a wise collaborative will give the mayor the seat at the head of the table.

The broader the base of participation, the more effective the solutions. Enduring structures require strong partners from civil society and the provider community to remain engaged during political transitions, nurture the network, and ensure its effective continuation. Regularly convening and working through tough issues when they arise ensures that plans are not static concepts left on the shelf but are used as frameworks constantly evolving.

Cities are innovating in new and exciting ways, and some are succeeding. This book explores firsthand experiences in ten cities across the globe that reveal strikingly similar challenges and strategies that have been employed to overcome street homelessness. The message is this: Homelessness does not have to be a fixture of contemporary urban life. From ending veteran's homelessness to eliminating entrenched encampments, resettling refugees, and housing a multitude of rough sleepers during the COVID-19 pandemic, cities have shown it can be done. This book is a starting point for sharing both successes and failures, because both will point the way.

1 The Transformation of Homeless Services

The landscape of services that address homelessness has expanded and matured over the past three decades. Homeless-service providers have increasingly shifted their focus toward the underlying causes of homelessness by complementing "three hots and a cot"—hot meals and a bed only—with employment and treatment services, along with harm reduction options that ease barriers to participation. Permanency support, such as counseling and resources for accessing housing in tightening markets, has become better coordinated and often integrated into case management in the shelters and on the streets. And, by seeking out high-risk households, prevention efforts have held tenuous situations together to avoid the disruption of homelessness.

Cities worldwide are responding to this crisis of mass street homelessness with differing amounts of energy and success. Sometimes it is simply the charitable sector providing overnight shelter and beds. In Athens, shelter services are provided largely outside city government by local charitable organizations, such as Athens-based PRAKSIS, and international relief groups, such as Doctors Without Borders. Shelter services that allow residents to stay without packing up each morning tend to be reserved for the elderly, disabled, or female-headed families with children. Edmonton's shelters largely discharge people each morning. In Mexico City, the municipal shelters often act as permanent homes for the elderly, in the absence of move-on services that can help people ultimately find permanent housing. In other cities, complementary daytime services like drop-in centers and food pantries supplement clients' daily needs and provide intervention. This is the case in Bogotá, where a central site, Bakata, provides clients with emergency shelter, daily meals, substance-abuse treatment, and employment services, but just a modest number of beds. To step up to a more service-rich shelter, clients must demonstrate adherence to the rules and show progress toward stability.

Municipal services often fill gaps or meet urgent needs, such as warm beds available in winter months. For example, Nashville's homeless-management team and other city departments transform into a shelter-delivery service as temperatures dip to winter levels and workers push aside spreadsheets for bedsheets to convert a designated public building into a 150-bed overnight shelter.

It is the rare city that provides the vast majority of shelter services. New York City, with a rich array of shelter options tailored to meet varied client needs, is one such example. Most cities offer a mix of both municipally operated facilities for special populations, such as victims of domestic violence, and shelters operated by nonprofit providers with some government support. In Houston, Baltimore, and Los Angeles, municipal facilities fill in critical gaps not filled by the patchwork of privately funded shelter operations.

This jumble of service offerings renders a coherent and coordinated service system difficult. A rational approach would allow each person's needs to be individually assessed before referring them to an appropriate provider for care. But in most cities, there is no central governing authority with the power to direct all providers. People show up on the doorstep they know about, and providers accept or reject them based on established capacity and eligibility criteria. Efforts to serve more-challenging clients can be thwarted by reluctant operators who do not want to disrupt their facilities with volatile individuals. Better collaboration among providers on serving priority clients and on sharing information about bed availability would result in a more efficient system.

Nonetheless, creative planning and effective use of skills have translated into increasingly successful outreach to people on the street. Why would a person choose to stay outside on a cold winter night when a bed is available in a shelter? Even in New York City, with a legal right to shelter, many are still found sleeping outside. Whether because of an inability to make sound decisions or a bad history with uncaring people, life on the street can seem the better choice for many. Outreach workers, however, are offering innovative strategies for restoring trust, stabilizing treatment, and providing alternatives that are appealing for people whose street homelessness is so habituated that rough sleeping has become their preferred way of life. As with shelter operations, street outreach can be pursued by a mixed patchwork of public and nonprofit providers, each defining their own mission and geography. Accountability for overcoming street homelessness is improved when each provider participates in a system that accepts responsibility for the whole, thereby coordinating both resources and placements.

A BRIEF HISTORY OF MODERN HOMELESSNESS

Early on, the most common official response to homelessness in cities was opening emergency drop-in facilities and overnight shelters and providing those in crisis with the bare essentials. Some cities offered a less humane approach, providing only substandard shelter in the hope that those asking for help would devise their own solutions, or simply leave. Cities also resorted to police action. Using existing statutes on the books against vagrancy, loitering, and public urination, police enforced cities' quality-of-life statutes as a primary tool against street homelessness. The enforcement of these minor offenses led to the overrepresentation of people with histories of homelessness in the criminal justice system.[1]

The settlement house movement, started in the United Kingdom and spreading to Europe and the United States, took root in the late nineteenth century by bringing food, shelter, and education to high-poverty areas plagued with homelessness.[2] The growth in social welfare systems progressed gradually from community-based organizations staffed by volunteers to government provision of cash assistance, food aid, and housing benefits. Services targeted primarily to women and children were creatively diverted by some local providers to assist families in preventing and overcoming homelessness. Evolving social policy in much of Europe centered on poverty, employment, health, education, and housing, with each country developing its own economic and social regimes. Responsibility to look after the homeless was tucked into agencies responsible for social welfare or housing but was rarely given its own department.

These early efforts largely bypassed single men who remained on the streets or isolated in neighborhoods full of homelessness, such as the notable Skid Row in Los Angeles. Men without homes were largely itinerant and unseen. Too often, police stations became overnight shelters, housing the homeless cheek by jowl with those detained for criminal activity. Barracks-style shelters for men were introduced over time through the support of the nonprofit sector. These shelters continued to be funded by contributions from the community and, increasingly over the decades, have been supplemented through subsidies from national, regional, and local governments.

The recognition of homelessness as a social problem occurred incrementally, the timing varying by country. In the United States, public tolerance eroded over the mass degradation of the people on the streets and in welfare hotels in the late 1970s and early 1980s.[3] Heightened public concern lagged by about a decade in Bogotá and Edmonton.[4] In the 1990s, the problem of homelessness in both Athens and Paris intensified around the same time and impacted a more diverse range of people. Those on the street expanded from people traditionally experiencing social exclusion to include able-bodied individuals unable to find work, refugees, and women with children.[5]

Advocacy organizations protecting basic human rights often sought a remedy through the courts, which sometimes resulted in crucial protections of human rights and at other times led to inflexible mandates that impeded well-balanced approaches to managing the problem. Or toothless edicts were issued without sufficient authority or resources to guarantee legal or humanitarian rights. None of these court decisions provided a path to addressing the causes of homelessness, much less long-term solutions.

The homeless population has continued to evolve over time. Homelessness in the early twentieth century was predominantly characterized by middle-aged male drinkers, but transforming economic, social, and demographic conditions have altered the composition. The social movements of the later twentieth century largely removed families with children from the streets, providing them shelter if prevention strategies failed at securing them homes. Also, increasingly mobile workers in a global economy and the influx of migrants and refugees have transformed many urban populations, altering both available housing and the policies to support affordable options.[6] Globally, political and social unrest pervades many regions and leaves many without sufficient housing. It is not uncommon to find many people with advanced professional degrees from their home countries of Syria and Afghanistan in the shelters of such European cities as Paris.

Unaccompanied children and youth, elderly, ethnic minorities, and migrants are increasingly found on the streets or turning up at shelters.[7] More homeless families appear as a burgeoning city life puts pressure on the low-income rental market at a time when public investments in social housing, housing allowances, and rent control are weakening. With nowhere else to go, homeless people sleeping in cars has become so commonplace that cities like Los Angeles are starting to adopt safe-parking policies.[8] In New York City, a third of homeless families with children have at least one working adult, and 20 percent of the single adults in shelters are working.

The degree and extent of legal and social protection for those at risk of homelessness differs by city. Children receive the greatest protection, but even that varies. A parent is not allowed to live with a child on the street in Edmonton, and a refusal to accept shelter will trigger child-protection action that might separate the child from the parent. But in Mexico City, the emphasis is on keeping families together, regardless of housing. Even so, only a small percentage of individuals at risk of homelessness in the cities examined in this book fall through existing safety nets and, among those who do, many manage on their own or with the help of family and friends.[9]

As explained above, the moral authority and financial responsibility for providing shelter was originally in the hands of charitable organizations, with governmental support slow to follow. Homelessness remained largely unclaimed as a social problem well into the twentieth century. Without the statutory responsibility to manage the problem, and few financial resources to achieve programmatic goals, municipal players were handicapped in terms of having the knowledge and ability to overcome homelessness. Elements of this inadequacy remains present in statutory schemes today.

Figure 1. "If only the homeless problem was about only being homeless." By Joe Heller, courtesy of Cagle Cartoons.

The obligation to provide shelter is limited in some places to residents of the country, disqualifying undocumented individuals. In Paris, national funds may not be used to support noncitizens. Even where the nation has shouldered responsibility to shelter people, limited services and difficulties of enforcement leave many unhoused, as in Athens. And across the United States, national funding is allocated only to supplement active local efforts. The McKinney-Vento Homeless Assistance Act of 1987 provides supplemental funds to cities like Los Angeles, New York City, and Houston that adopted management practices and evidence-based programming. The distribution of McKinney-Vento funds is based on a fixed national allocation, unrelated to need, that is woefully inadequate to the task. Without sufficient federal or state support, residents continue to look to their mayors for solutions to the homeless problem in their communities.

Cities around the globe continue to bear witness to the pervasive suffering and despair of thousands living unsheltered and thousands more living in some form of temporary setting. In Los Angeles, tens of thousands have taken up semipermanent status on the streets, setting up temporary shelters in public spaces, or simply lying prone on sidewalks. Homelessness is associated with shorter life-spans, higher rates of mental illness and trauma, and more frequent exposure to violence and abuse.[10] Despite the overall growth of economies globally, this tragedy in cities persists.

THE EVOLVING RESPONSE TO HOMELESSNESS

Cities everywhere benefit by growing evidence of what works in the battle against homelessness. A field of knowledge is gradually developing that allows a more accurate understanding of the causes of homelessness, and of effective means to prevent it. Some research is demonstrating strategies and supports that help vulnerable people find housing and remain there. For example, an international review of homeless strategies concluded that eviction prevention, landlord mediation, and housing advice programs are associated with a significant reduction of homelessness.[11] Building on proof of the effectiveness of housing subsidies in keeping people housed, Paris focused on eviction prevention and larger housing subsidies to pay rent, which led to a 30 percent decrease in housing evictions over ten years, contrary to the national trend. Paris also implemented a program of coaching and mentoring assistance to help homeless and formerly homeless people gradually return to work. Edmonton and Houston have adopted, and Paris is piloting, a "Housing First" approach to delivering services, dispensing with the philosophy that clients need to be "housing ready" before steps are taken to find them a home. Housing First, which is often synonymous with supportive housing, has been proven effective and adopted internationally.[12] Cities that relied historically on the family and homeownership as the primary response to housing needs—including Athens, Mexico City, and to some extent Bogotá—are infusing new elements into their homelessness response. These include "Safe Havens" to bring people off the streets and better links between emergency and housing systems. Mexico City and Bogotá deploy prevention services in a few of their highest-need districts.

Understanding the causes of homelessness is important, and knowing the common pressure points that can dismantle a life or multiple lives enables cities to intervene earlier to forestall more street living. For social welfare, as in health care, prevention can reduce the likelihood of a crisis. It is imperative to intervene when assistance is necessary, but these interventions must be effective, well implemented, and transparent.

Many evidence-based programs started local and were scaled up successfully to other places. New York City's HomeBase prevention program, which uses administrative data to identify risk factors and reaches out to families with offers of support services to stabilize precarious housing situations, has been replicated in the United States and internationally. The Safe Haven low-threshold shelter program has become a model for several of the cities examined in this book, though more rigorous evaluation is needed to back up the impressive outcomes being generated. Newer strategies are being tried continuously. Some of these efforts may be more relevant to some cities than to others. Each pilot effort builds upon and complements other strategies already in place.

While evidence of prevention and permanency accumulates, there is surprisingly little rigorous evaluation of what works for sheltering and program services to support individuals while they are homeless. Many of these services are born in times of crisis, are initiated through charitable organizations, or simply have such a long-standing presence in the urban landscape that they continue unquestioned. Cities around the globe act to open shelter beds and conduct street interventions in the absence of strong evidence of what practices are most effective. Without more rigorous study of long-term outcomes, however, there is no confirmation that these interventions follow the most effective practices.

The continuum of services is just as important. Outreach without shelter beds is an act of frustration. Shelters without housing placement options become quickly backed up and do little to provide relief on the streets. No single approach is so extraordinary that it obviates the need for any other model of care. Rather, each creates a broader array of options as diverse as the people on one street. They include:

- Homeless outreach teams that actively engage with the chronically unsheltered and service-resistant and motivate them to come inside shelter or directly into housing, and that work collaboratively with their local police departments to recognize that homelessness is not a crime and that behaviors that may be seen as illegal are simply acts of desperation to survive. Outreach has been found to be effective at improving housing and health outcomes, even among those with the toughest mental health and substance abuse problems.[13]

- Drop-in and service centers that provide numerous services under one roof, making it easier for both those who seek services and those who provide them.[14]

- Safe Havens, which embrace a philosophy of harm reduction, offer the most chronically homeless, self-reliant, and service-resistant individuals an alternative they find more desirable than living unsheltered. This promising emerging practice is not yet supported by rigorous evaluation. However, Safe Havens do employ motivational interviewing, an evidence-based treatment that provides an effective way to engage a person and help them to make positive change.[15]

- Goal-oriented shelters for single adults with robust services and clinicians to support the care often provided in other settings such as hospitals, psychiatric facilities, and alcohol and drug rehab programs, and that also offer job training.[16] Although the services embedded in these shelters often have a strong legacy of evidence, evaluation of their effectiveness within the shelters has not been done.

- An array of Housing First or housing-led policies, such as Rapid Re-housing, rental assistance, and supportive housing, that move people to permanency and support them in safely staying there.[17] The promising practice of Rapid Re-housing is ready for more definitive study. Critical Time Intervention is an evidence-based case management program designed to help the severely mentally ill live independently.[18] This program is utilized in some rehousing programs, and New York City's latest supportive housing contracts encourage its use. Priority access to a permanent housing subsidy for families bolsters housing stability and improves family and child well-being, including food insecurity.[19]

- Prevention programs that accurately identify the local precipitators of homelessness and intervene with relevant and responsive interventions. Evaluations of the New York City HomeBase prevention program found that it can reduce shelter entry (by one to two families per ten entrants, or from 18.2 percent to 9.3 percent) and average numbers of nights spent in shelter, should homelessness occur. There is also evidence of cost savings, and that empirical targeting of services can increase effectiveness.[20]

While the direct costs of these strategies are greater than that of either doing nothing or doing the bare minimum, results data show that over time these new approaches are having a demonstrably positive impact and can save money.[21]

Housing is *unquestionably* a critical factor in any discussion of strategies to end homelessness. There are many who argue that the only appropriate response to homelessness is to create affordable housing and include appropriate support to assist people in maintaining their housing. Further, many argue that spending scarce dollars on shelter strategies such as those presented in this book perpetuates the institutionalization of homelessness but does not bring cities any closer to ending it.

Consider how an effective and comprehensive public health strategy both invests in hospitals and community-based treatment to respond to illness and supports research on prevention and cures. Similarly, an effective and comprehensive social welfare strategy should invest in both community-based services to respond to homelessness and in affordable housing and interventions that will either prevent homelessness or act fast when it occurs. Cities and mayors should respond effectively to the immediate need and invest in longer-term solutions.

If cities lack the legal authority or service capacity to address fully the causes and consequences of homelessness, how can the evidence of what works be leveraged? A better approach would be for cities to move from this disjointed patchwork of often ill-defined services to a coordinated system of care whereby clients rationally receive the most appropriate service through a shared system of assessment and intake, with a commitment to measuring impact backed up with rigorous evaluation. The stories from these ten cities reveal that the challenges are only sometimes met with success. Yet the path is becoming clearer for replicable practices that can achieve a unified vision for achieving real progress toward ending rough sleeping.

The hard work of establishing the organizational willpower to move city officials, nonprofits, and the community toward an accountable and evidence-based way of doing their work remains the challenge everywhere, and is explored in the following pages.

2 Engaging People on the Streets

Most people, upon encountering an injured person, would call for help and provide comfort to the person until help arrived. And most of those injured would recognize their situation and accept such assistance. But what about victims whose wounds are much deeper and less visible, and who themselves may not be aware of their own plight? How likely is it that someone walking by a person sleeping rough would stop to get them help? Would the person in need accept the help? If the passerby did stop, would there even be a place to call? Situations like these are common occurrences in cities across the globe. The average person walking by may hand out cash or food or, so overwhelmed by the magnitude of human suffering witnessed day after day, and unsure of what to do or whether a call would make a difference, may simply ignore the person.

This reality of urban life in cities around the globe is undeniable, causes pain for many, and cries out for more urgent action. Many urban dwellers are affected: those in need of help believe they have nowhere to turn; those who see the suffering wonder why, in a world with so much wealth, more can't be done for those with so little; and those who see only human detritus on their doorstep demand its removal.

Figure 2. On the streets of Bogotá, outreach workers employ nonthreatening techniques to meet rough sleepers "where they are." Bloomberg Associates.

No matter how much or how little a city does—regardless of whether agencies provide housing, shelter, or other services—the homelessness situation persists, seemingly unabated, and appears only to be increasing. Even in New York City, with its *unconditional* right to shelter, a right that has led to the creation of a complex network of facilities that safely accommodate more than 70,000 adults and children every night—more than 120,000 different individuals over a year—an estimated 3,588 persons were sleeping rough, according to the city's 2019 one-night point-in-time street count.[1]

To put a fine point on it, even in one of the world's wealthiest and most progressive cities, where any person without a home is entitled to a place to stay, thousands every night choose to sleep rough. How better to underscore that it requires more than simply the availability of shelter to engage effectively those who sleep on the streets or in parks, transit facilities, and other public spaces of the urban landscape.

It would be overly simplistic, however, to conclude that, because homelessness persists universally, effective responses do not exist. Cities and communities are not resigning themselves to accepting the idea that public spaces not meant for human habitation nonetheless act as such.

To effect change in individual behavior and in social conditions, the challenge of homelessness must be looked at from fresh perspectives, as cities around the world have begun to do in the past decade. Even those in law enforcement have found better, more-effective tools than arresting those who may be violating the law but are doing so because they have no viable option.[2] These cities have begun to see those in crisis not as a problem to be managed but as people to be served; strong coalitions have developed innovations that enable these individuals to make better choices and achieve better outcomes. Signs of this shift may be found in Los Angeles, where the mayor's office and United Way are introducing new service models, building strong coalitions across the public and private sectors, fostering community and citizen engagement, and attracting an infusion of fresh funds; in Bogotá, whose social service agency is using neighborhood-specific strategies that incorporate marketing plans to address special populations; in Athens, where service providers, specialized by need, are rethinking how they deal with street homeless people to provide a more rounded, planned menu of options; and in Houston and Edmonton, whose leaders have invested heavily in a Housing First model with coordinated entry.

This chapter shares strategies from various cities undertaking ways to engage those who live on the streets, with a focus on motivating these individuals to trust those who connect with them to make their lives better. City workers and volunteers are also learning how best to intervene when people are no longer able to act in their own best interest.

PATHS TO LIVING UNSHELTERED AND REASONS FOR
RESISTING ASSISTANCE

Convincing individuals to come inside requires an understanding of what services may be available and, even more important, how these options may best be communicated to those experiencing homelessness. What to the outsider or passerby appears as a crisis demanding immediate action is often accepted as a long-established norm to the person sleeping rough, the disruption of which is anything but desirable. Critical for those seek-

ing to effect a change in this situation and in the unsheltered person's out-
look are patience and a willingness to listen, a demonstrated appreciation
of and respect for the individual and why they may reject offers of shelter
and assistance.[3]

Offering information about shelter services, even providing transportation to these services, is not as simple as it sounds. While many unsheltered individuals lack information and would be receptive to offers of
help, many others—usually the most entrenched and high profile—know
help is available, yet refuse. It may seem irrational for someone living on
the street to turn down an offer of help, especially when it comes from a
professional trained to provide care. Street living to most people is undesirable, but to the person who is there—the client—their perspective may
well be just the opposite. Although the client may not find living an
unsheltered life ideal, the street is preferable to their perception of, and
often actual experience with, the alternatives.[4]

Motivating those living without shelter to seek assistance depends,
therefore, on how those offering help perceive them, as well as on how the
clients view themselves and those engaging with them. Is the rough
sleeper perceived as a social nuisance to others, or as a person in need
whom society seeks to serve? Seen as the former, they are unlikely to
respond positively; seen as the latter, they might, and often do.[5]

Who, then, is this person? The popular press often presents this person
as older, male, unemployed, with mental health and substance abuse
problems; in fact, however, this person can be of any age and may have
faced any of a myriad of life circumstances. While, for many, experiencing
homelessness is a short-term crisis soon resolved (and, thus, often not
seen by others), in many cities a significant and perceptible number of
people are living unsheltered who have been doing so for some time, often
for several years. The path that has led these individuals to experience
chronic homelessness may be paved with their own mistakes, bad choices,
and transgressions; or it may be a result of circumstances, possibly trau-
matic, over which they had little control. Over time, undoubtedly, it is a bit
of both. In most cases, it is a long path that has formed over time by a
series of compounding events.[6]

These chronic homeless have most likely attempted unsuccessfully to
resolve their situation, with the possible results of additional trauma and

a sense of betrayed trust. Sometimes this betrayal derives from the very institutions society has created to assist them. Foster care and hospitals, for instance, rarely plan effectively for their clients' needs beyond the institutions' primary mission. Sometimes well-intentioned caregivers promise more than they can deliver. Many who are unsheltered perceive shelters as unsafe, or at least less safe than the street. Whether these situations arise out of willful neglect or because of funding inadequate to achieve their stated mission, the result is the same: individuals who need help doubt that it can be delivered.[7]

Further compounding the distrust are communities—especially those without enough shelter space to meet the need—that respond to homelessness with criminal enforcement against behaviors common to the circumstances of rough sleeping, such as public urination when there is no bathroom, trespassing in a park to seek a safe place to sleep, consuming alcohol or taking drugs in public when denied a private space or access to a facility to alleviate the addictive illness.[8] In many cities and countries, public institutions created to respond to homelessness set eligibility criteria that exclude many of the people they could, and should, be assisting. In the United States, public housing authorities routinely deny housing to those with prior arrests or convictions.[9] In Greece, the city of Athens provides transitional housing structures but, by law, has prevented access to those with addictions or mental health disorders or migrants without legal immigration status.[10] Los Angeles and other cities in California have appealed to the US Supreme Court to overturn a lower court ruling that declared homeless encampments legal when no alternative shelter is provided by the city.[11]

UNDERSTANDING THE CLIENT

For many experiencing homelessness, the root cause of their predicament extends back years, to childhood events associated with the two places that should have provided them safety and helped prepare them for adulthood—home and school. It is all too common in their personal histories for chronically homeless individuals to have not completed high school and, as children, to have experienced trauma—physical or psychological or both—in their home. These childhood experiences may or may not have been intended, whether by child, parent, or school; often they arise out of ignorance, a misunderstanding, or a lack of resources to address the need. The onset of psychotic behavior often comes as the adolescent mind is developing, but it is rarely recognized for what it is, particularly when the child is living in an environment with limited, if any, support at home.[12] Few public schools have access to counselors trained in social work or psychiatry. Children who are most at risk often live in impoverished households. When the first symptoms of psychosis arise and the teenager acts violently, the school responds with discipline, often by suspending or expelling them. Now a greater burden at home, the child is often disciplined again. The two places meant to nurture a child have turned on them because of behaviors they often cannot control and may not even understand. When this happens repeatedly, the child or teenager no longer feels safe at school or home. Whether they run away, enter the child welfare system, or wait until they reach majority status, the damage has been done. Having been let down by those whom they should have been able to depend on and trust more than anyone else—their parents and teachers— why would they, after years of suffering and having successfully developed their own survival strategies, now trust a stranger offering help?

Many different storylines explain why individuals or subpopulations become homeless, depending on a person's age and background and the locality and time period. Risk factors for street homeless, or at least common characteristics of those visibly homeless in the ten cities described in this book, are provided in chapter 6, on prevention. Solutions are best matched to attending needs.

BREAKING THROUGH—TURNING "GO AWAY" TO "PLEASE HELP"

The practice of addiction treatment teaches that addicts know they are addicts, and that telling them to "just say no" belies the science of addictive disorders. While the nonaddict rationally sees the drink, the needle, the pill, or the pipe as accelerating an addict's demise, to an addict they are necessary tools for survival. And until an addict is sufficiently self-motivated to pursue sobriety, no amount of tracing the connection between addiction and fatality will be persuasive.[13]

Many psychotic disorders also result in the creation of an alternate reality where what seems irrational to the outside observer is completely rational to the person living with the disease. Responding to very real voices and stimuli that others cannot see or hear and acting in manners generally perceived as antisocial (be it hoarding or lashing out violently) make complete sense from inside the mind of a person suffering from schizophrenia or paranoia.[14] These are not diseases unique to or common among the unsheltered, as one may see in the Best Picture Oscar–winning *A Beautiful Mind*, which tells the real-life story of the late Nobel laureate John Nash and his decades-long struggle with the demons inside his mind. But for those who lack the education, resources, and supportive family and friends that Nash had, mental illness can build seemingly impenetrable walls around the ill person. Breaking through begins by acknowledging the *reality* being experienced by those who are suffering from disorders of the mind. Suffice it to say that it is of no use to suggest to a person who has found a way to survive on the street—by successfully *managing* their addiction and their mental health—that they need to find shelter.

Improving the odds for engaging an unsheltered person requires a willingness to see them not as problems but as people and as clients. Those engaging with them must understand how they view themselves—as resourceful and resilient, innovative and entrepreneurial, capable and independent; but also as untrusting and scared. How could they not have all of these qualities? Every day they must develop an effective strategy for obtaining or maintaining conditions that most housed people take for granted, such as where to sleep, eat, bathe, and keep valued possessions safe and dry.

There is no course or book on surviving homelessness. Those who are homeless must figure it out. Often they do so by creating their own independent communities of those they do trust, a universe parallel to the world in which housed people live. As a teenager in New York City, Liz Murray chose the streets over an abusive and neglectful home (and nonetheless stayed in school and, though homeless, gained admission to Harvard). She speaks eloquently to the communities that form and the trust that arises among those living on the streets.[15] When a street person is offered the "opportunity" to leave the street and all the person has worked so hard to create and achieve, it should come as no surprise that the most likely response is at best skeptical and at worst flat-out dismissive.[16]

While it is possible to break through and help someone, doing so is rarely simple, easy, or quick. Breaking through takes a dedicated and patient individual—and often a team of individuals—willing to withhold judgment and to listen, show respect, lend support, and motivate. In short, willing to build a meaningful and trusting relationship. Mutual trust has to be earned through a continuous series of encounters and actions between two people who over time build a relationship. To the passerby, the series of encounters between an outreach worker and a client may seem counterintuitive, especially when the conversation ends and the unsheltered person is still on the street. Yet this is precisely how trust is built. When someone asks to be left alone, we have to respect their wishes as a first step in building a relationship and earning their trust. Coercing them to get help against their will is not an effective strategy, but is only to be considered when danger is imminent and the client's illness impairs them from recognizing it.[17]

One of the basic tenets of successful engagement of those living unsheltered—critical to building trust—is thus to do what the person asks, within the bounds of clinical appropriateness and professional conduct. Often, the very first thing an outreach worker hears when they meet an unsheltered person is, "Can't you just leave me alone?! Can't you see I'm fine?!" After quickly introducing themselves and checking to make sure there is no immediate danger, the outreach worker will do precisely that, leave them alone. (For cases where the unsheltered person is in imminent danger, see below.) In this way, the outreach worker builds a foundation of trust by demonstrating that they respect the person's autonomy and won't force them to do anything unless danger is clearly present. By walking away, the outreach worker is establishing a relationship that over time will enable them to provide meaningful help. Should this really be so surprising? The danger of accepting rides from strangers is common knowledge. Rarely does proposing marriage on the first date lead to a marriage. These are the rules of the road, self-evident to those with homes. Why would the rules be any different for the person living on the road?

This laissez-faire approach does often work. According to 2019 data, New York City outreach teams assisted 2,753 unsheltered individuals to leave the streets and subways for a better alternative.[18] While a placement does not necessarily mean the person placed will never return to the streets, it is another step forward. Ending a person's homelessness is a marathon, not a sprint, usually preceded by weeks if not months of preparation. Reaching the finish line, achieving a placement, takes an average of forty encounters.

Patience and listening are critical practices of effective outreach engagement. Equally important is appreciating how small achievements contribute to larger successes. The outreach worker's goal is to assist an unsheltered person to move to a more appropriate living situation, but that is usually not how the journey begins. Rather, the first move may be helping the client obtain a lost piece of identification, such as a social security card or birth certificate, or helping them obtain a doctor's appointment or a new pair of socks. Whatever the need, success for the outreach worker depends on their ability to see themselves as their client's advocate.[19]

EFFECTIVE ENGAGEMENT TECHNIQUES

The professional approach to engaging the unsheltered—often referred to as homeless outreach— has steadily evolved from rudimentary and well-meaning efforts of untrained volunteers to data-driven and evidence-based techniques applied systematically by professionals hired and trained specifically for this work.[20] What was mostly a random activity conducted on the margins of the service delivery system is today, in many cities, a core municipal service often enhanced by the coordinated efforts of public transit systems, police departments, and business associations.[21]

Homeless outreach first became a major activity of local governments in the New York City metropolitan area about a decade after the city's right to shelter was established in 1979. Outreach arose out of an acknowledgement that, although shelter was available on demand, thousands of homeless individuals were voting with their feet and choosing to sleep on the city's streets, parks, subways, and transit facilities rather than in shelters. In providing homeless outreach, the city recognized that it had to do

SEEING THE WHOLE PERSON

Muzzy Rosenblatt

A young boy, only six years of age, watches as his father is taken away in handcuffs, even though the father has asserted he has done nothing wrong. His mother gathers all the money she can find and runs down to the police station in an attempt to gain her husband's freedom. She succeeds, and when both parents return, they tell their son to pack a bag, one bag, as they both do. The next morning they leave their home with only what they can carry and head to the train station. They never look back, and they never return.

The year is 1938 and the country is Austria, having just fallen to Nazi rule. The train from Vienna takes the little boy and his parents to Trieste, Italy, on the Adriatic Sea. With the little money they still have, they board a ship sailing to Lisbon, Portugal, a neutral nation in the war overtaking the European continent. They spend almost two years waiting in a resettlement camp—a temporary shelter—hoping for a way to a better life, and a new home. Life is hard. The boy refuses to eat. His mother tries, unsuccessfully, to take her life and end the interminable wait. Finally, after nearly two years, they receive visas to emigrate to the United States, having been sponsored by a distant relative. They arrive in New York City and double up with family while the parents look for work and the boy goes to a school where everybody sees him as different; he does not even speak the language.

That young boy was my father. And although I am a child of a family that experienced homelessness, it was by coincidence that I chose this work.

I was waiting tables a year out of college when, in March 1988, I put down my apron and—believing in public service—went to work for New York City mayor Ed Koch. Helping to accelerate his monumental affordable housing program, I soon added to my portfolio the opening of homeless shelters, and prisons.

The city was building record amounts of housing, shelters, and prisons. And the more I learned about each of these systems—housing, social services, and criminal justice—the more I came to realize that each was often serving the same person. Yet, actually, none were doing that at all. All of these systems were reacting to problems, but none of them saw the whole person. Wanting to understand the people we were trying to serve, I went out on the street to speak with them, and listen to them, and learn from them. And in them, I saw people no different from my father and grandparents. Lost, frightened, alone, confused, untrusting, and struggling to be understood.

Over more than three decades I've continued to have these conversations while serving under three mayors and helping to establish the first municipal agency in the nation dedicated to serving people experiencing homelessness. I continued even after moving on to running a nonprofit doing the same thing, just closer to the client. I've been privileged to be a part of an ever-evolving and maturing network that helps thousands move from homelessness to home. Most of all, I am inspired by the resiliency and hopefulness of the people we serve. And, if I've learned anything from them—and from my father—it's that we will succeed in ending homelessness only when we stop seeing people as problems, and instead focus on who they are, why they are in these situations, and how we can serve them better.

more to motivate people to avail themselves of the shelter and services being offered and that, if the customer wouldn't or couldn't find the service, the service needed to find the customer—and make the *sale*.

Since 1993, New York City has run a municipal agency dedicated solely to homeless services delivery. That agency—the Department of Homeless Services—contracts with nonprofit social service agencies, each of which is responsible for conducting outreach in a specific geographic region of the city. Combined, they cover every public space in the city. In 2018, the city budgeted close to $100 million for street homeless programs and increased the number of outreach staff from 191 in 2014 to nearly 400 to cover the entire five counties of the city 24 hours a day, 365 days a year, as well as the entire subway system (with 472 stations).[22] In addition, from 1995 to 2020, the New York Police Department operated a dedicated Homeless Outreach Unit, whose entire mission was to address the needs of homeless individuals with a primarily non-law-enforcement orientation. The unit, comprising close to a hundred police officers wearing nontraditional uniforms, operated nonstop and, as often as not, worked alongside, or in coordination with, nonprofit agencies.[23] In addition New York State's Metropolitan Transportation Authority (MTA) provides round-the-clock homeless outreach at its major stations and terminals (among them, Penn Station and Grand Central Terminal), as does the regional transportation agency, the Port Authority of New York and New Jersey. Finally, many business improvement districts, which offer enhanced services to complement those provided by the municipality (such as security, sanitation, and economic development), have elected to invest in homeless outreach teams dedicated to their geographic catchment areas, often by contracting with the same nonprofit agencies under contract to the municipality.[24]

Investment in dedicated resources for homeless outreach is becoming more prevalent in cities around the globe. From Baltimore to Bogotá and from Athens to Edmonton, cities are responding to their unique street homeless circumstances with increased attention and focus on engagement efforts. Baltimore has established a homeless outreach unit within its police department. Bogotá's police and security forces coordinate with homeless outreach workers to serve and protect those on the street who may be victims of crime or exploitation by sex or drug traffickers. In Athens, the Center for Reception and Solidarity of the Municipality of Athens (KYADA) deploys teams that offer counseling, social support services, and shelter referral to people living on the street. In response to rough sleepers camping in the city's vast network of forest parkland and transportation corridors, Edmonton ran the Homeless on Public Land Initiative to coordinate efforts to address rough sleeping in encampments. The program involved stakeholders from numerous city departments, including the Edmonton Police Service and Fire Rescue Services, and provided housing locator resources to dedicated parkland outreach teams.[25] More and more cities realize that the response to street homelessness has to be coordinated across multiple departments, including both social service and law enforcement agencies. From a client's perspective, this is important because their willingness to accept help is closely tied to their perception that they are being "met where they are" both in terms of location and their unique needs.[26]

The best practices of homeless outreach embrace the philosophy previously articulated: to succeed in assisting the unsheltered, outreach workers must be dedicated to building a relationship of trust and respect with their clients. They must always be perceived as putting the client's needs first. Outreach workers' job is not to clear the streets of homeless people. Their job is to help homeless people leave the streets. This subtle difference in orientation and attitude is critical.[27]

The objective is always to assist the client in leaving the street for more appropriate housing, and, while some types of placement will be more likely than others to lead to positive long-term stability, any placement is positive. That said, as noted earlier in this chapter, the outreach worker cannot expect to achieve a placement on the first encounter, at least not one likely to last. Rather, the goal of every engagement is to progressively acquire knowledge so as to forge a genuine bond with the client. The more the outreach worker can enable the client to feel in control of the relationship, the more likely a success will occur. The more the client believes the outreach worker to be helping them achieve their objectives, the more likely the client will stay engaged with the outreach worker. Branding is important too. The nonprofit BRC (Bowery Residents' Committee) in New York City has recognizable orange vans and logo. The outreach workers, too, are widely known. Bogotá has bright, light-blue vests for its workers that bear the tagline "Bogotá Mejor Para Todos" (Bogotá Better for Everyone). Mexico City outreach workers don Day-Glo pink jackets. These easily identified vans, vests, jackets, and other markers help give clients comfort if the face of the worker approaching them is not familiar. Those who wear the special clothing also communicate to the public the extent of efforts to help people on the street. At the initial encounter, clients often ask to be left alone. In complying with that request, the outreach team makes a positive first impression, shows respect for the client, and improves the likelihood that future encounters will enable the relationship to grow. Not understanding "No" or "Leave me be" lowers the chances of ever developing a productive relationship with the client.

Outreach workers typically deploy in teams of two or (at most) three, for safety and effective engagement while also not presenting the client with an overwhelming force. One outreach worker takes the lead in initiating the engagement, while the other listens, observes, and takes mental notes on the client's appearance, physical condition, and possessions, while also assessing both the environment and the client's connection to it. Workers should ascertain where the client may be residing and what makes the space attractive. Are there individuals, institutions, or places in the area where the client may access food (as at pantries or soup kitchens), income from panhandling, illicit or off-the-books income, or even drugs? These observational elements are valuable in assessing the client's vulnerability and needs.

The way the outreach team approaches and engages with the client, in or out of uniform, will either reinforce or undermine the message the team is trying to communicate. Approaching on foot, always leaving the client a clear path to walk away, reinforces that the relationship is not coercive and reduces the risk that a client feeling threatened may lash out in self-defense. Outreach workers should always approach the client at their physical level and not stand or lean over them in a manner that can be perceived as threatening or overbearing.

Often clients may want help but not be in a place where they can speak freely, either because of their relationship to other clients or simply because they would prefer to speak about their personal needs in a private setting. Therefore, it's also desirable for the outreach team to have an easily accessible office where clients can appear on their own terms whenever convenient to them or during scheduled "office hours" when workers will be available, should the clients request assistance.

Outreach workers' success can be enhanced by establishing contacts in the areas where clients are known to frequent: other people who have independently developed relationships with those living on the streets, such as local merchants; maintenance and security staff of buildings, parks, or plazas; and local police officers.

Effective outreach does not require advanced formal education, and effective frontline outreach workers need not have a college degree. Engaging peers in outreach who have a shared experience with people currently on the street can quickly build legitimacy. However, once an outreach worker establishes a relationship with a client, offering additional professional resources often accelerates progress toward placement. Practically speaking, outreach workers should be supervised by a licensed social worker, and the program should have within its network a licensed psychiatric professional (doctor, nurse, or nurse practitioner) who can, if called upon, assess and evaluate more-challenging or fragile clients. Similarly, a primary care professional is useful, particularly as one of the most common first requests from clients is attention to a physical ailment that, if left unattended, may become a barrier to housing placement.

ACTING AGAINST A CLIENT'S WISHES, FOR THEIR OWN WELL-BEING

The key focus of outreach work is grounded in the motivational. Interviews of street homeless individuals reveal that the outreach worker should be both a networker-navigator and an advocate. Clients identify being treated respectfully and feeling valued as the most important aspects of these outreach services. This finding emphasizes that effective outreach involves not simply what is offered but also how it is offered.[28] The value unsheltered individuals feel comes from outreach workers patiently building trusting relationships with them over the long term. That trust building requires listening, developing personalized strategies, and ultimately helping support a client's desire to walk away from years of surviving a life unsheltered and move toward healing, transforming, and thriving in an appropriate residential setting.

These strategies work most of the time, but not always. Sometimes, despite the best outreach efforts and most creative techniques, the client continues to refuse help and, often, their health deteriorates right before the eyes of the outreach team.[29] When it becomes apparent that the client's illness is so debilitating that their chronic lack of self-care puts themselves and others in danger, more extreme actions may be warranted, and are usually permitted under the public health laws of many jurisdictions. Individuals may, for example, appear unaware they are inappropriately dressed for the elements and are at risk of freezing to death or overheating. Or an individual may be unaware they are covered in their own urine and feces, with open sores that are infected, risking greater infection; or a known diabetic may be unable to secure insulin and may risk losing, or have already lost, digits or limbs to amputation. Or, an individual's psychosis may be so profound that they acknowledge hearing voices that tell them to harm themselves or others.

Whether to act in a person's interest, but against their stated desires, by compelling their involuntary removal and treatment requires case-by-case determination. The decision cannot be made simply on the basis of a general diagnosis of an addictive disorder or a severe mental illness, as most individuals with these diagnoses are fully capable of making decisions and acting upon them.[30]

Any decision to remove an individual from a public space because of their inability to act in a safe manner often requires context. How long has the person been in this condition? How much have they deteriorated? Have they lost or gained weight? Started or stopped hoarding? Are they taking their medication and attending to personal hygiene? Are they aware of their environment and dangers present? The outreach team, and the knowledge of the client they have documented over time, is critical to answering these questions and making the determination. For this reason, the decision to remove someone involuntarily often must be made by a clinician or health care professional, usually licensed by a regulatory authority that has trained and empowered them to decide whether to temporarily deny someone of their civil liberties. It is not a power of law enforcement, though it is standard protocol to have police assist in these actions to ensure the safety of all involved.

Creating a clear and well-balanced legal standard for when action should be taken, even against the individual's wishes, is critical because the rights of the homeless person must be protected, as well as their sense of self and their confidence that the outreach worker is acting on their behalf. The standard should also protect both the outreach worker and the community from accusations of criminalizing homelessness through cruel and unusual use of force. Respect for clients is crucial; however, when a client is unable to make responsible decisions that affect their own safety, then the client's survival and welfare—and that of the community—become the team's primary concern, even if it means outreach workers must act against the client's immediate wishes. Laws and practices on this matter vary by community.[31] Wherever the line is drawn, it should be well defined and clearly understood by the community of clients, outreach workers, health care professionals, and law enforcement officers who will be most impacted by its application. Only a medical or psychiatric professional familiar with the client and the general circumstances of homelessness can make an accurate evaluation. And when that occurs, it may be beneficial to have law enforcement professionals in place to support the effort and ensure safety.[32]

THE EVOLVING ROLE OF LAW ENFORCEMENT

The role of police in homeless outreach is both evolving and, understandably, controversial, because the line between aiding a person in distress and enforcing the criminal code is blurred, both for the person sleeping rough and for the police. Whose rights should prevail and what should those rights be—the homeless person's abrogated rights to self-determination or the community's rights and responsibilities to keep its own safe? Bringing in law enforcement requires balancing the community interest in social order with a recognition that punitive measures will not solve homelessness. As urban police forces move away from criminalizing homelessness, attention is turning toward nondiscriminatory enforcement of laws to assist those who are living unsheltered gain access to the services they need.

Based on the sheer size of the municipal police force compared to that of other city teams, those living unsheltered are more likely to encounter police officers than other public servants. The evolution of police work from strict enforcement of laws to outcome-driven, problem-solving policing is consistent with how police should be expected to interact with individuals living in public spaces. Most unsheltered individuals learn quickly the legal limits in their communities and strive to avoid trespassing on private property, violating curfews, or obstructing doorways and points of access or egress. As tensions subside, some police and other entities involved in law enforcement (such as prosecutors and judges) are exercising more discretion in not punishing people for being unable to find a place to live or for being afflicted with untreated mental health and addictive disorders.[33]

Yet these behaviors may still present community members with significant quality-of-life issues and may evolve into the sort of public safety issues to which police are often asked to respond. This puts law enforcement officers on the front line of what is primarily a social, not a criminal, matter. Recognizing this, police departments have begun to develop protocols such as partnering with homeless outreach organizations, as they do in Bogotá and Los Angeles, to developing their own homeless outreach units, as they have in Baltimore; or both, as in New York City from 1995 until 2020 and as Baltimore was moving toward in 2020.[34]

Where minor infractions of local nuisance laws are present—for example, consumption of alcohol in a park or other public space—police are often forced to take an aggressive approach toward people with addictions who often have no other place to drink. Complaints by the public, and resulting enforcement of public nuisance laws, may also be rooted in an exaggerated fear of homeless individuals. Yet it is often the people living on the street who are the most vulnerable and who, rather than posing a real threat to public safety, are the ones in need of law enforcement protection. Studies show that homeless individuals are at greater risk of victimization than the general public, and those living with severe mental illness on the street are more likely to be victims of violence than to be perpetrators.[35]

Coordination and collaboration between well-intentioned police and homeless outreach workers have proven effective. When New York City first established its Homeless Outreach Unit, many of the officers in it had master's degrees in social work, psychology, or public health. Further, in order to incentivize appropriately motivated officers to volunteer for what some might see as an undesirable or career-breaking assignment, it was designated as a required stop for officers seeking eventual appointment to the department's elite emergency services units, the unit called to respond to various emotional disturbance cases, including hostage taking and suicide attempts. Thus, it is in the interest of all to ensure that police officers are trained appropriately for interactions with those who are homeless, and that they know about the resources available in the community. Well-trained and well-intentioned police often are an outreach workers' best ally because they help to maintain a safe environment and can enforce rules.[36] The safe environment can make it easier for both clients and providers to have time and space to develop the trusting relationship needed to move forward. Also, enforcing rules sometimes serves to motivate the unsheltered person to accept the outreach worker's offer of services—as in, the proverbial good cop–bad cop scenario.

ENCAMPMENTS: COMPOUNDING THE CHALLENGE

As both the incidence and prevalence of unsheltered homelessness intensifies, so does the frequency of encampments—communities of similarly situated, unsheltered individuals who, due to scarcity of options and greater safety in numbers, choose to make a particular area their shared living space. While usually staking claim to abandoned and neglected areas in remote parts of cities, as evidenced throughout Los Angeles and particularly on the city's Skid Row, more and more of these encampments are establishing themselves in central urban areas.

Usually they are in violation of local ordinances that prohibit the erection of structures without permits or the obstruction of public thoroughfares such as sidewalks. However, once in place, efforts to remove them, though legal, often pose a political liability. New York City's attempt to do so in Tompkins Square Park in the 1990s led to a riot that resulted in numerous substantiated cases of police brutality and a complete restructuring of policing tactics, and left both the department and Mayor Ed Koch politically damaged. The park had been taken over by squatters, punks, drug pushers, and over a hundred homeless people, making it unruly day and night, littered with belongings, and generally inaccessible to the public. When the local community board convinced the Parks Department to institute a 1 A.M. curfew, those in the park refused to adhere to it and a police riot ensued. In 2017, Baltimore mayor Catherine Pugh experienced a similar challenge in the park opposite City Hall. Through a comedy of errors, scores of symbolic tents were erected by advocates as a homeless protest; then, however, the park evolved into a permanent encampment when the tents were occupied by people who actually had no homes. When it became clear that the encampment was not going to go away, the city offered the residents an unoccupied public school property to move into as a makeshift shelter. As most accepted a move to the shelter, the tent city encampment was effectively removed, but other tent cities have appeared elsewhere in Baltimore.

Encampments often get on public officials' radar when the damage spills over to people who live and work nearby. In Bogotá, officials had long struggled to manage an occupation known as El Bronx, a multiblock neighborhood of abandoned buildings near the urban core that was a center of self-dealing and addiction and had exploited many against their will, with drug dens, prostitution, and gun and human trafficking. Pressure on public officials to intercede in the overt lawlessness and private control of public spaces increased when the area became the favored spot of visiting youth attending weekend party blowouts. Many prior efforts by the mayor to retake the area were thwarted by corrupt police who gave advance warning to the occupying leaders. Shortly after his reelection in 2016, Mayor Enrique Peñalosa collaborated with the police forces of neighboring towns to mount a the raid and successfully liberated El Bronx, providing shelter and services to its victims while prosecuting those who had harmed them. As the case of El Bronx shows, a coordinated strategy is necessary to peacefully dismantle an established encampment. Bogotá officials involved homeless outreach organizations and prioritized access to shelter resources so that those in the encampment were offered acceptable alternative places to stay.[37] The buildings are now long gone, together with the accompanying graffiti portraits of Padre Nícolo, a beloved local priest, and Pablo Escobar, the notorious source of the residents' addictions.[38]

While the circumstances in El Bronx were unique, in general, once a decision is made to dismantle a particular encampment, a specific date must be set and communicated to the residents. This affords the outreach teams sufficient time to do their work (build relationships, engage clients, and the like), while confirming to encampment residents that whether they accept services or not, they will have to move by a certain date. In short, it empowers the clients to make choices and feel at least partially in control of their circumstances. Over the weeks leading up to a removal, as outreach teams engage, some clients will accept services. Others will wait to see if the threat is real before pulling up stakes. Credibility is thus critical; it is imperative that once a date is set, it is enforced. On the stated date, with police and property managers present, outreach teams will make one last effort. Most clients who took the wait-and-see approach will leave, either to accept services or to find a new location. Because of the extensive effort and advance notice, rarely is it necessary to arrest anyone for trespass, though there might be cases of involuntary removals for safety. Once all residents of the encampment have left, the area should be cleaned of any remaining debris by the property manager, secured, and routinely patrolled to ensure the encampment is not reestablished.

Much information is gleaned from the many efforts undertaken to meet the individual needs of each person living unsheltered. Outreach programs can better position themselves to advocate for the many people they serve by collecting and analyzing the data derived from this work. Cities can assess the types of placements to which clients better respond and prioritize efforts to achieve more of these placements. Careful records kept by outreach workers can be used to determine if there are times of day, periods of the month, or seasons of the year when clients are more receptive to assistance.

The efforts of homeless outreach teams should become more highly visible to the community at large. Whether driven by feelings of compassion or consternation, urban citizens tend to make homelessness one of the most prevalent issues of public concern. As detailed in chapter 8, municipalities should consider public-awareness campaigns that let their constituents know what is being done, the achievements made, and how the public can help other than by giving out food and money. Annual point-in-time street counts staffed by community volunteers, local homeless helplines, and 311 call centers that encourage neighbors to phone in when they see someone who may benefit from an outreach team all further public awareness that the most vulnerable in the community have not been forgotten.

The culmination of these efforts is to bring these people inside. Months of engagement can be wasted if, at the point the person finally agrees to accept a bed, no placement is available. The ability of outreach workers to coordinate who is prioritized for shelter and housing resources is critical to success. With this final step, much depends on whether the municipality has a range of placement options available for outreach workers to access, options that are explored in the next chapter.

3 Sheltering Options That Work

The terms *homelessness* and *homeless shelter* took their place in the bureaucratic and public policy lexicon in the 1970s; however, the social conditions these terms address have existed for centuries. One need only go back to biblical times and the exodus from Egypt to appreciate the impact of displacement. Today, homelessness is woven into the urban landscape, beneath the underpasses of Los Angeles and Houston, in the subways of Paris and New York City, and in the parks of Athens and Nashville, to name just a few. Whether in doorways, tents, parked cars, or makeshift shanties, rough sleeping is ubiquitous. While no standard international definition of homelessness exists, and there is no universal approach to counting those on the street, all countries report that rough sleeping is an integral fixture of modern urban life.[1]

Most policy makers, and even most advocates, speak of the situation as if homelessness were a temporary challenge or one having emerged only recently. Although the Ending Homelessness Act of 2019 was pending in the US Congress at this writing, the very concept of ending homelessness has become a recurring mindset. Language matters, and how we define a challenge shapes how we respond. Many cities have opted for quick responses to basic needs but have not accepted reality:

despite decades of evidence, homelessness is a chronic societal condition and, as such, necessitates a comprehensive, strategic, and permanent response.

Most municipalities respond to homelessness with immediate, short-term remedies as they would in the case of a fire, flood, or other natural or human-driven disaster causing the temporary displacement of families (many of whom would eventually be able to return to their homes). New York City responded to a new wave of homelessness in the 1970s in this fashion, unfolding hundreds of cots on drill floors of abandoned military armories. Today, nearly a half century later, most of these buildings are still being used as shelters, albeit in lower population density and with improved services.

Such responses befit a time-limited emergency or a crisis, but not a decades-old social condition. New York City established its Department of Homeless Services (DHS) in 1993 with a sunset provision of five years, confident that no more time would be needed to resolve the crisis. More than a quarter century later, DHS is now a permanent component of New York City's municipal bureaucracy, with a fiscal year 2019 annual operating budget in excess of $2.1 billion.[2]

Although cities speak in a language that connotes a short-term need for shelters, the evolution in the design and operation of homeless shelters increasingly recognizes their permanence in the fabric of city and community life. This chapter spotlights some of the many initiatives under way in cities around the globe that represent this evolution in thinking about responses to homelessness go further than providing a roof, bed, and meal. Instead, these new undertakings acknowledge that homelessness, as a product of many events and conditions, requires a multipronged approach to sheltering society's vulnerable.

Shelters occupy the core of municipal response to homelessness. No matter how strong and trusting a relationship an outreach worker builds with a client, success depends on the availability of an appropriate place for the unsheltered person to accept. Outreach efforts may be for naught if there are no beds acceptable to clients, as mentioned in the previous chapter. While the goal should be to have housing affordable to all, the reality is that the supply-demand imbalance is extreme and won't be resolved in the short-term, if ever. Stable housing unquestionably improves an individual's ability to manage their lives. However, there are individuals—sheltered and unsheltered—who have physical or behavioral health issues, or both, that put them at risk, jeopardizing their ability to succeed and thrive in traditional housing. Therefore, it becomes essential that municipalities consider offering forms of transitional living facilities as a bridge between homelessness and home.[3]

NONPROFITS ENTER THE SHELTER OPERATING FIELD

Historically, shelters were run either by the local government or by a faith-based institution; many still are. However, as the nature of shelter services has evolved, many cities—including New York, Los Angeles, Athens, and Baltimore—have turned to nonprofit organizations that have experience in such fields as behavioral health and workforce development to provide these services within the shelter setting or, in some cases, to take over all aspects of shelter operations. Edmonton contracts with nonprofit organizations to provide government-funded shelter services, though some nonprofits deliver additional services funded by private donors or charities. The relationship between government agencies and nonprofit service providers operating under contract to provide shelter can be complicated, and often conflictual. Competing philosophies on how best to provide services, the ability of larger providers to exert undue pressure, weak accountability mechanisms in contracts, and the simple inadequacy of public subsidies all converge to create barriers to unified municipal action.

To establish a coordinated approach to a comprehensive service array, local government leaders can use their authority to persuade the community to coalesce around a well-articulated and shared vision for guiding public contracts. Creating such an environment lays the groundwork for negotiating outcome-based contracts that best use public-sector dollars. A shared-vision approach to outcomes reflects the community's collective will rather than unilateral government dictation of policy. In this way, the contracting organization uses taxpayer dollars to leverage the collective community vision for service-delivery outcomes. Other local charitable funding organizations might similarly adopt the approach for their financial support as well. In the most advanced version of this practice, the government partner procuring the service establishes an effective performance-based contract that clearly spells out the population to be served, the practices to be followed, and the outcomes to be achieved.

Individuals who choose to live on the streets and in subways often base their decision on negative experiences in poorly run and maintained facilities. Compassionate care requires serving many different types of people with diverse needs and levels of stability, including those who would prey on the vulnerable with methods both physical and psychological. Even the best-run shelters can pose real risks to the most fragile, weak, and vulnerable, which is why conscious decisions about a client's needs must be made by those who connect the unsheltered to shelter. Perceived safety is not the only barrier clients face. Some are overwhelmed by the services, structure, and rules. For longtime self-reliant individuals, structured service shelters are off-putting and offering them can be counterproductive. As with homeless outreach work, effective shelter workers must know their clients and be able to cater to their specific needs, abilities, and desires. A shelter system that recognizes and can meet this diversity is more likely to be an effective resource to a municipality's long-term efforts to address the needs of those living unsheltered.[4]

Ascribing responsibility for being homeless to those who refuse what's being offered does not take the full picture into account. In cities where the only options are bare-bones shelters, emergency rooms, and detoxification for those with an addictive disorder, living on the streets and subways can seem preferable. Yet those who refuse shelter are often labeled "service resistant" by policy makers. Some cities have begun to create models of care that respond to the preferences of individuals who have rejected shelter, understanding that the right service and structure for them has yet to be established. In creating models informed by the preferences of the unsheltered, cities such as Los Angeles with its Bridge Housing, Houston with its Service Centers, Paris with its Halte de Nuit (Night Stop), and New York City with its Safe Havens are effectively responding to the needs of both the unsheltered and the communities where they publicly reside. These cities are assisting people off the streets and into better living situations and, in so doing, helping them move closer to the ultimate objective of a home of their own.

THE ACCESSIBILITY OF DROP-IN AND SERVICE CENTERS

As the name suggests, drop-in centers and service centers are designed to be easily accessible, on a client's terms. The intent is to offer the client access to the services they want without obligatory engagement in other activities. The model's objective is to expose clients to other services. A client may initially come to the center only to bathe or eat a meal. Once inside, however, they may encounter a nurse or a doctor, apply for a public benefit, or simply socialize with others they know from the street.

The functions of drop-in and service centers overlap and may blur. The most significant distinction is that drop-in centers offer respite, allowing clients to sleep by providing chairs (though not beds) for them to do so. Many drop-in centers operate twenty-four hours a day, allowing clients to come and go at their convenience, and may even offer lockers where they can secure certain belongings. Service centers are more likely to have limited hours, so as not to create a false perception that clients may linger or reside there. To confuse things further, the titles can be used interchangeably, and other titles can be used, such as *navigation* or *resource center*, or *one-stop*. The distinctions notwithstanding, what matters most is not what these programs are called but rather how they are designed: these models offer a barrier-free environment that embraces a stages-of-change approach to working with clients. The expectation is that, after a period of time coming to the center for what they *want*, the client will be further motivated to seek out what they *need*.[5]

As with homeless outreach, the effectiveness of drop-in and service centers depends as much on how they deliver their services as what services they offer. The initial challenge is getting clients to come, and one effective strategy is to base the homeless outreach staff at the center, building upon the trusting relationship these staff have with their clients. In this approach, the outreach worker may escort the client to the center or may schedule a time to meet with the client there. Once at the center, the outreach worker can introduce the client to the services it has to offer and slowly transition the client to these services, either when the client requests them or by using the power of suggestion.[6]

The center's design also plays a critical role in its success. The concept of barrier-free access manifests on several levels. The center should not be hard to find or so remote from where clients are congregating that the time and effort to find it becomes a disincentive. Similarly, it should have its own entrance from the street, so there is less confusion for the client. Even if it is colocated with other services, the center should have its own door through which only those seeking the center's services will enter.

Given that the individuals arriving will have diverse histories, needs, and challenges, security protocols should be followed, but in a nonthreatening and nonauthoritarian manner. Rather than employing uniformed security officers, center staff that serve as greeters and take on a concierge-style function can also be trained in a broad array of nonthreatening security techniques and even be licensed as security guards, without dressing the part. For example, it is not uncommon for clients living on the street to carry items they should not need inside the center. Knowing this and asking clients to present them for safekeeping by center staff (who will provide a receipt, secure the items, and return them if asked—unless they are illegal—when the client leaves) is a trust-building and pragmatic approach to both motivating clients to come to the center and ensuring that others are safe while they are there. A similar approach can be taken with clients' medications. Alternatively, Los Angeles has experimented with "amnesty lockers," where clients can safely secure items not permitted in the facility (such as weapons for personal protection or drugs) before they enter.

While the barrier-free, low-demand qualities of the drop-in and service center models make them appealing, two elements limit these centers' value for clients' long-term—and sometimes immediate—needs. The first is limited hours, and the second is the absence of beds in which to sleep.

Some drop-in centers are open only during the day, requiring clients to leave before night to find a place to sleep. To help surmount this shortcoming, many drop-in centers have established partnerships with small community-based (often faith-based) organizations that offer to accommodate people in overnight makeshift shelters, often by setting up cots on the floors of community centers. This model, which has been used in New York City for decades, is practical only for fairly stable clients who have no mental or physical health issues that might put them at risk, as often these overnight accommodations are staffed only with volunteers. Further, the two-stop structure compels a client to continuously cart their belongings back and forth as they move between the two locations, the proximity of which is not always close or convenient (though some jurisdictions provide transportation). This hybrid model also depends on close coordination between staff at the two facilities. Once the client leaves the center, there is no certainty they will arrive at the overnight shelter, increasing the probability they may return to the street.

To better contend with these challenges, some drop-in centers operate on a twenty-four-hour basis. This approach not only addresses the coordination and travel issues noted above but also enables clients to come and go at any hour of the day or night, better meeting the needs of individuals who may not be able to utilize such services during the day. Operating around the clock provides clients with an easily accessible alternative to living and sleeping in public spaces. For some, the drop-in center offers a safe place to sleep, whatever the hour may be, which encourages greater use.

Whether open twenty-four hours or only during the day, drop-in centers commonly allow individuals to sleep only in chairs, their heads resting on their folded arms atop a table or reclining in a corner against a wall. The safety of the drop-in center can be preferable to sleeping on the streets; but by design, the centers do not operate as shelters and do not offer clients the ability to lie down. This poses a real problem. Sleeping upright contributes to circulatory problems, such as "homeless feet," a condition in which the uninterrupted upright condition of the body causes fluids to gather in the feet, ankles, and legs, which then tend to swell, impacting blood circulation. Other common health challenges such as dehydration, when combined with the swelling, can cause the skin to ulcer or crack. This subsequently leaves clients vulnerable to infection, particularly those who may be reluctant or unable to bathe. For these reasons, it is quite reasonable for clients to choose to sleep in doorways on the streets, on park benches, or on the subways in New York City or a night bus in Paris. They may use a sleeping bag or blankets or simply lie atop a heating vent on the sidewalk. For the sake of their health, clients will forgo the drop-in center in exchange for having the ability to lie down.[7]

SAFE HAVENS PROVIDE A BED OF ONE'S OWN

Recognizing the limitations of drop-in and service centers, in 2006, New York City developed a new model called Safe Haven that provides the unsheltered with both a low-demand model and a bed they may consider their own.[8] The overwhelmingly positive outcomes have encouraged other cities such as Los Angeles to adopt and adapt the model.

The New York City Mayor's Office, in collaboration with the local non-profit BRC (Bowery Residents' Committee), developed the Safe Haven program to offer a continuum of services—outreach, shelter, treatment, job training, social services, and housing—to vulnerable and unsheltered adults. Analyzing its outreach data, BRC identified a significant cohort of individuals with a history of chronic homelessness within Manhattan (one of the five boroughs that make up the city) who were not willing to accept existing housing and service options. To respond to their needs and wants, BRC developed a new residential service model based on the Housing First philosophy, which prioritizes the provision of permanent housing to people experiencing homelessness. The underlying theory was that the unsheltered homeless are more likely and able to pursue personal goals and improve their quality of life if they have their own home. Housing First does not require people to resolve their challenges or to graduate through a series of service programs before they can access housing, nor does it require participation in services.[9]

Similar to Housing First, the Safe Haven model applies a come-as-you-are philosophy that does not require, as either a prerequisite or co-requisite, the participation in any form of service or treatment. This is sometimes referred to as a bed-first model. Safe Haven was specifically designed for chronically homeless individuals who had not been successful in, or had refused to try, other structures, models, or environments, but who were willing to leave the streets and subways to work on securing permanent housing.

A Safe Haven's physical configuration is quite similar to that of a shelter. It is similar to a drop-in center in that it has few rules and a low-demand operational structure. As such, Safe Havens are often referred to as drop-in centers with beds, or shelters without rules. Neither characterization is entirely accurate. Residents seeking admission are assigned a bed and a locker; thus, the program has less of a revolving-door experience than do drop-in and service centers. And because the program is designed specifically for individuals who have been unsheltered for significant lengths of time (the chronically homeless), they are less likely to have other options. Safe Haven participants differ from the shelter population, who are more likely to have a support system and to use shelters as one of several living arrangements they navigate.

As Safe Havens are designed specifically for chronically homeless individuals who have been living unsheltered, clients seeking admission cannot simply arrive; instead, they must be referred (and often are brought) by an outreach worker who has verified the client's chronic homelessness as well as their appropriateness for the program. Once admitted, clients are assigned a bed and a locker and can come and go freely, leaving their belongings behind, and not be subject to a curfew. Many of the most effective Safe Havens are run by entities that also operate the homeless outreach program in that area. Although this coincidence is not necessary for the model's success, it allows for seamless continuity and transition of care, as well as a complementary culture and philosophy. Safe Havens are part of a natural progression that starts with homeless outreach and continues with drop-in centers and service centers. Each shares the same philosophical tenets of an adaptive, low-barrier service approach to meet client needs and readiness to engage.

NEW YORK CITY'S SAFE HAVEN

Having piloted the model in 2006, BRC opened New York City's first independent Safe Haven in 2008; by 2010, three were in operation with a combined capacity of nearly two hundred beds. BRC analyzed seven years of data from these three Safe Havens (July 1, 2010, through June 30, 2017) and found that, of the 1,790 unique individuals served, nearly half (841, or 47 percent) achieved some form of positive outcome. Most secured housing, while other positive outcomes included moving to a residential rehab, treatment, or skilled-nursing facility that could best meet the client's needs. Clients achieved these outcomes on average within 298 care-days, with only 8 percent returning to the homeless services system during the period of study.

These positive outcomes highlight the Safe Haven model as a popular alternative among many living unsheltered. However, demand for these beds has exceeded supply. By 2019, more than 1,000 Safe Haven beds

Figure 3. El Puente, a Safe Haven in Los Angeles, California, that is part of A Bridge Home and practices harm reduction and barrier-free access to shelter to make it as easy as possible for people to leave the streets. Office of Mayor Eric Garcetti.

had been established, and the city had allocated funding to bring online an additional 250.[10] The model has been deployed in other cities, sometimes by other names. The city of Los Angeles recognized that, while it was rapidly investing in and building permanent supportive and affordable housing to meet the needs of rising homelessness, there was also an immediate need for community-based shelters in most, if not every, council district in the city. To meet this need, it invested in a variety of shelter models under the umbrella program of "A Bridge Home." Among the first was El Puente, a project designed for the chronically homeless that opened in 2018 and embraces the low-barrier model. Globally, Athens, Paris, and Mexico City have also developed preliminary plans to open Safe Havens that employ the BRC model.

BEYOND EMERGENCY RESPONSE

While drop-ins, service centers, and Safe Havens have offered successful alternatives to shelters, they are not a replacement. Shelters are an integral part of addressing homelessness by providing options other than living unsheltered for those who have been displaced from prior living situations, whether because of eviction, release from incarceration, discharge from a hospital or long-term treatment facility, or some other circumstance. And, in communities where there is an extreme shortage of affordable housing, shelters are a necessary alternative.

Shelters are as important to many communities as a hospital. Ultimately, those seeking shelter or health care will leave the facility to achieve better outcomes and move forward with their lives. For some, undoubtedly, the need to return will present itself; when it does, those individuals should feel welcome to return. In either the shelter or hospital scenario, these facilities should be places where those in need are sure to receive all the care necessary to heal and gather strength.

For shelters to succeed, they need to provide structure, ensure safety, and offer an array of services. As shelters evolve away from emergency response to centers of transformation, attention should be paid to the service model, the physical design, and building up an organizational entity qualified to operate the program.

EMERGING SERVICE-MODEL SHELTERS

As has been acknowledged in prior chapters, complex and diverse circumstances lead an individual or family to finding themselves without a home. They might have experienced a fire or be fleeing from domestic abuse. They could be driven by economic factors, such as unaffordable rents or loss of income. A prolonged physical or behavioral health condition, or a lengthy period of institutionalization or incarceration, might have led to loss of income and home. Any one or an unlucky combination of these root-cause factors may force people with no alternatives to turn to a shelter for help. Whether that shelter has the ability to address the specific issues that precipitated the loss of housing becomes critical to determining how quickly and effectively housing can be restored and maintained.

Since the beginning of the twenty-first century, the concept and design of a homeless shelter has evolved from a place of temporary respite, providing only the basic necessities of food and shelter, to a place of healing and personal growth, offering robust social services provided by social work and psychology professionals and tailored health services provided by psychiatrists, nurses, and addiction counselors.[11] These services transcend traditional case management activities that generally attend to more administrative and transactional activities; instead, they focus on addressing the underlying factors that led to a person becoming homeless, factors that must be resolved if the individual is to be discharged successfully to housing—that is, in a condition in which they can maintain and thrive in the housing.

Shelter services may include individual and group addiction therapy, diagnosis and referral to treatment for mental health disorders, job training and workforce development activities, and counseling on financial management, among others. These services are often built on the "Stages of Change" model of behavior modification, using evidence-based practices such as "motivational interviewing" and "critical time intervention."[12]

Enhancing a shelter with these services adds to its program costs; however, evidence shows that these transformative services move more clients into housing, and do so with shorter stays in shelters and with lower incidence of homelessness recurring.[13]

Some cities have organized certain shelters around specific root-cause issues; for example, designating one or more shelters for individuals focused on finding and retaining employment, living with a mental health disorder, recovering from addiction, or obtaining medical recuperation and support. New York City contracts with nonprofit organizations to operate service-rich program shelters for single adults, sometimes leveraging the health care system and philanthropic contributions to provide the financial support for these enhanced services. Paris is piloting a program called First Hours that allows long-term homeless to work at their own pace, believing that *rapid reemployment* will facilitate *rapid rehousing*. Athens and Houston are discussing similar approaches, though Athens already provides a special shelter for formerly homeless seniors. By making these types of investments in shelters to meet specific needs, cities create environments more conducive to better outcomes.

Among the various types of shelters that have emerged to serve specific needs are the following:

Employment shelters. For some, overcoming homelessness involves the combined challenges of finding and keeping both a job and a place to live. Multiple barriers impede this effort, including lack of employment history and preclusions that bar employment and housing options on the basis of prior criminal or behavioral records. Considerable work is being done to assist such individuals with supported work environments and tailored housing assistance in order to create a pathway to independence.

Mental health shelters. The global prevalence of mental illness, often with co-occurring substance abuse, in the population of those sleeping rough has necessitated refined models for engaging shelter residents with on-site medical professionals to provide counseling and support services and to dispense and monitor medication.

Substance abuse shelters. Evidence-based substance abuse treatment regimens have widely been incorporated into shelters.

Domestic violence shelters. Fleeing an abusive partner is a common precipitator of homelessness, and a safety risk for individuals as they cope with finding an appropriate alternative place to live. Counseling and support for victims in secure environments are critical components of assisting their transition to healthy alternatives.

Youth shelters. Young people who find themselves homeless are often fleeing abusive or unsupportive homes, or are aging out of foster care without adequate transition to permanent housing. Their challenges are magnified when they come of age without the support of family and community. These shelters are designed to welcome and support their development.

Family shelters. A frequent precipitator of family homelessness is the stress placed on overcrowded housing by the addition of new children. Family shelters create safe and nurturing environments for young families.

SPOTLIGHT ON INNOVATION: ATHENS

Through an Athens' pilot initiative, able-bodied workers out of a job and languishing in city shelters would be given a chance to work their way into housing. City officials recognized that many of those in adult shelters had extensive employment histories but, because of the country's economic crisis and high unemployment rate (over 20 percent), could not find work. They proposed that these shelter residents be allowed to renovate abandoned residential properties into permanent housing in return for being given priority to live in the properties. If carried out, the project could reclaim abandoned city properties, provide sweat equity that would reduce the properties' renovation costs, and give shelter residents both skills training and work. Once completed, the refurbished property would enable individuals to exit shelter for housing, freeing up capacity in the shelter so that others could enter and be served.

As with many initiatives not launched until the end of a mayoral term, however, the fate of this work is uncertain. In August 2019, Athens elected a new mayor and the pilot project was shelved. The hard work of program design and resource allocation can be lost if the opportunity of the political moment is not seized and irrevocable actions are not timely taken.

PHYSICAL DESIGN AND OPERATION

How a shelter is designed has a significant impact on its success.[14] A shelter has to be safe and welcoming, and it should demonstrate respect for the dignity of those who live there. This requires investing in furnishings and equipment, including technology, that give the facility the feel of commitment and comfort, not that of an institution. There should be sufficient space to support activities appropriate for the provided services, from classrooms for job training or group counseling to offices for individual counseling and exam rooms for on-site medical staff. While the space must be clean, safe, and offer a reasonable amount of privacy, if the shelter appears more attractive than housing currently available in the community, there may be less motivation to move if there are no time limits imposed on shelter stays.

A careful balance should be maintained to provide a shelter space that both draws people on the street inside and motivates them to progress toward more independent living. The shelter stay is one of mutual obligations, with shelter management obligated to provide a safe and clean environment and support services and shelter residents obligated to act to the extent of their abilities to overcome their homelessness. Shelter rules must support the mission. For instance, shelters that compel clients to reapply daily for a bed or to leave the building during the day do not create an environment or operate in a manner that supports and reinforces their goals. Rather than set clients up to achieve success, they set them up to fail. Such rules undermine the sense of stability and belonging crucial to helping someone who is homeless achieve goals. Clients who may have nowhere to go during the day become vulnerable on the street to forces that may undermine their success, such as a drug use or alcohol relapse or arrest. Clients should be encouraged to leave the shelter and engage in activities that support their growth and goals, such as seeing a doctor, attending an outpatient program, or going on a job interview or to school. But they should not be punished for their efforts by then being locked out of the shelter for the entire day, leaving uncertain whether they can return the following evening.

The evolution of shelter services and environments has incorporated critical knowledge concerning the underlying causes of homelessness, allowing cities to adopt practices proven to engage clients and to direct them toward greater permanency through a safe and stable home, practices explored in the following chapter.

4 Developing an Affordable Housing Strategy

With the resurgence of city centers late in the twentieth century as hubs of economic opportunity, culture, and innovation, people began moving back in from the suburbs, filling available living spaces, gentrifying neighborhoods, and driving up housing prices. A stark example is Colombia, the third-most populous country in Latin America, where people flooded from the unsafe countryside to cities in the late 1970s. Bogotá, the country's largest and most populous city, swelled from 2.38 million residents in 1970 to almost 11 million in 2020, a growth each year of between 2 and 9 percent.[1] This trend toward city living is increasing the global demand for affordable urban housing.

The upswing in urban living follows years of disinvestment in social housing by many national governments, which has put many low-income people at risk of displacement because of escalating costs. Canadian social housing production, for example, peaked in the early 1970s when it represented 10 percent of all new national housing production. By the mid-1990s, the national government had slowed investment, and, by the early 2000s, there was little new production in social housing.[2] In the United States, pleas from California governor Gavin Newsom and mayors from the state's thirteen largest cities to increase federal funding to combat the affordable housing shortage were rejected by the federal government in 2019 on the grounds that state and local policies should play the driving role in reversing the shortage. [3]

In the absence of sufficient national housing support, municipal governments are under pressure to protect residents who face huge rent burdens and possible eviction. Tenants look toward local government leaders to implement policies that make housing affordable; for example, limiting rent increases, protecting tenants from eviction, subsidizing housing construction, providing rental assistance, or building more government-funded housing. In general, a household that spends more than 30 percent of its income on housing is considered rent burdened.[4] A Pew Charitable Trusts report in 2018 concluded that 38 percent of renter households in the United States were rent burdened in 2015, a 19 percent increase from 2001. The share of renters who are severely rent burdened—that is, who spend more than half their income on rent—increased by 42 percent during that same period to 17 percent.[5] Consider the greater Los Angeles metropolitan area, one of the most expensive housing markets in the United States. A 2020 report from the Joint Center for Housing Studies of Harvard University found that nearly 56 percent of renters in Los Angeles in 2018 were rent burdened.[6] In Baltimore, a 2016 Abell Foundation report found that over half of renters (57 percent) were paying more than 30 percent of their income on rent and 33 percent were paying more than 50 percent.[7] The frustration with high rents resonates across the country, especially in New York City, where a political party was created around that sentiment, aptly expressed in its name: "The Rent Is Too Damn High."

Similar struggles have occurred in Europe and Canada. Between 2010 and 2016—a period of wage stagnation and growing income inequality—the cost of housing for poor households increased on average more than 20 percent in most European Union countries.[8] Comparably, one-in-five Canadians spent more than half their income on housing costs and utilities in 2016.[9] In Edmonton, 38 percent of households spent more than 30 percent of income on rent and utilities; 18 percent spent more than half of their income on these necessities; and 13 percent lived in overcrowded conditions.[10]

The precariously housed—those on a fixed income who can barely afford rent each month—often have no resources at hand to deal with life's

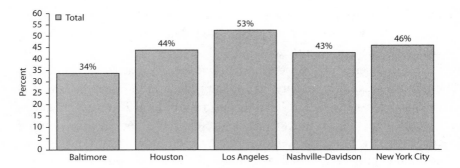

Figure 4. Percentage of children living in households with a high housing cost burden in selected cities. From National Kids Count Data 2018 (a project of the Annie E. Casey Foundation).

unexpected expenses. A high-housing-cost burden is too often associated with eviction and homelessness. Such a burden impacts low-income renters in two ways. First, they pay so much of their income toward rent that it becomes an unsustainable financial burden or creates unsustainable living conditions.[11] Second, the higher the percentage of income spent on housing, the less the renter has available for other necessities such as food and health care. When emergencies come up, such as loss of employment or high health care bills, resources are diverted and rent payments missed. The higher the housing cost burden, the more tenuous a person's housing stability becomes, and any sudden change can result in an episode of homelessness.

YOU CANNOT BUILD YOUR WAY OUT OF
HOMELESSNESS, BUT . . .

In response to these urban pressures and the inadequacy of national responses, cities are increasingly devising innovative solutions for expanding the supply of affordable housing. Unfortunately, however, few cities are able to implement housing strategies at a scale large enough to make a measurable impact on homelessness. New York City built or preserved almost a half million units of affordable housing from 1999 to 2019, a decade during which the homeless population continued to grow dramatically. Those half million units weren't enough to keep pace with the growth in the number of homeless, especially among families. And it is unlikely that cities will be able to launch the housing development required to keep pace with the needs of those on the verge of homelessness. One simple dynamic lies behind this inability. With a fixed amount of federal housing development dollars to invest, cities face a trade-off between the size of a subsidy per unit and how many units should be built. Most city housing strategies opt for stretching investment dollars to develop units that require income levels out of reach for many people. Without doubt, these housing projects do provide relief to low- and moderate-income households, but the units built are largely unaffordable for the poorest residents.

A municipal housing plan that seeks to alleviate the current level of homelessness must set aside protected resources for homeless-system partners to access for their clients. Despite considerable knowledge about strategies for expanding affordable housing, little is said about whether or how to target that housing construction for homeless prevention or to overcome current episodes of homelessness. Yet cities are peppered with efforts to do just that, albeit with mixed success.

The largest sticking point in this policy debate is whether set-asides within the supply of affordable housing will *incentivize* homelessness as desperately poor individuals calculate the suffering they are willing to tolerate to secure a better life for themselves. At the same time, some in the community argue that the affordable units should be preserved for people who have been struggling on their own without the help of shelter services and who therefore should not be penalized by those who are currently homeless being allowed to jump over an affordable-housing waitlist.

These debates and tensions swirl around the discussion of what avenues are available, and what policies and programs should be put in place, to facilitate housing the homeless. The standards set for housing assistance eligibility thus must reflect the desire to avoid the moral hazard of jumping the queue through the shelter system and, at the same time, ensure that the allocation of this scarce resource targets those most in need.

Three broad categories of actions have been tried. They are:

- Housing navigation services and supports that ease the process of finding and securing an apartment and address modest barriers to moving

- Rental assistance strategies that help tenants pay for apartments available in the community
- Development solutions that create incentives and set-aside units in new building construction for people who are at risk or formerly homeless

These actions rarely exist in isolation. The first two can be thought of as demand-side solutions that include numerous strategies to empower people to obtain, or maintain, housing that exists in the market. The third is a supply-side solution to create additional affordable units targeted to the homeless.

HELPING CLIENTS COMPETE IN THE HOUSING MARKET

Shelter is meant to be temporary, a step toward the goal of helping shelter residents move into the most appropriate form of housing. Barriers to moving out of shelter are high, however. Shelter residents need to fill out housing applications, pay the first month's rent on top of a security deposit, pay to move their furniture into the new apartment or to buy new furniture, and, perhaps the most challenging hurdle, find a viable unit and convince a landlord they are an attractive tenant.

Providing moving assistance to those in shelter is critical, and many cities have become remarkably adept at identifying the supports needed to ensure a successful transition from the street or shelter into housing.

Service providers can develop permanency plans for clients that set expectations for the apartment search. Case workers often guide residents through the paperwork needed to support applications and help them set goals for visiting available apartments. Beyond that, many housing support organizations also expedite the process by generating lists of available units with affordable rents. Providers may also help with moving expenses, such as purchasing furniture and starter packs of kitchen supplies and toiletries.

Because of the differences in housing markets and cultural expectations from city to city, the approach to navigating the rental market for the homeless varies. Vacancy rates in New York City are consistently low (3.63 percent in 2017; 1.15 percent for units renting for less than $800 a month), making it very difficult to find something affordable.[12] As a result, the city has had to turn to an intermediary—for-profit brokers—to develop relationships with landlords in order to secure apartments for homeless clients. In Paris, one of the most expensive cities in the world, the government is implementing various programs, including renting apartments directly from landlords and reintroducing rent-control measures, in an attempt to make existing housing affordable and available to the people experiencing homelessness in the absence of sufficient social housing.

The overarching goal of finding apartments is the same across cities, but the implementation differs based on the particular market challenges and housing dynamics in each city.

New York City compensates brokers for units they bring to the shelters' attention that are leased by shelter residents. Over the years, the city has implemented various versions of the "broker's bonus" in an effort to bring more private-market housing to the disposal of homeless clients. As of 2020, New York City is targeting both brokers and landlords by offering a broker's fee equal to 15 percent of the annual rent and a landlord bonus of $4,300.[13] There is constant debate within the City about whether these solutions are cost-effective and how much, if anything, should be offered in bonuses. Because the city offers rental assistance at a fixed amount, the landlord bonus is an attempt to compete in a very tight private housing market by increasing the overall amount landlords receive. While there have been attempts to determine how many additional apartments a given bonus incentivizes, without a comparison group of landlords and brokers who do not receive the bonus, it is challenging to ascertain the impact. As it is not feasible to implement the program in only part of the city to study its effects, there has been no reliable analysis of the cost-effectiveness of offering bonuses.

Paris expanded its rehousing efforts in 2007 into the private market. The Louez Solidaire (Solidarity Rent) program entices private-sector landlords to rent apartments to the city to be used for people living in shelters, refugees, and young people leaving child welfare. In Europe, this program design, called rental intermediation, offers vulnerable households a way to rent from landlords more easily through a third party. The city guarantees that landlords are paid the rent and for any damages incurred. In addition, rent is low and the renters receive social support. By

2018, the program had housed more than three thousand people, and the national state was extending it across France.[14] In 2019, Paris reintroduced rent-control measures after a previous attempt in 2015 was overturned in court. The revised measure caps the amount of rent allowed and serves as a strategy for controlling increasing housing costs in the city.

In both New York City and Paris, the government had to engage landlords and use the private-sector stock of apartments to meet the demand for housing for the homeless. The scale of the need is so vast that the social sector and government combined have been unable to build enough housing.

Rather than working with private-market landlords who are seeking to maximize rent and profits, a small pilot program in New York City partnered with nonprofit affordable-housing providers that received government subsidies or tax abatements in exchange for agreeing to limit rent increases. The program, Come Home NYC, developed by the national nonprofit Enterprise Community Partners, incrementally ramped up from 2014 through 2016, and addressed landlord concerns as a way of enticing affordable-housing developers to accept homeless clients. The main components of the program include assistance in finding and leasing to tenants, support for tenants once housed, and a fund to cover missed rent or damage to the apartments.[15]

The New York City municipal government incorporated some lessons from the pilot program in its rental assistance program, Living in Communities (LINC), including, in particular, the creation of a security fund to provide additional financial support to landlords for unpaid rent or damage to an apartment. LINC vouchers provided to more than eighty-five hundred households between 2015 and 2017 were targeted toward the entire housing market.[16] In 2019, the LINC program became the Family Homelessness and Eviction Prevention Subsidies. Affordable housing, with rents that are both fixed and lower, is a better long-term strategy for the homeless than market-rate housing. Because scarce affordable housing is also in high demand among other low-income individuals and families, a private-sector rental strategy that targets only affordable housing is insufficient. Efforts are under way to better position the formerly homeless to compete in this limited-supply market.

PRIORITY ACCESS TO RENTAL ASSISTANCE
AND PUBLIC HOUSING

To move into housing from a shelter, individuals and families need support in paying rent, whether temporarily or indefinitely. In the absence of rent-controlled affordable housing, some US cities issue housing vouchers that provide a certain amount of money each month to subsidize market-rate rents. The federal Housing Choice Voucher Program, an outgrowth of Section 8 housing, is managed locally, usually by the public housing authority. Setting aside an allocation of these vouchers for the homeless, done through local discretion, is often a contentious issue due to the low availability of vouchers compared with the high need. Supply is also shrinking, as annual federal appropriations are being stretched to cover existing vouchers with escalating rents. Waiting lists are long, and many qualified applicants may never receive a voucher.

The same high demand applies to public housing authority properties and social housing. Turnover rates are extremely low, and set-asides of units in publicly owned and managed social housing follow the same dynamics as those for housing vouchers. A central resource carefully allocates the units to ensure they go to individuals in greatest need. The rudimentary surrogate for need is the status of being homeless, or the length of time a person has been homeless, which creates a perverse incentive to stay unsheltered long enough to qualify.

In Paris, applications for social housing are prioritized through a scoring system, with households receiving points for criteria demonstrating different levels of need, such as the number of persons in the household, forcible eviction, or disability. Homelessness receives the highest number of points by far of any criteria—17 extra points if the person is residing in a homeless shelter and 25 points if an outreach team documents them as living on the street.[17]

New York City faced a crisis point in 2003 with ever-more-constrained funding from the federal government for rental vouchers, a waiting list for public housing of more than 100,000 individuals and families, and a homeless population rising to 40,000. Acknowledging that there would never be enough vouchers to keep pace with demand, the city government chose to disassociate the federally funded resources from the shelter system and create a locally funded rental-assistance program designed to address the unique homelessness situation.

Several considerations came into play and competed for attention. Who would be eligible? How many vouchers would be required to meet the need? How long would residents receive support, and how much would it cost? Then–New York City mayor Michael Bloomberg wanted a program that encouraged work, and in 2004, his administration launched Housing Stability Plus (HSP), a five-year housing voucher for shelter residents that decreased in value by 20 percent each year. To help fund the voucher, the city could tap the federal Temporary Assistance for Needy Families (TANF) program if the shelter resident was on federal public assistance, thus limiting eligibility for the voucher to those qualifying and in compliance with that program. Compliance requires that the resident be employed (at a below-poverty level) or be actively searching for employment. As the name suggests, the program offers time-limited cash assistance.

During its first nine months, the HSP voucher proved an initial success by placing 2,850 New York City households in permanent housing.[18] However, many tenants did not earn the increase in salary commensurate with making up for the decreasing voucher amount and paying the rent. And those who did increase their income often lost eligibility for public assistance and, therefore, were no longer qualified for the voucher. In addition, the living conditions of the apartments being rented were not subject to the same controls as in other federally funded rental assistance programs, and substandard units were rented while unscrupulous landlords made side deals with tenants asking for additional rent on top of the voucher.

After monitoring the impact and results of the housing voucher program, the city changed course, launching a new program in 2007, Work Advantage, that addressed many of the problems with Housing Stability Plus. The new program, targeted toward shelter residents working at least twenty hours a week, was intended to last for one to two years. The city added an inspection mandate for new apartments and required landlords to sign an agreement that rendered side deals illegal. During its tenure from 2007 to mid-2011, the program housed more than 45,000 people.[19] It ended abruptly when New York State governor Andrew Cuomo withdrew the program's eligibility for matching state and federal funds under

TANF. The city, unwilling to bear the program's entire cost, ended it. As a consequence, homelessness accelerated. During the years that Work Advantage was in place, the number of people in shelter remained below 40,000.[20] In the years that followed, without a subsidy beyond Section 8, the number of homeless in shelter increased to an all-time high above 60,000 in the winter of 2014.[21] Since then, despite the reintroduction of a rental assistance program and various rehousing efforts, the number of homeless in New York City has remained above 50,000.[22]

These iterations of various programs generated an environment where creative city solutions could be developed, evaluated, and adjusted. In 2014, when New York City mayor Bill de Blasio launched the LINC rental assistance program, responding to advocates' demands by creating a wholly city-funded rent subsidy for the formerly homeless, it built on lessons from earlier programs. Such efforts to tap into the private rental market and facilitate access to already-built apartments found some success in tailoring solutions to the difficulties that market competition poses for low-income home seekers.

Apartment search, moving support, short-term rental assistance, and ongoing case management have been combined in the quickly expanding practice of Rapid Rehousing. Using a combination of approaches, Rapid Rehousing intervenes to move people quickly from homelessness to housing, often with temporary, light case management. The goal is to identify the person or family's housing needs, find appropriate housing, provide move-in assistance and short-term rental support, and follow up with minimal case management.

The Rapid Rehousing model was expanded nationally as a demonstration project supported by the US Department of Housing and Urban Development (HUD). A formal evaluation published in 2016 by Abt Associates showed that only 10 percent of families that were part of the study returned to homelessness within one year of exiting it.[23] However, three-quarters of the households moved at least once in the twelve-month period, indicating that the families were not stably housed, which is a risk factor for future homelessness. The evaluation also found that Rapid Rehousing was 40 percent more effective in preventing clients from returning to homelessness when administered in areas with vacancy rates above 5 percent.[24] While these data give one pause over the power of the approach, by contrast, a continued stay in shelter for a longer period without a structured permanency strategy both costs more and perpetuates the trauma of homelessness. After the launch of this multicity demonstration, the use of Rapid Rehousing has expanded and is a promising practice that cities will, and should, continue to refine.[25]

SUPPLY SIDE: BUILD BUILD BUILD

National, regional, and local incentive strategies are being structured to induce private developers and nonprofits to expand the supply of affordable housing units. Mayors have taken the lead in pulling together a mix of governmental funds and private development dollars to bring more affordable units into neighborhoods squeezed by gentrification and displacement. Within this context, mayors must make tough policy choices over whether to require set-asides of units for the formerly homeless. Although the involvement of local developers often demands strong balance sheets, successful strategies that include the once homeless are emerging.

One shift at the national level in the United States has been away from direct funding of construction of units to house the very poor toward tax credits to incentivize private development for low-income renters. The Low-Income Housing Tax Credit has become the primary source of federal support for affordable housing development, producing over 3 million units since its enactment in the Tax Reform Act of 1986. The tax credit offsets taxes the housing developers would otherwise have to pay. The credits can counterbalance development costs, reducing the overall expense of the building, and, as the law stipulates, can ensure lower rental payments. States and cities still may be required to add additional public funds to further subsidize the lowest-income households.

One avenue to securing these funds is local revenue raising. Although this is a straightforward—albeit sometimes politically fraught—solution, the impact can be significant if cities target an affordable-housing portion for the homeless. In November 2016, Los Angeles voters approved Proposition HHH, which authorized the city to issue $1.2 billion in general-obligation bonds to develop housing and facilities for the homeless, along with affordable housing for those at risk of homelessness. A total of

Another strategy encourages development through inclusionary housing, which uses building codes or zoning regulations to increase production of affordable housing. Inclusionary zoning (IZ) policies, for example, link the production of affordable housing to the production of market-rate housing by requiring or incentivizing new residential developments to make a certain percentage of the housing units affordable to low- or moderate-income residents at below-market rates. According to estimates, 80 percent of IZ policies in the United States are mandatory.[35] Many of these mandatory policies have "in lieu of" provisions that allow a developer to pay a penalty, usually to an affordable housing fund, so that it can build fewer affordable units. Voluntary or incentivized IZ policies typically allow the developer to build more units than conventional zoning would allow, and other policies grant fast-track permitting that lets developers build more quickly.

Several European countries have incorporated some inclusionary practices into comprehensive land-use planning. However, when the capacity of public social housing or public subsidy of affordable housing cannot meet the demand, it is increasingly necessary for localities to craft additional policies that regulate, through mandates or incentives, the development of affordable housing by private- or civil-sector organizations. In some countries, inclusionary housing is also necessary to counteract an unintended consequence of public housing developments—racial segregation. The laws are only a tool and still require aggressive participation from local officials to encourage and enforce the development of affordable housing.

New York City has a two-part inclusionary zoning program. The voluntary component offers housing developers a density bonus (i.e., permission to build more units) in designated areas of the city for building affordable housing units onsite or in another location. Affordable housing is available to households earning 80 percent of the area median income (AMI). The required mandatory inclusionary housing component calls for a "share," a number of permanent affordable housing units to be carved out for any new housing development in medium- and high-density areas that have been rezoned to promote new housing production.[36] The developer can choose among four options that require fewer affordable housing units to be carved out if the AMI requirement is lower, versus more affordable units if the AMI is higher, and the options range from 40 percent AMI to 135 percent AMI. The fifth option allows developers to pay into an affordable housing fund if the project does not exceed twenty-five units. In 2016, New York City went even further and required that developers who used certain tax abatements to build luxury buildings allocate their community set-aside units for the homeless sheltered in that community. Some developers balked, refusing to comply or to withdraw from the tax program; others, after much reassurance and support from the city, agreed. New York estimated in 2018 that roughly 750 homeless households would find new housing through the pilot program.

Baltimore's inclusionary planning law has created very few low-income units since the law was enacted in 2007. A bill introduced in 2016 that would have strengthened the law was voted down.[37] In a promising move in mid-2020, the city requested proposals from vendors to analyze the current inclusionary housing law and recommend strategies to increase its effectiveness.[38]

Inclusionary housing is a key tool that holds the potential to expand the number of housing units and, by doing so, reduce homelessness. Cities or regions can also encourage targeted zoning changes and incentives to build denser housing and better utilization of existing space. In the city of Los Angeles, officials have proposed the development of accessory dwelling units (ADUs), or tiny secondary homes, to house persons who are homeless. These solutions are less costly to build, often prefabricated, and can be clustered on public or private land or even located in the backyard of a single-family home. The city used a $100,000 grant from Bloomberg Philanthropies to study the concept and eventually won a $1 million grant to pilot the model from the same organization as part of the US Mayors Challenge. Meanwhile, in 2017, Los Angeles County was already embarking on its second small-scale ADU pilot to fund construction of up to six new units, or preservation of unpermitted units, to house homeless individuals and families.[39] To encourage ADUs by easing restrictions to their development, the state of California enacted legislation in October 2019 intended to help localities use this innovation to increase their affordable housing supply.[40] The Los Angeles city and county models will focus on installing ADUs in the backyards of family homes. City homeowners will be given a stipend of between $10,000 and $30,000 and will be allowed to charge the resident a modest rent to be paid with income or a government-subsidized voucher.

Another creative solution involves cross-subsidizing affordable housing with payments for shelter services. Since public financing is slanted toward the immediate need of shelter over the longer-term need of housing, many cities are using shelter funding to better target homelessness prevention. One New York City nonprofit found a way to use shelter funding to also help pay for permanent housing for the shelter residents. BRC opened a model in 2018 that was developed to house both a shelter and permanent-housing residence in a building owned by the nonprofit. BRC uses surplus revenue from the market-rate shelter rent to subsidize the operating deficit caused by extremely low rents paid by the formerly homeless households to whom it rents the low-income housing units. Also, rather than spending public funds to rent a building for shelter from a private landlord, the money is now invested in a BRC-owned building that will continue to be used for the homeless.

Canada has shown how the national government can play a significant role in addressing homelessness. In 2017, Prime Minister Justin Trudeau set a national goal to reduce chronic homelessness by half in ten years. To achieve this, Canada developed a national housing plan that includes a $15.9 billion National Housing Co-investment Fund to generate up to 60,000 new housing units and repair up to 240,000 units through a combination of direct subsidies and low-interest loans.[41]

Although many cities do not have sufficient funding or the right tools, an impressive range of innovations has emerged as cities formulate housing strategies in an effort to tackle homelessness. Cities can make a difference, as this chapter demonstrates. Local housing plans are integrating homelessness strategies into policies on affordable housing that break through policy silos. Cities are balancing short-term solutions with more ambitious long-term planning that includes finding homes for those with severe barriers to housing. And, numerous mayors, while being held accountable for their local plan, are advocating for more resources from national or regional governments to support the most vulnerable.

5 Supportive Housing to Target Complex Needs

A comprehensive housing plan considers both affordability and the many reasons why a person may be living unsheltered. Homelessness brought on by an economic crisis can be solved with affordable housing, but chronic homelessness requires more than simply a place to stay. It requires additional support to ensure a person stays housed. Daniel Broome lived on New York City streets for years with substance-use problems before finally moving into a home. "I'll never forget," Daniel said during an interview with Breaking Ground, a nonprofit that operates nearly four thousand units of supportive housing across the city, "when [outreach workers] came to get me the day before a big snowstorm and said 'you're going home.'"[1] For the chronically homeless, or people with severe mental illness, depression, or substance-use disorders, more-intensive housing options are needed. Supportive housing is an evidence-based model of permanent, affordable housing that combines on-site services and supports to leaseholding tenants who need assistance to live successfully on their own.

Permanent supportive housing (PSH) is an innovation that grew out of a grassroots movement of community-based nonprofits in New York City in the 1970s and 1980s. PSH was driven by the need to organize a chaotic and inadequate array of government services for the community's frailest members. Groups serving the homeless and mentally ill saw the need for an immediate, independent, and supportive environment for the city's most vulnerable people who require more intensive services in addition to housing. New York City service providers not only came up with the model for supportive housing but also leveraged a funding stream from the Single Room Occupancy (SRO) Loan program to finance the bricks-and-mortar component. Providers matched that program with another city program that sold the SRO buildings to nonprofits for $1 instead of tearing them down. With the city in fiscal crisis, homelessness on the rise, and the closure of psychiatric hospitals leaving patients with nowhere to go, innovation ensued and supportive housing was created.

Supportive housing expanded nationally in 1987 after the federal government enacted the McKinney-Vento Homeless Assistance Act, which authorized more than $1 billion in funding for long-term comprehensive services and housing dedicated to addressing homelessness.[2] This funding ignited a new era of programs and housing interventions to stem homelessness nationally. The new law established funding sources for emergency food and shelter grants for the homeless and included a supportive-housing demonstration program for transitional and permanent housing. Over the years since, US cities have relied on this funding to finance shelter services, outreach efforts, and supportive housing.

Three years later, in 1990, New York City and New York State signed the landmark NY/NY Agreement, which expanded supportive housing for the homeless and mentally ill by 3,615 units through a combination of new construction and rentals.[3] This agreement marked a systematic shift in homeless housing away from volunteer and faith-based organizations toward government-funded supportive housing. Since then, the practice of pairing bricks-and-mortar construction—leveraged by low-income housing revenue streams—with on-site social service contracts has proliferated globally.

Dennis Culhane, a researcher at the University of Pennsylvania, conducted a large-scale analysis in 1999 of homeless people placed in the NY/NY supportive-housing program. His matched-pair study involved seven systems of care, from shelter services to Medicaid and criminal justice, and demonstrated the cost-effectiveness of supportive housing from the savings across these systems. He found that the homeless were each accruing public costs of more than $40,000 annually by accessing the seven systems. After these residents were placed into supportive housing, their public costs were reduced by $16,282 per person each year. At the time of Culhane's analysis, the cost of supportive housing for each resident was $17,277, producing a net cost of just $995 per unit each year.[4] A modest incremental investment produced stunningly improved outcomes for these individuals.

By the beginning of the twenty-first century, fueled by decades of growth, funding, evaluations, and success, supportive housing had become a critical element in a comprehensive housing strategy, not only in the United States but also in Canada, Europe, and elsewhere.

When Mayor David Briley assumed leadership of Nashville in 2018, supportive housing as an effective solution to homelessness had a strong evidence base. After his first year in office, Mayor Briley created an ambitious affordable housing plan called Under One Roof 2029 with the goal of increasing affordable housing by 10,000 units in ten years. The housing plan included a supportive housing and service center to be built in the downtown area. Nashville's Downtown Homeless Service Center and permanent supportive housing complex was slated to serve the chronically homeless. The first-floor service center would function as a coordinated entry point and provide showers, public restrooms, and case management services.[5] Lacking capital investment from the state or federal government, Mayor Briley found ways to finance the $24 million project using city resources such as a land swap, bonds, and tax revenue. The city had already selected a contractor to build the center when Briley lost the mayor's office to John Cooper in the September 2019 election. After initial skepticism during a reevaluation of the Under One Roof 2029 plan, the new mayor confirmed his commitment to the supportive-housing component of the plan, which is expected to be completed by 2021.[6]

WHAT EXACTLY *IS* SUPPORTIVE HOUSING?

Supportive housing is affordable permanent housing with additional wraparound services, often on-site. Although initially developed for the chronic and street homeless with mental illness, supportive housing has expanded to serve other at-risk homeless populations such as families with children, people with histories of incarceration, and youth aging out of foster care. It allows tenants to decide where to live and what services to use. Choice is important because it gives tenants ownership of their lives. Tenants have leases and the same rights as any citizen when it comes to eviction or other housing concerns. They are expected to pay rent, take out the trash, and cook and clean for themselves, although in some instances, meals are provided. As units are meant to be permanently affordable, rent is usually capped at a percentage of the household's income. In the United States, many people who are homeless and coping with severe mental illness qualify for Supplemental Security Income or Social Security Disability Insurance, and a portion of that federal income is used to pay rent. Different types of housing vouchers or rental assistance can also supplement rent to ensure affordability.

There are many permutations of supportive housing, differing as to which population is served, what services are offered, how clients are admitted, and how the program is funded. Many models of supportive housing are publicly funded but administered through nonprofits experienced in providing housing and services to the homeless. In the United States and Canada, nonprofit providers are critical to the success of supportive housing, offering services that vary greatly across cities and programs. For example, the Nashville model was designed specifically for people experiencing chronic homelessness. New York City's Walton House, which opened in 2018 and is run by the nonprofit Jericho Project, was developed to serve veterans and young adults by offering such amenities as a computer room and technology workshops. Although most follow the basic model, housing providers in different cities target supportive housing and services to their specific populations, which garners community support for the project.

Because housing in general, and supportive housing specifically, is expensive, national investment is essential. Government support ranges from construction financing to ongoing rent payment assistance and social services funding. Many affordable-housing developers and nonprofits own the buildings and provide ongoing services. Multiple levels of government have buoyed city efforts to expand supportive-housing capacity through financial supports or tools. For instance, the federal Low-Income Housing Tax Credit offers tax breaks to developers, investors, and nonprofits for direct investment in low-income housing. By agreeing to build affordable housing, private investors receive a dollar-for-dollar credit against their federal tax liability.

Supportive housing comes in two models: congregate and scattered site. *Congregate* supportive housing generally takes the form of a stand-alone building with a majority of the units reserved for the homeless population, though it may include some low-income residents. More-recent projects tend to be new construction designed specifically for the population to be served, such as veterans, families, or those with severe mental illness. A less frequently deployed model provides supportive services through a local storefront to *scattered* apartments—a mix of living spaces in different buildings throughout the community. Under the scattered approach, a nonprofit holds the property lease and subleases to the tenants. In New York City, a nonprofit holding a state or city contract rents private-market scattered-site apartments on the tenants' behalf, and case managers visit tenants in their apartments.

Some policy makers and individual providers have a philosophical preference for the scattered-site model because it favors fuller integration into the community through independent apartments and it is also more expeditious to find and rent apartments than to finance and construct a new building. But there are also drawbacks to the scattered-site model. Changes in the rental market, such as increasing rents or intolerant landlords, make it difficult for the nonprofit provider to rent the same apartment for many years. Being scattered contributes to social isolation for some tenants, who might otherwise thrive in a congregate model where on-site support is always at hand. And delivering services to multiple locations is inefficient. Typically, scattered-site case managers visit, at most, once a week and often once a month, and this infrequency can be a challenge for tenants who need more support. As rental markets tighten and housing prices increase, the scattered-site model becomes less and less desirable.

IMPLEMENTING THE MODEL

Different cities and providers identify different compilations of services necessary for their residents to succeed in supportive housing. In Los

Angeles, supportive housing has become a necessary tool in the city's battle against homelessness. Supportive services include everything from health care to job training, education, and community-building activities. Los Angeles mayor Eric Garcetti signed the Permanent Supportive Housing Ordinance in 2018 to cut down on the regulatory red tape that often delays building new supportive housing. The law aimed to reduce the timeline for development of supportive housing to less than one year, a process that previously could take up to five years. With a dedicated funding stream identified through Proposition HHH, the city is aggressively tackling barriers preventing the development of more supportive housing in an effort to reach its goal of 10,000 more units.

Beyond regulatory hurdles, however, political or community backlash can often delay or derail projects entirely. Frustrated by the slow progress in building homeless and supportive housing, in late 2019, the Los Angeles County Board of Supervisors began requiring that public agencies partner with the private sector, submit progress reports to the county, and develop a comprehensive community outreach plan to mitigate some of the continued delays.[7]

New York City has a variety of supportive-housing models, including True Colors, developed in collaboration with the musical artist Cyndi Lauper and geared toward lesbian, gay, bisexual, and transgendered youth with services such as benefits advocacy and money management. Since the city's large investment in supportive housing in 2005 (for 9,000 units), more evidence has emerged on what interventions are most effective at working with hard-to-serve populations. As a result, with homelessness on the rise in 2015, the city developed a plan to fund, build, and support 15,000 additional units over a fifteen-year period. Drawing on the growing evidence base in social services, the New York City request for proposal to fund services for congregate supportive housing asked providers to demonstrate their ability to implement evidence-based or evidence-informed practices, including but not limited to person-centered planning, motivational interviewing, and recovery-oriented and trauma-informed case management.[8] The city increased the amount of service funding available, and, rather than leaving it up solely to the nonprofits to determine the mix of services, providers in New York City have to demonstrate how they plan to incorporate these promising program models.

Houston has committed federal, state, and local funds toward supportive housing and Housing First. With about 1,500 units of supportive
housing, the city identified the need for 2,500 more and continued to
work toward funding and creating more units to close the gap. In January
2019, Houston funded a residential building to accommodate the chronically homeless with alcohol addiction that offers wraparound support
through licensed chemical dependency counselors and life counselors
available onsite.

Although the services provided in supportive housing are as diverse as
the cities and the residents, standardization to ensure fidelity to model
elements that produce results is necessary. For this reason, the Corporation
for Supportive Housing and other national groups have defined the characteristics that should be present in all supportive-housing programs; for
example, that programs should target the homeless or those at-risk of
homelessness, be affordable, provide tenants with a lease and supportive
services, and connect tenants to networks.[9] Not all programs described as
supportive housing follow these standards, however. The US Interagency
Council on Homelessness recognizes there are many design iterations and
cites the core components as affordable housing with voluntary services
and no time limits on residency.[10]

As supportive housing expands to new countries and new populations,
much more is being learned. As long as cities have rigorous systems in
place to measure results, the adaptations that successfully reduce homelessness and keep people housed supply considerable evidence to the field.

With slightly less than 3,000 supportive-housing beds, the city of
Baltimore is exploring multiple pathways to innovation.[11] The city pursued a creative pilot program in 2019 to serve vulnerable homeless
through a form of supportive housing. The Baltimore Housing Authority,
Mayor's Office, and a local nonprofit worked together to house up to fifty
chronically homeless individuals and families in vacant public housing
apartments in need of repair. Since federal funding was unavailable for
sufficient repairs, city organizations shared the cost to rehabilitate apartments and used housing vouchers to pay the rent. Additionally, the nonprofit Health Care for the Homeless was brought in to provide services to
help attend to the residents' wellness needs.[12] With the goal of delivering
immediate results and some relief to homeless residents in Baltimore, the

Housing Plus Pilot program is one example of working across city divisions to create necessary housing through a mix of available resources.

HOUSING READY VERSUS HOUSING FIRST

The typical path to available housing for the homeless is like ascending a staircase, from living on the streets, to shelter, to temporary housing, and then, to the last step, achieving permanent housing. Housing is seen as a reward for compliance and progressive improvement. Social service delivery systems treat people first and, as they stabilize, address their underlying causes for homelessness. Eventually, clients become what is referred to as *housing ready*.[13] While seemingly logical, in practice people's behavior does not often follow an upward or linear trajectory. The traditional pipeline from street to housing does not always work, and in reality, those who are unable to progress or overcome their challenges are left without housing. As homelessness increases, the problem becomes more unwieldy. Cities struggle to find ways to bolster options along the housing continuum, but are too often able to focus only on the immediate need to house people in shelters.

In response to the lengthy, often cumbersome process of qualifying the homeless for housing—becoming *housing ready*—a clinical psychologist and practitioner in New York City, Sam Tsemberis, created the nonprofit Pathways to Housing in the 1990s and developed the Housing First model. Using a distinctive theory of change, Housing First has grown into an overarching philosophy adopted by many cities and supportive-housing providers globally.[14] The initial program had a simple premise: house homeless individuals struggling with mental illness without requiring them to be housing ready. Housing First does not require engagement in treatment, yet offers services the person may use once they are housed. The philosophical underpinning is that homelessness can be most efficiently ended by providing people with access to affordable housing even before goalposts toward housing readiness have been met. Some consider the Pathways model similar to scattered-site supportive housing since both employ rental apartments in the community and offer onsite services in the tenant's apartment. However, the Pathways model offered care through Assertive Community Treatment teams, which is a costly model involving a team of providers including nurses and psychiatrists who are available 24/7.

The Pathways to Housing program was rigorously tested using the gold standard of evaluation, a randomized controlled trial (RCT) that *randomly* assigns participants into either an experimental group or a control group while studying outcome variables over time. The longitudinal study followed participants, assigned either to the Housing First program or to typical treatment care for four years. The results, published in the *American Journal of Public Health* in 2004, found housing stability for 80 percent of the Housing First participants compared with 30 percent housing stability for the control group after two years.[15] These results showed that homeless individuals with mental illness could in fact remain in a stable home if given an apartment coupled with voluntary wraparound services.

The Housing First concept gave rise to numerous questions, including whether the program reduces substance use and whether being housed early increases resident's participation in mental health treatment. Other, more independent evaluations followed the first to confirm replication of results.[16] One of the first independent studies, conducted by HUD's Office of Policy Development and Research in 2007, analyzed thirty-three US programs and determined that nine programs reflected the model and an additional fourteen contained some Housing First elements. The study team selected three programs, including the Pathways program in New York City, to evaluate their outcomes and found promising results: 84 percent of participants retained housing after one year. Of those, 43 percent remained housed the entire year and 41 percent left at some point but returned.[17]

The Housing First approach is easily adaptable in different cultures and political contexts because of its focus on the rehabilitative qualities of housing as the first and most important step in addressing homelessness. In 2009, Canada implemented one of the world's largest demonstration projects, known as At Home/Chez Soi. The project, which cost over $100 million, was funded by the national government and followed more than two thousand residents with mental illness over four years. The final results, published in 2014, showed that Housing First participants had higher rates of housing stability (62 percent) compared with those who accessed the normal array of housing services (31 percent).[18] France adopted a similar model in creating its program, Un Chez-Soi d'abord Programme, which selected four cities, including Paris, as test sites from 2011 through 2016. Using a randomized controlled trial, the pilot produced evidence showing improved housing stability for participants.

Because permanent supportive housing is aimed at the most vulnerable, many of these programs subscribe to a Housing First approach and do not require residents to be in treatment prior to moving into housing. Supportive housing has also proven cost-effective, an important factor in its adoption, and can even produce savings where the costs of unhoused chronically ill can be astronomically high. From New York to Chicago to Los Angeles, the program has effectively reduced the use of homeless shelters, hospitals, emergency rooms, jails, and prisons. An RCT study conducted in Chicago from 2003 to 2006 saw a 29 percent and 24 percent decrease in hospital days and emergency room visits, respectively, for the experimental group in supportive housing; the evidence helped to establish a budget justification for supportive housing.[19] Similarly, a 2017 RAND Corporation pre-post study of a PSH in Los Angeles found that residents used fewer public resources after being placed in housing, resulting in a 20 percent program cost offset for the county.[20] PSH programs that target higher-need individuals often end up saving more because those residents tend to use more costly services prior to housing.

WHO ARE THE RESIDENTS OF SUPPORTIVE HOUSING?

Once supportive housing is up and running, the housing operators (often nonprofits) have to ensure that apartments are occupied and that approaching vacancies are backfilled. The process for identifying and selecting tenants is often controversial, as effective targeting is crucial if a city seeks to maximize the use of supportive housing. Some cities, like Houston, have already launched a comprehensive coordinated system to identify those most in need; others, like Baltimore, are still in the process.

Supportive housing works best for people who have multiple needs, such as housing instability, no or low income, serious and persistent health problems, or mental health or drug addiction challenges, or both.

MAKING CHOICES

Tamiru Mammo

I was with a group visiting a shelter in Bogotá when we met Eva. She was distinctive for her elegant wardrobe, black gloves, meticulously applied makeup, and warm smile. Eva, a resident of the shelter, was a magnet for staff and other clients who happily greeted her with kisses and hugs. She was gendered male at birth, but identified as a woman for much of her life, and, because of that, was stigmatized.

After living on the streets for several years, Eva eventually decided to go into a city-operated shelter. The city of Bogotá uses a step-up shelter system whereby people living on the street start out by entering a crisis day shelter. When a resident stabilizes, follows rules, participates in the programs, and reaches certain milestones, they progress to nicer facilities, with more amenities, fewer restrictions, and greater privileges, all with the ultimate goal of transitioning to independence.

Eva had reached the final shelter step, the Comunidad de Vida, a beautiful campus with manicured lawns, client-tended gardens, and art classes. In this program, residents receive continued access to medical and mental health treatment, group therapies, employment assistance, and life skills training, all with the expectation that they will go off campus and look for a job. The Comunidad de Vida prepares and supports their residents' transition into permanent housing and independence.

Progressing through the shelter system, Eva remained stable and happy, preparing for hormonal therapy and dreaming of eventually getting transitional surgery. However, she had been in the shelter system for years. It became a place where she could belong and thrive, and she had a wide support system of staff and other clients. Outside this place, the world was not so supportive. Her family had disowned her. There are still many people in the community who will not accept a transgendered woman, and threats of violence are real.

Eva was hesitant to move out, but the city was already rationing the at-capacity shelter programs. I felt conflicted about the best course of action for the client versus a government with limited resources. The goal of transitional housing should be to move people on to permanent housing and reintegrate them into society. But what happens if the larger society is not ready to accept the person? What if Eva could instead have gone right into supportive housing, building a community of support where she could remain and not have to face another potentially disastrous transition? Bogotá provides some support to residents discharged to permanent housing, though it has not adopted a supportive housing model. Regardless of the model of permanence, some former shelter residents will struggle to make this transition, as the services are not one-size-fits-all. The societal factors that drive a transgendered person, a survivor of domestic violence, an LGBTQ youth, or a person living with HIV/AIDS to the street will not be fixed by the time they move on.

I worry about what happened to Eva. I don't know where she is or how she is doing. Providers and cities are faced with these difficult decisions of how and when to ask people to move; I am not sure there are always right answers.

Government agencies, which have a vested stake in the success of the housing, frequently choose to identify the appropriate tenants to fill vacancies rather than leaving it to the housing operator. However, housing operators are often required by lenders to fill units quickly since vacancies mean lost revenue. The New York City agency that oversees homelessness refers three clients for each vacancy, allowing the housing provider to select the one that fits best with the program model.

Does supportive housing serve individuals most at risk? New York City media often investigate whether on-site managers are selecting the most stable, compliant candidates rather than those who would benefit most from the support.[21] There is no evidence to show that providers or the city are intentionally filling units with higher-functioning residents; indeed the opposite result is guaranteed by the city-mandated requirement that applicants be chronically homeless with a serious mental illness or substance-use disorder. As resources are limited and supportive housing is in short supply, targeting the housing for those on the severe end of a spectrum is the best use of this resource.

GROWING GLOBAL SUPPORT FOR SUPPORTIVE HOUSING

The Canadian city of Edmonton has also been at the forefront of under-standing the critical role of supportive housing. In 2005, the city's Community Plan on Housing and Supportive Services identified support-ive housing as a means to tackle homelessness.[22] Even so, Edmonton has struggled to create new units. Its Ten-Year Plan to End Homelessness, released in 2009, identified the need for 1,000 more units of supportive housing. By 2018, only 226 had been completed.[23] The challenges in exe-cuting Edmonton's supportive-housing vision are numerous, including zoning and density restrictions.

Community pushback is another major global barrier. For example, Holy Trinity Riverbend Anglican Church in Edmonton worked with a nonprofit organization in 2013 to propose a supportive-housing development, known colloquially as the Terwillegar project. The project was scrapped after intense opposition from the community, including a mounting legal challenge from a nearby homeowners' association. While community opposition can build quickly in reaction to such proposals, a city can work more closely with affected communities to head off such reaction, as by, for instance, making common spaces in the proposed building available for community meetings or by including a mixed-use development to provide affordable housing units to surrounding neighborhoods. Holy Trinity, through better community engagement, reconfigured the Terwillegar project to house families instead of single adults and to include a community space, day care, and a café. In 2019, the project did move forward. To combat the NIMBYism (not in my back yard), Homeward Trust, the nonprofit responsible for coordinating and implementing Edmonton's homeless plan, developed a "good neighbour" clause in its funding agreements to mitigate community concerns before and after development. The clause creates a process for community engagement that ensures residents' concerns are being both communicated and addressed.

Community fears are often overcome once the housing opens and neighbors can engage with the project through volunteerism or local activities. A Brooklyn, New York, development built in 2009 with 116 supportive-housing units, the Schermerhorn, also houses a practice area for the Brooklyn Ballet and a performance space for the community and

Figure 5. Hogar CDMX, a homeless housing complex for families, opened in Mexico City in 2017. Bloomberg Associates.

residents. Evidence from the Furman Center at New York University found that supportive-housing facilities can be correlated with increased neighborhood property values and stability when an improved building replaces an abandoned building or vacant land.[24]

A concerted focus on street homelessness in June 2016 by Mexico City mayor Dr. Miguel Ángel Mancera led to the creation of a citywide strategy that included robust prevention, intervention, and permanency programming. A key part of that plan was the development of Mexico's first supportive-housing program in 2017, which was designed to move homeless families from the streets, through a brief shelter stay, and into housing.[25]

With a limited budget for the project, the city was forced to be creative. Mexico City's secretary of social development, José Ramón Amieva, pushed staff to look for several properties that the city could purchase for a low price, or at no cost, and convert into supportive housing. They ended up selecting a formerly prestigious hotel that had fallen on hard times and was functioning as a hot-sheet hotel and then went into tax arrears. With

44 units and a capacity of up to 84 persons, this hotel became the city's first foray into housing with supportive services.

The former hotel was transformed into the site for the program Hogar CDMX (CDMX Home). Now clean and bright, the building includes a modern new facade designed in collaboration with prominent Mexican architect Emilio Cabrera. The original, light-filled atrium covering the four-story courtyard around which the rooms sit has been fully restored, and the individual units each carry the name of local flora. The city created a model with short-term leases and a goal that tenants should not stay there for more than one year. Rental contributions are saved and returned to the tenant at the point when they move on to a fully independent apartment in the community. Hogar CDMX also includes on-site social services and child care help to support, stabilize, and strengthen parenting skills.

Mexico City considers Hogar CDMX an example of supportive housing; however, there are two key differences between this program and the more traditional model implemented in the United States, Canada, and Europe. First, the short-term nature of the tenancy, up to a year, classifies Hogar CDMX as transitional or bridge housing rather than supportive housing, which is intended to be permanent. Second, Hogar CDMX does not employ a Housing First philosophy. Reflecting a relatively high-threshold model, some units remain empty for lack of tenants *ready* for the required move to housing.

To date, results at Hogar CDMX have been mixed, with only half of the tenants served from 2014 to 2018 transitioning into independent housing, and the other half having returned to shelter or left of their own accord without reporting a forwarding address. The facility managers have identified the need for more social work, drug treatment, and mental health services if the dual goals of lowering the admission threshold and improving permanency outcomes beyond Hogar CDMX are to be fully realized. Yet, though this Mexico City program is not traditional supportive housing, Hogar CDMX does represent an important milestone. At this writing, the city's first effort at dedicating housing and services to the homeless was being reevaluated and could be tailored to more closely align to the supportive-housing model.

KEY OUTCOMES AND OPPORTUNITIES

With more than 350,000 beds in different settings in the United States and others planned, the supportive-housing design and expected outcomes are evolving.[26] Various studies conducted across the United States and Canada have looked at such outcomes as housing stability, return to shelter, mental health, and quality of life. The studies use different sample sizes and formats. Some are pre-post studies that measure the impact of the intervention, while others are randomized controlled trials or a matched comparison group study that examines specific populations such as youth or those with serious mental illness. Due to the program's prevalence and the number of positive evaluations, permanent supportive housing is included in the US Department of Health and Human Services' tool kit of evidence-based practices, which provides guidance on replication and cites over 180 studies, reports, guidelines, and resources.[27]

As the street homeless often do not have health insurance, emergency costs are frequently not reimbursed and public hospitals often bear the cost. If the PSH can reduce costly emergency room visits, a compelling budgetary argument can therefore be made. A number of studies have assessed what other systems accrue in savings due to the stabilizing effect of PSH. A New York City Department of Health study calculated an average of $10,100 in annual cost savings, mostly due to reduced use of inpatient psychiatric beds. While some costs like shelter and emergency medical services are reduced, other costs, like access to food support or drug treatment, may increase. The cost-benefit data have been particularly helpful to cities when making a budgetary argument for funding supportive housing. New York City, Edmonton, and Los Angeles often cite the cost-effectiveness of supportive housing in their presentations to city council and budget officials in an effort to fund more beds.

Evidence on the health outcomes of supportive housing is mixed. A research committee in 2018 reviewed multiple studies and data and concluded that there was not enough evidence to demonstrate that permanent supportive housing helped to improve health outcomes.[28] Among the many reasons for this, consistent data are lacking, in part due to medical and privacy concerns. However, some evidence does show that chronic conditions stabilize in a Housing First model with on-site services and that hospitalizations related to psychiatric conditions are reduced.[29]

Outcomes for the homeless criminal justice population in supportive housing are also mixed but promising. For example, a 2012 study of a reentry program in Ohio found that participants were 43 percent less likely to be rearrested for misdemeanors and 61 percent less likely one year later to be incarcerated than the comparison group, but there were no cost savings.[30] The 2017 RAND study in Los Angeles found decreases in the number of people arrested and jailed, but an overall increase in jail days and costs.[31]

Researchers have also questioned whether supportive housing reduces chronic homelessness on a macro level. The findings are encouraging, showing that when more PSH is added, there is a steeper decline over time in chronic homelessness.[32] The number of different studies conducted across subpopulations is encouraging, even though not all of them are rigorous. When examining the impact of supportive housing on the quality of life for residents, the sample sizes are often small or self-reported. Additional rigorous research beyond self-assessments is needed to establish a case for the effect of supportive housing on residents' health outcomes and well-being. The sustained positive housing retention results are often enough, however, to justify supportive housing over shelter or other, less humane and more costly options.

THE PATH FORWARD

There is a global push in the homeless field toward permanent housing solutions and for supportive housing over temporary or transitional options. Coastal cities such as Los Angeles and New York, with exceptionally high numbers of homeless, were early adopters of new models to intervene in the growing homeless epidemic. With evidence of positive results, variations on supportive-housing and Housing First models intended to serve the most-entrenched homeless are now spreading to Houston, Paris, Edmonton, and Mexico City, among other cities. Building supportive housing is hard. It takes time and requires significant up-front funding often obtained through creative methods; plus, support must come from providers, the community, and the public. For cities, it can be politically challenging to commit to a long-term plan to address homelessness when leadership changes, as in Nashville, where the new supportive-housing initiative was developed and precariously sustained over the course of three different mayoral administrations in eighteen months. However, more than thirty years of practice has shown that supportive housing is a critical part of the solution. Having an adequate supply of appropriate housing for people experiencing homelessness is one reason that Houston has been so successful in reducing its homeless numbers.

More recently, the US government has supported regional collaborations in setting up a coordinated entry process for assessing everyone who is homeless, determining their relative level of need, and then prioritizing those most in need for available resources, such as supportive housing. While the overarching goal seems simple, meeting the goal is complicated in practice and requires fractured service-delivery systems to all row together. Later chapters consider a systems-level approach in depth. Many large US cities are in various stages of implementing a coordinated entry process, all with the goal of allocating scarce resources in the most effective way possible.

6 Prevention That Works

Most at-risk people manage through various means to remain sheltered, as demonstrated by administrative data from New York City and additional evidence, mostly from the United States, Canada, and Europe, showing that in a given year the overwhelming majority of individuals and families who live in poverty and struggle to keep affordable housing do not end up on the street or in a shelter.[1] Homelessness is so uncommon that a seminal 1990 study, based on a phone survey of adults in the United States, found that 7 percent risk being homeless during their lifetime, with 4 percent staying in shelters, 1 percent sleeping rough, and 2 percent staying in shelters and sleeping rough. A more recent US study that uses data collected in 2012–13 confirmed the rarity of this occurrence, showing a 4.2 percent lifetime prevalence of homelessness.[2] Even those data overstate the problem to some extent, since the occurrences are less frequent over two to five years and since people typically experience periods of homelessness lasting less than a year, never to be repeated.[3] Another survey of Canadian and US households, published in 2007, found a similar lifetime prevalence of homelessness in the United States (6.2 percent) and a higher rate among Canadians (8.2 percent). However, the five-year prevalence of homelessness was 4.6 percent to 1.3 percent for US and Canadian residents, respectively.[4]

The key point is that homelessness is relatively rare and most occurrences resolve quickly. But this does not negate the fact that millions of people will be impacted over their lifetime or that, in recent years, hundreds of thousands of people annually experience homelessness for at least one night. It likely takes more effort to stably rehouse a person or family than to take the necessary steps to prevent them from losing their home. The challenge is to ascertain who, in fact, is most in jeopardy of becoming homeless.

Who are the people experiencing homelessness in the cities that are the focus of this book? Can cities examine characteristics of these people to draw any useful conclusions about the risk factors? A direct, practical way to start is to analyze the characteristics of a city's homeless population, survey these people, and work backward to understand how those attributes are associated with structural determinants (macro factors), personal-level experiences or vulnerabilities (micro), and the interaction between these factors.[5] The causes of homelessness are complicated, but ascertaining who *might* be in danger can be done by using data to make assumptions and testing those assumptions.

The pattern of homelessness risk varies by group and by place. Universally, men are more at risk than women of becoming street homeless; single individuals are more at risk than families.[6] In the United States and Europe, factors that increase risk include being poor, having been homeless before, lacking full-time work, living alone or in a single-parent family, and being in a minority group or an immigrant, having been a victim of domestic violence or eviction, and having been discharged from an institution—a hospital, jail or prison, or a substance-abuse program—without an identified home. [7]

Risk factors for homelessness are better understood in some cities than in others. Bogotá, Los Angeles, Mexico City, and New York City have conducted detailed analyses of risk factors to develop models for efficiently targeting prevention services. Other cities, such as Baltimore, Edmonton, Houston, Nashville, and Paris, do not use modeling to predict client homelessness, so the prevention programs cut a broad swath and rely on staff assessments of risk to prioritize and provide eviction prevention services or, in the cases of Houston and Nashville, utilize Rapid Rehousing programs as well. Athens has no homelessness prevention program.

In Bogotá, the homeless clients are predominantly young, male, and addicted to either *basuco* (freebase cocaine) or alcohol. There is also a community of "recyclers," who pull their own carts and sleep in them, many of whom have families and homes in the countryside. In other places, such as Mexico City, family conflict, mental illness, substance use, physical disability, social exclusion, discrimination, and lack of economic opportunities are major risk factors for homelessness.[8] Many youths on the streets abuse paint thinner, among other substances, and some of them spend significant time peddling for substance-use money but have a place to sleep, while others are completely without a place to sleep.

Paris has a growing proportion of rough sleepers who are young migrants without the asylum or refugee status necessary to qualify for public benefits. Some homeless there are Romany, an ethnic group whose members frequently face discrimination and often stay for a period of time and then move on. Also scattered across Paris are "traditional" French homeless, who tend to be older and either alcoholic or mentally ill. Drug users, some homeless and some not, also congregate on the city's streets.

The large majority of rough-sleeping people who congregate in the central historic part of Athens are male, many are migrants from countries outside the European Union, and most are chronically homeless. More than half of them are actively using drugs. The sheltered population is mixed, with the city providing temporary accommodations for families, female victims of domestic violence, and the elderly; however, there is an insufficient supply of emergency shelter beds for single adults in shelters operated by municipal and nonprofit providers. Overall, homelessness is largely a recent phenomenon in Greece and is associated with economic crises. The Greek Statistical Authority reported a 25 percent increase in homelessness after the first financial crisis between 2009 and 2011. A 2016 city survey showed that 71 percent of rough sleepers in Athens had become homeless during the 2011–15 period.[9]

This variation in demographics across cities amply makes the point that a local prevention program must be tailored to the specific population. The root causes must be explored; for example, did a person's abuse of alcohol or drugs lead to homelessness, or did the person start using drugs as a coping mechanism after living on the street? Surveys about health and economic challenges, service history, and personal history, including why or how the person moved onto the street inform well-designed strategies.

Identifying common factors associated with people experiencing homelessness is a good start, but it is not necessarily predictive. Persons who are members of families outnumber single adults among those experiencing homelessness in New York City, but this statistic doesn't mean that having a family is a risk factor for homelessness. New York City and Los Angeles have identified risk factors and validated their models, factoring in magnitude and combinations of risk factors, in order to predict which households or singles are most likely to become homeless in the absence of preventive intervention. Bogotá and Mexico City have analyzed data to propose risk factors for homelessness, but they have not conducted rigorous analyses to verify these findings.

In general, even among the groups most in danger of becoming homeless, the percentage who do so is modest. One study of youth aging out of foster care found that 19 percent experience a shelter stay within ten years, about half of them doing so within two years of their exit.[10] For individuals released from prisons, 12 percent sought shelter within two years.[11] Over time, these subpopulations on the street can add up and constitute high percentages of the homeless. Nonetheless, most do not end up on the street. A snapshot in time of the homeless population in the United States might show large percentages of people who are veterans or those evicted from public housing. But such findings in fact reflect the high ratio of veterans in the general population and the commonality of being evicted or living in public housing among those who are poor. Some characteristics prevalent among the homeless population, such as receipt of public housing support, can actually serve as protective factors shielding people from homelessness. For example, public housing rental vouchers in the United States have been shown to significantly reduce homelessness among recipient households, compared with those not receiving this rental support.[12] However, this does not mean that persons who receive housing vouchers never become homeless, as there are many other risk factors that may push people onto the street.

Given the rarity of homelessness and its relationship to a certain level of bad luck, ensuring that prevention strategies reach the right households poses a major challenge, because distinguishing the potentially homeless household or person from the rest of those in the neighborhood suffering from the stresses of poverty is difficult. It may be more difficult than finding the proverbial needle in the haystack—more like finding the right piece of hay in the haystack—since those who lose their housing have many of the same characteristics as their luckier counterparts.

Considering that only a small percentage of any one group ends up homeless, and given that public resources are limited, programs must be well designed and workers must be efficient at identifying those at risk and choosing the proper services for them. A classic challenge that cities face is structuring service offerings that help individuals within their jurisdiction without luring people from other locations that do not offer such services.

WHERE, WHEN, AND HOW TO INTERVENE ALONG THE CONTINUUM IN A HOUSING CRISIS

Homeless prevention programs can cast a wide or a narrow net. Intervention and support at the full-population level to provide housing supports would address larger systemic failures, often lying outside a city's control. For a city with limited resources, this type of effort would be very thinly spread and likely be inefficient or very expensive. Waiting to intervene too far along the continuum of housing insecurity will shrink the group to be served, but the crisis will have escalated and the costs of intervening become higher and more precarious.

Once precariously situated individuals and families are identified, policy makers and practitioners must decide what to do. The key goal of prevention programs is to help these people stay housed. If this fails, prevention efforts can still quickly target those arriving at the shelter door, quickly rehouse individuals who have recently entered the shelter system, or divert people exiting institutional systems from winding up on the streets.

Homelessness prevention can be characterized as primary, secondary, or tertiary.[13] To put it simply, primary prevention aims to address the risk factors of homelessness well before they happen. Efforts to keep people housed may broadly include social housing, education, job training, child care, access to health care, and income support. Primary prevention can also be part of a targeted intervention strategy that uses data to identify those falling into at-risk status and provide support before a potential crisis strikes.

The goals of both secondary and tertiary prevention strategies are to ensure that homelessness is brief and does not recur. This seems counter-intuitive as, once a person is out on the street, the homeless prevention opportunity would appear lost; however, duration and frequency of a homeless stint can be risk factors for future homelessness. Secondary prevention involves targeting people who are just approaching the crisis-response system or are at the shelter door. The aim is to stabilize an individual or family. It could involve eviction prevention, emergency mediation, cash to offset unpaid bills, or legal services. Or the situation might require diversion into Rapid Rehousing (explained in chapter 4). Secondary prevention can also include diversion efforts targeting people discharged from hospitals, mental health facilities, jails, and prisons, which pose high-risk situations for housing instability, especially among single adults.

Tertiary prevention seeks to eliminate repeated spells of homelessness, recognizing that those who have been homeless before face the highest risk of homelessness. This strategy seeks to slow the progression or mitigate the effects of a particular condition once it has become established.[14] The Housing First program (detailed in chapter 5), for example, seeks to end homelessness by providing permanent, affordable housing and supportive services to help a person achieve stability, health, and well-being— essentially to prevent them from ending up on the street again.[15] Hence, it is prevention too. In this example, the intervention has a dual benefit, which suggests that homeless-service providers should consider the potential advantage of prevention options as additive rather than mutually exclusive. To go further, tertiary prevention should be an essential criterion for evaluating the quality of any intervention that moves a person experiencing homelessness into housing permanence.

In the US health care system, the Centers for Medicare and Medicaid Services (CMS) is the federal agency that oversees and administers public health insurance programs such as Medicare and that partners with states in administering Medicaid, the Children's Health Insurance Program, and Health Insurance Marketplace. CMS often uses value-based programs to incentivize Medicare payments to hospitals.[16] As part of its Hospital Readmission Reduction Program, for example, CMS lowers Medicare payments to hospitals with excess readmissions to encourage health care providers to improve care coordination and post-discharge planning.[17] The US Department of Housing and Urban Development does not have a comparable program to incentivize greater adherence to housing goals. National governments might consider the possible effectiveness of value-based programs such as those that have proved effective at CMS that encourage tertiary prevention or penalize a lack thereof, such as when repeated episodes of homelessness occur for an individual or family.

NEW YORK CITY HOMEBASE COMMUNITY PREVENTION PROGRAM

Targeted community prevention is efficient in that it uses data and evaluation to gauge who is at highest risk of homelessness. The HomeBase Community Prevention Program, established in 2005 by the New York City Department of Homeless Services, reaches out to and assists households experiencing a housing crisis. The program began as a pilot in six of the fifteen communities with the highest shelter-entry rates in the city, which together accounted for half of the city's shelter entries. Street addresses were collected from shelter clients who entered the shelter system immediately preceding the pilot.

Once the neighborhoods were selected, the next step in building the program was to meet with partners in the field who worked with at-risk families and individuals in order to learn more about the community dynamics. That information, paired with additional analysis, was used to map the life courses of the families in the five years before the onset of homelessness. The process required collaboration between practitioners, researchers, and three city agencies.

Using this collaborative input and existing predictive models, program organizers developed a new model for identifying families at highest risk. They found, for instance, that a young woman about to give birth to her second child while doubled up with another family member was among those at highest risk of entering the family shelter system.

Once geographic concentration and family characteristics are established, proper targeting is key. The implementation of HomeBase was closely monitored to verify that community-based providers correctly engaged the right households. Every week, the city shared lists of people coming into shelters from each catchment area and informed providers of who was missed. In monthly reports, the city compared profiles of those coming into shelter—age, family composition, reasons for homelessness—with those being served by HomeBase to inform emerging community trends. The total number coming in monthly from each HomeBase community was compared with the number for the same month the previous year, and year-to-date data were compared with the previous year's, to gauge whether the services provided were reducing numbers. These data were also compared with trends in the other nine communities of highest need that did not implement HomeBase, and with citywide trends. Constant communication between the city and providers to calibrate and refine client outreach and selection improved the strategy's efficiency.

When the program began, no evidence indicated which services it should provide. The program took a flexible approach to developing the model during implementation, with flexible funding to address a range of circumstances that were not always reimbursable from existing funding streams. This approach led over time to informed outreach strategies and an ultimate alignment of service-recipient profiles. For example, knowing that the imminent birth of a second child was a risk factor, some community providers started to hold community baby showers, targeting the grandmother, who was often the primary tenant, as the connection to the pregnant daughter. Engagement would flow from there. The pilot based on this approach proved successful, with program communities seeing a 20-percent reduction in rates of homelessness compared with the other nine communities.[18]

Having thus gathered evidence that this was a promising model, organizers decided to subject it to the most rigorous evaluation. The city's Department of Homeless Services commissioned a randomized controlled trial, and researchers from Abt Associates split the study group into those who were enrolled by HomeBase for services (the experimental group) and those who were not (the control group) and followed study participants between 2010 and 2012.[19] There were three major findings: (1) HomeBase reduced by half the number of study households needing shelter compared with the control; (2) the program reduced by 70 percent the average number of days in shelter among study participants who entered shelter; and (3) every dollar invested in HomeBase saved the city $1.27.[20] New York City also commissioned a report to look at the community impact of HomeBase, which found that it reduced shelter entries between 5 percent and 11 percent in communities where it was operating.[21]

This type of refined analysis is necessary in crisis prevention interventions, where only the most at-risk households should be served. This work started at the beginning of the twenty-first century, and in the two decades since, advances in data analytics have opened up more doors to using extensive administrative records to help identify risk.

ADVANCED ANALYTICS IN LOS ANGELES

Following the New York City HomeBase model in attempting to identify the highest-risk households to target with assistance, several other localities are advancing sophisticated uses of data and predictive analytics to more precisely locate the highest-risk households. Predictive analytics involves the use of statistical models to forecast the future based on demonstrated patterns and relationships found in current and past data. In Los Angeles County, researchers with the California Policy Lab and the University of Chicago Poverty Lab used data to create a model predicting who among single adults accessing certain county systems was at highest risk of first-time homelessness or of returning to homelessness.[22] Those systems, serving 1.9 million people a year, include health care and mental health care, substance abuse treatment, probation, the sheriff's department (incarceration), social services, and the homeless-services system.

Los Angeles County officials started with a list of 75,786 persons who experienced homelessness in 2017. The county's 2017 annual data showed that 33,634 (1.7 percent) of single adults using county services, out of almost 2 million individuals with service histories, experienced a new homeless spell in 2017, and that 14,481 of them (0.7 percent) experienced homelessness for the first time.

The predictive analytical exercise then attempted to look back into the five-year history of services to identify the combination of predictive factors that signaled an increased likelihood of becoming homeless. As there are multiple risk factors that contribute to homelessness, risk cannot be distilled down to a couple of indicators.[23] The most common risk factor among the cohort for those who became homeless proved to be contact with three or more county agencies, which would indicate complex household needs. Most frequent among those agencies were public food-purchasing assistance (i.e., SNAP), cash assistance, public medical or mental health care usage, and contact with the criminal justice system.

The resulting algorithm, when applied to the baseline data to determine if it could accurately forecast who became homeless, correctly predicted repeat homelessness with 46 percent precision and, for first-time homeless, with 34-percent accuracy.[24] While it is close to being operationalized by the local government, this highly effective screening tool may well mark a global milestone for accurately identifying households at risk of homelessness.

If the first element of consideration in shaping a prevention program is efficiency, the second is assessing the effectiveness of the provided services. An important goal of this initiative will therefore be to contact people prioritized as at risk and offer them intensive case management and support to stabilize and keep them housed. The Los Angeles Homeless Services Authority and Los Angeles County will be studying which tailored client interventions for the targeted group are the most effective in preventing homelessness.

PREVENTION IN MEXICO CITY

Programs similar to New York City's HomeBase model have been developed in Mexico City and Bogotá. In general, however, prevention efforts must be tailored to the local social services available to those at risk of homelessness. As New York City residents have a legislated right to shelter backed by a social commitment to relatively high levels of services, prevention can be blended into alternative models of service delivery. Localities where the shelter system and services are less developed may configure prevention in a lighter-touch, less expensive way.

Figure 6. Children's artwork from the Espacio SI homelessness prevention program in Mexico City. Marco Lara Orozco, SIBISO CDMX.

In Mexico City, the Espacio SI (System of Inclusion) prevention program was launched in 2016 in the east-side borough of Iztapalapa, a *delegación* with concentrated poverty. The program targeted youth and the elderly at high risk of living on the street in eleven neighborhoods with high social vulnerability. Workers operated in schools and in the streets, conducting informational workshops to contact constituents, identify households at risk of homelessness, and offer referrals to city services. In early 2018, a second prevention program site opened on the city's west side. Between both sites from 2016 through 2018, more than 15,000 contacts were made, with connections to 34,000 services. However, only 850 households were identified as being imminently at risk of becoming homeless, based on the profile information gathered. Only 473 households eventually received comprehensive supportive services in the Espacio SI prevention centers. Although it is a good sign that Mexico City outreach teams cast a wide net, a great deal of their effort was devoted to providing light-touch or referral services for the many, while the desired comprehensive supportive services reached only a few.

In this case, despite the positive outcomes of connecting vulnerable households to supportive services, better use of data would have informed the city as to whether it was targeting the most-at-risk households, and whether it could have used the time of Espacio SI's staff more productively. Unfortunately, those data were not available (as is true in most jurisdictions without advanced integrated administrative data systems), and workers were left to make their best judgment and offer self-identified drop-in access to services.

Efficiency contributes to a better use of limited resources. While cost-effectiveness is not the only rationale for homelessness prevention, the city benefits if the cost of keeping people housed can offset some, if not all, of the expenses of such costly services as shelters, criminal justice, and emergency health care that would otherwise be incurred.[25] In some cases, a city may not bear a great deal of the direct costs of homeless services, making it hard to justify the price it has to pay for more-intensive community preventive measures to offset costs to the benefit of national, state or provincial, county, or other regional governments. This makes efficiency even more important, but ideally, not at the price of effectiveness. Finding the right people at the right stage of need, and shaping an effective intervention, requires skillful, evidence-based targeting, engagement, and service provision, especially for cities whose resources are tightly constrained.[26]

Historically, prevention efforts relied on experience, logic, and hope—hope because these efforts were often haphazard, did not seek to target the highest-risk households, or lacked a standardized logic model to guide the complicated work. Practitioners were not even sure if their well-intentioned efforts worked. Fortunately, recent homeless-prevention methodologies have received considerably more study, increasing the likelihood that well-developed models are being implemented with some success.

BOGOTÁ: SPOTLIGHT ON INNOVATION

The Secretariat of Social Integration in Bogotá currently implements a homelessness prevention program with a unique approach, using the eyes and ears of the community to target subpopulations at high risk of homelessness. This massive engagement effort builds awareness and support through community workshops, informational gatherings, and visits to schools and businesses to disseminate educational materials and create a system for referrals. Materials include brochures on such topics as how homelessness occurs, alcohol dependence, substance use, family violence, and the hazards of street life for youth. Outreach workers regularly go into the community to establish trust and serve as a reliable presence and community resource.

In developing this program as a pilot, the city conducted tours of the target neighborhoods in order to map social problems and needs, local assets for health and quality of life, and social actors through a process known as social cartography. Also, surveys were conducted of people living on the street and in the shelter system to develop an instrument to score risk and determine for whom prevention services should be prioritized. The city could then more efficiently identify at-risk individuals and families to target through its social service offices and civil society partners.

Bogotá strengthened its prevention activities by mobilizing important community stakeholders—community leaders, business leaders, members of community action boards, neighborhood organizations. Such social marketing, used in the neighborhood of Usaquén, educated the public and employed workshops to engage local residents to learn of or identify neighborhoods and blocks with concentrations of people using substances or spending a lot of time on the street. Then, residents co-developed neighborhood-specific strategies to engage and connect these vulnerable populations to city services. Mobilizing networks in the neighborhoods created a type of community protective force, providing eyes and ears to identify people at risk, recruiting support for referring vulnerable people to city services, and leveraging resources such as training or jobs. Bogotá has yet to formally evaluate the prevention program, but it proved popular in pilot communities and was expanded citywide in 2017.

PREVENTION AFTER THE FACT: QUICK ACTION IS CRUCIAL

Tertiary prevention strategies are quick interventions after a crisis hits that attempt to restore the situation as quickly as possible before there is no going back. Helping a family who prematurely leave their home for a shelter after receiving an eviction notice, but not an order, is a good example. Providing legal assistance that allows the family to return to their apartment is an effective tertiary prevention strategy.

Tertiary prevention can also include new solutions, but ones effected quickly before homelessness becomes chronic. Rapid Rehousing is an example of this strategy, as it seeks to move homeless people swiftly into permanent housing with supports to help them achieve stability. Rapid Rehousing shows promise in helping people move from homelessness or homeless shelters to permanent housing.[27] The long-term impacts of Rapid Rehousing and benefits to housing stability and well-being are less known.

The Nashville Family Collective model is a small-scale Rapid Rehousing program for families that uses a two-generation approach, addressing both parents and children. It is supported by United Way of Greater Nashville, the Siemer Institute, the Nashville Mayor's Office, and the Tennessee Department of Human Services. The two-generation approach posits that the well-being of parents and children is interactive: parents are healthy if their children are healthy, and vice versa. Interventions must simultaneously create opportunities for and meet the immediate needs of the family.[28] The Family Collective program employs intensive case management to stabilize housing or divert families into permanent housing (using public housing vouchers) and provides employment navigation, financial assistance, and financial counseling for families experiencing homelessness or at risk of homelessness. Program participants receive assistance for two years. The program has served more than 1,207 households since its startup in 2014, housing 539 families, potentially preventing 516 families from becoming homeless, and taking an average of one hundred days to find housing for them.[29]

Houston's Rapid Rehousing program is a key part of the city's homelessness strategy, serving as its primary housing intervention for (non-chronic) homeless youth, single adults, and families with children. From January 2015 to January 2019, the city housed 4,084 individuals, of whom 3,671 obtained permanent housing. Houston also sought to revamp case management and pool financial resources to better serve young-adult clients with a lower caseload ratio and for a longer period of time. In addition, the city is exploring whether it can address the continued housing instability of persons housed through Rapid Re-housing by providing longer-term housing subsidies.

In the array of services to the homeless, prevention has been the final frontier. The growing body of literature supporting prevention, along with more technologically advanced methods of prediction, could enable other cities to cross this frontier. Localities should continue to pursue strategies to prevent homelessness or to make it brief; without those efforts, the work to move people off the street will never end.

7 Systems-Level Thinking

Clear from the vast international array of efforts to tackle homelessness, some thwarted by internal divisions, is the hard truth that real and lasting progress cannot be made without acting collaboratively on system-wide reform. Getting people off the streets cannot be achieved from the confines of a shelter system. Each player with a piece of the solution must be brought to the same table to coordinate a strategic response. Only a complete, coordinated, and well-managed array of programs at scale can deliver on the promise to end homelessness.

Many cities whose experiences are described in this book have deepened their approach to homelessness by pursuing evidence-based practices and refining models of care. At the core of municipal services, however, remains a siloed array of emergency services and shelters. An overlay of competing political and structural barriers drive fault lines through what should be a coordinated continuum of services. A clear example of this division is in Mexico City, where heads of independent agencies providing social services, youth services, health, urban development, and housing each hold a piece of the portfolio of services for homeless people. Forming a coalition government often involves concessions to opposition and minor parties through appointments of party leaders to head agencies, leaders who are often active hopefuls for the mayoralty. Political goals can thus go before program goals. In Paris, housing and social services are separate camps headed by elected *adjoints*; and, while agencies can work well together, they can also be set against each other by agenda priorities established by the strong national government. This national-versus-local dynamic plays out elsewhere, with local leaders unable to garner support from organizations funded by national programs. In Athens, for example, fiercely independent nonprofit organizations and thousands of volunteer citizen groups often work without supervision or coordination. The city of Nashville has a strong network of homeless-service providers who have stepped up to the plate over the years, but as the homeless population has diversified, city officials have struggled (due in part to limited resources) through multiyear efforts to formalize partnerships and collaboration.

Promising new approaches are emerging that successfully bind disparate players together to solve these larger challenges. Edmonton, Houston, and Los Angeles are, with notable success, using systems-level solutions to refocus their homeless services across agencies. In the homelessness arena, these strategies share the following characteristics:

- Trusted and respected leadership that steers everyone toward a shared vision, and that allows the group to address and prioritize the individual interests of the partners at varying times

- Shared practice tools—for example, a plan and governance structure— that hold the people being served in the center and commit the partners to a more unified approach in addressing their needs

- Integration of data that allows knowledge to migrate across the siloed agencies, supporting a shared vision and facilitating collective priority setting and action.

- Respect for differences of approach and perspective that leverages, rather than diminishing, the diversity of skills and knowledge present at the table.

Generating successful collaboration, and sustaining it over time, is the key to making real, systems-level progress in preventing and overcoming homelessness.

THE NEED FOR A BROAD COALITION

Episodes of homelessness often result from the failures of many service systems. Single individuals cycle in and out of substance-use detox facilities, short- and long-term incarceration, homeless shelters, and the street. The homeless system is at the mercy of other institutions and their ability to transition a client from service to service. These other institutions may offer discharge planning, but ensuring stable housing at discharge is not at the core of their mission. When someone comes into treatment or incarceration precariously housed, they exit with even greater risk.

Too often, homeless shelters become the social service agency of last resort. If a particularly challenged family lingers in the child welfare agency, or a young person ages out of foster care, or an individual exits a time-limited domestic violence shelter, or someone exceeds an allotted stay in a mental health ward, the default can be to simply discharge them to the street or a shelter. Such discharges are not the norm; however, small percentages of large numbers of people end up having an oversized impact on the shelter system or the street. For example, eviction is one of the most common reasons that families enter the homeless system in New York City. Although a small percentage of those evicted from apartments become homeless, at over 18,000 evictions a year, that feeds a significant proportion of the shelter system.[1] Similar dynamics govern domestic violence programs and the child welfare system.

Even if a city's homeless system is effective and efficient, many factors beyond its control can still result in full shelters and crowded streets. For example, the influx of migrants, both from within national borders and from other countries, can suddenly strain a city's resources. Paris and Athens were barely managing the long-standing homeless populations on their streets when the cities were swarmed in 2015 with refugees from the Middle East and Northern Africa. Bogotá became overwhelmed with Venezuelan refugees in 2018, demanding the attention of managers to meet the sudden surge. Deinstitutionalization of the mentally ill in 1980 without adequate alternative accommodations resulted in thousands of vulnerable people on the streets across the United States. Even reform efforts to reduce jail and prison populations can, without adequate planning, put people at high risk of homelessness.

Curtailing homelessness at its roots requires multiple partners to actively participate in solutions. It takes systems-level action, with a unified approach and shared accountability. The more the public, nonprofit, and private actors within and outside the homeless-services system are engaged and aligned, the greater the collective tools and opportunity for success.

Even small efforts can create the foundation for future collaboration. In Athens, Mayor Giorgos Kaminis and his staff's desire to take action on street homelessness, starting with an estimate of how many were on the street, began a process of bringing many disparate partners together. Work was launched during an series of uncomfortable meetings. Logistical struggles on the ground reflected the disparate organizational structure of the ministries and agencies. In Greece, responsibility for homeless policy rests at the national level, with separate ministries addressing different homeless populations, including emergency shelters and day centers, shelters for drug users and accommodations for people with mental health problems, accommodations for refugees and unaccompanied youth, and shelters for abused women. At the local level, this translates into the municipal government running some shelters, while nongovernmental entities operate a grab bag of night shelters, day services, and street outreach.

From the start, representatives of Greece's national government, including the Ministry of Labor, questioned Mayor Kaminis's authority to take leadership on this issue, and the local nonprofit providers bristled at being asked to take on work by a municipality that did not fund their services. The city muscled through the planning and conducted its first street homeless count in 2017 with a combination of volunteer staff from different agencies. In a stroke of last-minute creativity, the mayor's project coordinator, Théodora Papadimitriou, broke up the teams from the different organizations who had each shown up intent on going out as a group under the banner of their agency. Instead, they were scrambled into multidisciplinary teams and sent into the night to navigate the streets and their own relationships with homeless individuals. This first street count helped build a foundation among people and across agencies. Staff began to develop a shared vision that became the source upon which trust was established. From that base, a local plan of action was created, followed by an endorsement and commitment from the various agencies to continue the street count as a national mandate.

WHAT SYSTEMS-LEVEL THINKING INVOLVES

Systems-level thinking is often considered the hardest part of any success-ful strategy. Committing to working at scale to overcome homelessness requires relentless attention to improving existing services and investing in the ways necessary to solve the problem. But the challenge to effective collaboration, as illustrated by the organizational barriers typical of Athens, Mexico City, Nashville, and Paris, is that each person coming to the table works for a separate institution, each with its own mission. Each individual reports to a boss who pays their salary and calls the shots. Each has a complete set of tasks and goals to satisfy in their day job.

Despite the silos, few big, thorny problems can be solved within the confines of a single agency. Tackling a problem as large as homelessness requires people and institutions to act across agencies to iterate solutions through nontraditional partnerships. Strategies that have effectively brought people to the table for the long term demonstrate what can create a culture of iterative problem solving and thereby successfully reduce homelessness. The six key principles, described below, are effective leader-ship, a shared vision, a plan, a governing structure, application of data, and a structure for ongoing effectiveness. The hard work up front of fos-tering a climate of collective commitment can exponentially yield ongoing effectiveness in communities.

Effective Leadership

A leader is someone with authority and respect who is willing to take on the challenge; someone to step up and call the team to action. Being a leader does not require taking on all the work, or being held solely respon-sible for the outcome. It requires the bravery to say what needs to be done to break out of bad practices and worse outcomes. A strong leader needs to rally all the partners to the table, bring out the best in all of them, encour-age and inspire everyone to do their part in overcoming the challenge.

At the municipal level, the chosen leader is most often the mayor. While a mayor may have little control in terms of budget or program with which to address the challenge, the mayor has the bully pulpit and the local grav-itas to convene partners to shape a shared vision or goal and to forge a plan. Whether motivated by a vision for a better city or called to account by residents for improving outcomes for people who are homeless, mayors hold more convening authority than any other city official over the array of necessary partners and wield more power. In city after city, mayors can best shoulder the task of creating a home base for tackling homelessness. Paris mayor Anne Hidalgo ran in 2013 partially on a platform of addressing street homelessness, and came into office with a comprehensive plan. Mayor Miguel Ángel Mancera of Mexico City declared a mission to tackle street homelessness in 2015, calling his administration to the table to develop ideas and a plan. Mayor Bernard Young of Baltimore created an independent municipal agency to lead the task in 2019, coordinating regional partners in lining up behind a unified vision. Over and again, mayors have stepped up to bring the many actors together in a manner that allows a shared vision to be articulated and implemented with accountability.

But what if the mayor isn't invested in the work or doesn't show up? Then the community needs to act on its own to bring the partners together. In the world of effective community organizing for systemic reform, collective-impact approaches identify the need for a strong backbone organization that can bring the effort along, gain the trust of partners, and provide the respected leadership voice for the community. In Edmonton, the independent nonprofit Homeward Trust has managed to sustain local efforts on homelessness through multiple changes in provincial and municipal leadership.

Should a mayor decide to join the efforts later, after the initial hard work is done, it is up to the community coalition to effectively integrate a strong mayor into the existing effort. This may require ceding some leadership control without completely handing over the reins. And, of course, for a mayor, showing humility and respect for existing efforts in order to keep committed partners engaged is critical to long-term success. Whether the mayor or the community organization holds the leadership role will fluctuate over time. A challenge for collective-impact models is making room at the table for a new mayor who embraces the challenge and chooses to exert energy and use political capital on the issue.

Illustrative is Los Angeles County, which faces a near-impossible task in overcoming street homelessness. The numbers are huge (44,214 rough sleeping countywide in 2019, with over 27,000 in the city of Los Angeles alone), the services are insufficient and, according to a gap analysis commissioned by the county, there are fewer than 6,000 shelter beds for singles at any point in time, while there are close to 9,000 new street homeless annually. The governance is complex: the county has most of the responsibility and resources, but has to coordinate with eighty-eight separate cities and an independent local entity that allocates federal homeless housing resources for the county. Large numbers of people sleeping in public spaces have long plagued the talented mayors who have worked in the beautiful Art Deco Los Angeles City Hall, just blocks from the notorious Skid Row. Without the tools and authority to tackle the challenge, one mayor after another has tried, or not, to move all the forces that must align to shift the culture of inaction.

The disorder in the Los Angeles environment became particularly toxic in the twenty-first century. Typical of complex service systems, authority for the various system parts that must work together was scattered, in the hands of individuals whose relationships with one another were strained by years of finger-pointing and blame-casting and whose institutions were controlled by competing political interests. With little effective coordination, conditions only worsened. The annual street count more than doubled countywide from 19,193 in 2009 to 44,214 in 2019.

As early as 2010, when homeless numbers were escalating, the United Way and the Los Angeles Chamber of Commerce, through a pioneering grant from the Conrad N. Hilton Foundation, launched a local effort to build a coalition of partners called Home for Good. Originally chaired by the Business Leaders Task Force, this group convened the systems players and public and private funders for monthly staff-level conversations. Although starting small, the conversations remained consistent, with the United Way providing a comfortable conference room and feeding participants a good, locally prepared meal. Home for Good grew over time to include the city, county, local continuum of care, researchers, nonprofit intermediaries, service providers, and advocates; and it emerged a decade later as a trusted, safe environment where real issues could be raised and resolved, and aligned strategies developed.

This Los Angeles convening of staff was supplemented with the Home for Good Funders Collaborative, created as a place where public and private funds could be sequenced and coordinated. This allowed for innovations to be piloted and then ultimately scaled and institutionalized. And attached to these efforts were action plans that set forth clear goals, annual milestones, and an outline of roles and responsibilities for various sectors. The pathway was thus laid toward creation of the city's Tenant-Based Supportive Housing program and the Single Adult Coordinated Entry System, which built a unified infrastructure across the entire county with a federated leadership in each region.

For the first time in memory, these developments created a new energy in the Los Angeles area that is laying out the possibilities for real change. Such change has not happened fast, and despite stronger relationships, has yet to produce a turnaround in the growing street homeless population. In 2016, two years after the start of his term, Mayor Eric Garcetti released his Comprehensive Homeless Strategy. It was developed in close coordination with Los Angeles County, which also led an intensive process to create a comprehensive plan. Mayor Garcetti announced a push for immediate solutions through an initiative called A Bridge Home, adding his considerable voice to the primacy of the challenge and importance of the commitment. The foundational work started by the United Way of Greater Los Angeles, combined with the energy and leadership of a new mayor and the county Board of Supervisors, provides the greatest hope for real impact that local stakeholders can remember.

This collaboration supported a successful campaign to pass two ballot referenda that will pump billions of dollars into housing and services, laying the foundation for a strategic campaign to overcome community fears of shelters and allowing Mayor Garcetti to meet short-term needs with shelters while implementing an ambitious housing plan. The various institutions' representatives have, in some cases, changed, yet the collaboration remains strong as members rotate in and out. This kind of sustained partnership, where egos are left at the door, new members are welcomed, and serious policy differences can be discussed without splintering the community, provide the makings of a serious long-term infrastructure capable of sustaining change. The effort has not yet stanched the flow of people onto the streets, but it is equipping the partners with a more robust and coordinated array of services than has been the case in the past.

A Shared Vision

The articulation of a clear and simple shared vision inspires people and institutions to work together. Participants come to the table with widely varying services and missions, likely defining their outcomes and objectives independently and even in contradictory ways. For example, without a broader lens, a homeless shelter may count every discharge to housing as a success; however, a precariously housed person may rapidly return to the shelter, or go to jail, or wind up in an emergency room for treatment of an exacerbated condition. Poor outcomes are no one's definition of success.

By tying everyone together, from the police officer on the street to the housing manager, in a shared commitment to safe and stable permanency for all community members, the system can recalibrate its goals and tasks in support of the shared mission in a way that aligns with the outcome. Resolving differing points of view with a shared vision that everyone can embrace, and facilitating a comprehensive integration of activities such that each player can see how their individual organization fits within that shared vision, allows the independent participants to act as a whole. A vision statement creates the North Star against which all actions can be measured and allows the coalition to judge whether they are getting closer to the goal.

Beware of getting overly ambitious. A solid vision statement respects the reality that past efforts have failed for lack of resources, insufficient coordination, or unforeseen challenges. A vision statement has to engender the trust and respect of the broader community.

Tensions inevitably develop between an aspirational goal (We can do it!) and the community's exhausted expectations. Inspired by the national movement to tackle homelessness, New York City set forth an ambitious plan in 2004 to reduce homelessness by two-thirds in five years. While the intent was aspirational, it became the public measure by which all homeless work was evaluated, making modest yet substantial progress seem inadequate. Between 2005 and 2009, according to the one-night survey of visible street homeless, the population was reduced by nearly half, decreasing from 4,395 to 2,328 individuals (even reaching the two-thirds goal in one borough, the Bronx). The US Interagency Council on

Homelessness and the National Alliance to End Homelessness have both recognized that innovations in New York City homelessness work across the board.[2] Yet the thrust of popular press reports highlighted how the plan fell short of the ambitious two-thirds goal, buttressed by scathing reports from homeless advocacy organizations. The passion that drove the leadership of New York City at the time to set the audacious goal was thwarted by the system's resistance to change, the refusal of legal advocates to compromise for the sake of progress, and the sheer magnitude of the need, which was not met with a commensurate amount of resources. The significant progress on many program fronts was simply drowned out by the headlines of an increasing homeless population.

Past failures can lead to a collective cynicism that homelessness cannot be overcome, an attitude exacerbated by soaring housing costs, continuing social service strains, and failures of prior efforts. Aspirational goals based in reality strike a better balance. The US Interagency Council on Homelessness adopted one simple and compelling vision statement to guide its work with localities in assisting veterans: "Homelessness should be rare, brief, and non-recurring." It's aspirational and allows for the knowledge that, for some, brief episodes of homelessness will occur. It invites good questions: How do we make it rare? Brief? Nonrecurring?

Another common vision embraces ending chronic homelessness. If homelessness is to be tolerated, then no one should be so for more than a limited time. Beyond that, their homelessness is chronic. For many years, the term *chronic* had no standard definition in the United States or globally. In 2015, the US Department of Housing and Urban Development created a regulatory definition, which recipients of federal funding have to meet, measuring "chronic" as any twelve months spent homeless over a three-year period.[3] In Edmonton, Alberta, at the time of this writing, chronic homelessness among single adults is defined as one year continuous or four episodes in three years, which is similar to the HUD definition. However, the Canadian federal government is in the process of amending that definition. Internationally, jurisdictions have varying definitions of homelessness or chronic homelessness depending on their local conditions (see the appendix). Should efforts aimed at preventing any person from falling into a chronic condition fail, those individuals whose homelessness has become chronic take priority.

Another strategy is to create vision goals for distinct subpopulations, such as the efforts undertaken to end homelessness among veterans described in the introduction. Galvanized by Mayor Annise Parker's leadership, The Way Home Continuum of Care in Houston started in 2012 with a clear, achievable goal of housing one hundred veterans in one hundred days and effectively ended veteran homelessness by 2015.[4] The city was then positioned to focus its efforts on all chronic homeless. Between 2012 and 2019, Houston put more than 17,000 homeless individuals in permanent housing and reduced overall homelessness by 57 percent.

The most desirable overall approach is to set a vision statement to reduce the total number of homeless and, at the same time, eliminate cases of homelessness lasting for more than a brief period. A vision statement calls for a clear set of metrics to describe the current state of affairs and invites discussion of strategies to reduce those numbers over time.

A Plan

A clear articulation of the initial set of actions to be carried out to fulfill the vision statement, set forth in a broadly shared document, creates a road map for partners to rally behind. Ideal homelessness plans include actions on prevention, intervention, and permanency, tackling the challenge from all angles. Winning endorsements from all or most of the organizations that have the potential to impact outcomes will signal that the community is behind the plan. Mexico City mayor Miguel Ángel Mancera released such a plan that involved interagency coordination across departments from children's welfare to training, employment, medical health, and mental health services. The list of participating agencies is impressive: the Secretariat of Inclusion and Social Welfare, the Ministry of Finance, the Secretariat of Urban Development and Housing, the Ministry of Labor and Employment Promotion, Integral Development of the Family, Comprehensive Attention to People in Street Populations, Legal and Legal Services Counseling, the Ministry of Health, and the Secretariat of Public Security. After its first street count, Mexico City enshrined its plan items in a formal mayoral administrative directive intended to endure political transitions.

In late 2019, Mexico City elected a new mayor, Claudia Sheinbaum, who reevaluated the strategies of the 2016 homeless plan. The new social integration director, Alumedena Ocejo Rojo, decided to continue the city's innovative prevention program and sought to move people off the street, engage them in treatment, and enlist more professional staff to better case-manage clients in their move toward permanence. The original inter-agency plan acted as a living document, guiding the city in adjusting homeless services to changing times.

Involved parties need to know who is responsible for implementing the plan. Paris mayor Anne Hidalgo's 106-point plan includes action items that are measurable, underscoring who is responsible for each objective and establishing a clear timeline. These are tracked by the deputy mayor, Dominique Versini, and are reviewed with the public and by the private partners that are part of the implementation collaborative.

The world changes, conditions evolve, some ideas work and others do not. Plans require updating as initiatives take hold and as constant moni-toring and attention provide evidence of impact. As a collaboration matures, there is less of a need for plan documents that are rallying cries than for documenting the evolution of commitments generated by part-ners iterating solutions. The role of the plan reflects the maturity of the group as the constant push-pull of institutional strengths and priorities is harnessed until the vision is achieved.

Making a single program work well is comparatively easy. Getting it right within the confines of a shelter or drop-in center pales in compari-son with the challenging and time-consuming work of negotiating to coordinate referrals, altering organizational culture, and even revamping practices that may work fine in-house but produce negative externalities for others. There must be accountability for all outcomes. Partners need to organize and be prepared for hard work over the long term, which will inevitably include uncomfortable conversations and new burdens and responsibilities.

Governing Structure

Under systems-level thinking, the organizations that directly and indi-rectly impact the number of people who may become homeless also need to be at the larger table and share accountability in the outcomes. To do this well requires ongoing partnership and commitment to iterative reform. Many different political levels can be represented at the table, though typically they include the city and region. Different service delivery partners also should be represented, such as behavioral health services and employment supports. A solid governance structure may typically involve public and nonprofit sectors, and often the private sector as well (particularly housing-related businesses), each represented by a person having authority to commit their organization or firm to delivering on its promises. The Los Angeles collaborative table includes city, county, non-profit, and regional partners. The Edmonton partners include shelter, housing, and mental health providers. Houston includes philanthropic organizations and city government agencies as well as regional players. Each city has a different configuration; what they share in common is a commitment to align efforts of their varied organizations behind a unified strategy of action.

Every system identified as a cause and a contributor to a solution needs to be part of shared governance. The health department takes the lead for an emerging health problem. The social services department responds to a surge in domestic violence. In this way, shared targets and a single plan of action unify the collective table. The collective allows information gathering, analysis, and insight that otherwise would not be possible. This information sharing should occur at the program level and may also be done at the individual level, with the appropriate confidentiality protections in place. An individual or family may have multiple independent interactions with the homeless or social services system, or with the criminal and health care systems, with each agency unaware of the others' actions. Individual agencies may be whittling away at what they perceive as the presenting problem, blind to other needs and responses that others are undertaking.

A collaborative effort can start with a big bang or with just two partners beginning and combining their time. The big-bang approach could be the appointment of a mayoral commission of stakeholders charged with devising a strategy for action, as in Mexico City. Initially, the commission might recommend policy and programs, and then evolve into an ongoing partnership for implementation and action. In Mexico City, a mayoral task force produced a comprehensive plan that was later incorporated in an administrative mandate overseen by the secretary for social integration.

The start-slow-and-build approach reflects a more careful investment in concrete actions among a core group toward effective working relationships that accommodate success and the addition of partners over time. This below-the-radar effort builds progress from the ground up. Nashville has integrated several different planning groups, formerly functioning in parallel (including some overlapping membership) with disparate strategies, into a single governance structure under the mayor's office in order to coordinate efforts and pool resources. In its first year, Nashville's new governance body increased federal continuum of care funding by 10 percent, secured a $3.5 million federal grant to prevent and end youth homelessness, and reduced the city's annual point-in-time street count by 14 percent.

Both big-bang and start-small approaches have merit. The goal of achieving systems-level reform requires the creation of a long-lasting, supportive environment where partners can contribute and that survives political ups and downs.

Perhaps the most important characteristic of such a collaborative meeting environment is that it be positive, constructive, and welcoming. Intergovernmental tensions and periodic disputes among partners will inevitably arise. But people will keep coming back if the commitment to positive reform and joint problem solving persists despite occasional disruptions.

Application of Data

The glue that holds a plan and partners together over time is the use of data to shine light on the magnitude and dimensions of the problem and how each obstacle should be addressed.

This systems-level principle is best applied when broken down into manageable objectives, achievable short-term outcomes that build momentum toward the longer-term goal. Many cities are incorporating such plans into their homelessness programs. In Houston, the charting of program or agency performance is approached at a systems level to gauge how the city as a whole is doing. Monthly key indicators facilitate conversations about whether the city is experiencing an increasing or otherwise different demand and where there are any gaps in services. Data inform assessments as to whether the plan is working or not, has the capacity to meet the volume needed for the community's desired solution, or is being shifted from one institution to another.

If a bad trend is surfacing, a conversation among partners can shift resources to reverse it and move forward more effectively. Among a large group of players, actions can be prioritized. Unified data systems and coordinated governance make it possible to identify where cases overlap, harness the thinking of experts across systems, and approach the person's case as a whole, rather than as disparate institutional problems. Without this big-picture focus, it will be unclear if the individual efforts are contributing to the shared goal of reducing homelessness. Even worse, a piecemeal evaluation may mask the possibility that one program's success is simply shifting the problem from one provider to another or from one system to another.

A data-informed plan requires staff from city agencies to calculate the size of the service population, as expressed in current statistics on those in shelter or on the street, any waiting lists for services, and the anticipated newcomers. And it requires a clear quantification of the source of the problem—not just how many are becoming homeless, but why. Pinpointing failures from feeder systems and identifying trends in the populations to be served allow the city partners to determine how services need to be recalibrated. Measuring the efficiency and effectiveness of programs is needed to inform the expected duration of the episodes of homelessness, and helps in estimating the magnitude of services that will need to be provided.

A diagnostic assessment must map the population profile and track multiple system dynamics over time. These broadly may include public housing or rental subsidy administration, income assistance, justice administration, child welfare, health care, immigration, and domestic violence. Understanding the upcoming trends in those fields and anticipating how they will impact the number of homeless can enable agencies to raise the alarm for preventive interventions that can forestall the events from happening, and can improve system preparations if they cannot.

Homeward Trust in Edmonton has done this kind of system flow mapping. The community guides the nonprofit, with a strong understanding that no one agency or program can eliminate homelessness. Homeward Trust has mapped committee structures in order to tap a broad group of

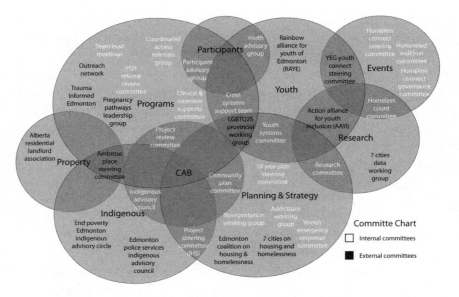

Figure 7. Edmonton homeless-sector committee map. Homeward Trust Edmonton, 2020.

homeless-serving government and community partners and apply elements of a RACI (responsible, accountable, consulted, and informed) management matrix. This balances the goal of broad engagement with specific tactics and execution of strategy.

Homeward Trust and its partners throughout the community establish crystal-clear targets. For example, the goal was set that, through assertive outreach and coordinated access to appropriate housing and supports, all rough sleepers would be engaged by 2018. In June 2020, there were 505 unsheltered individuals in contact with the city and on its by-name list.[5] Agencies outside the homeless systems also play an important role; for example, corrections, health care, and child intervention are expected to report at least biennially on the number of people discharged into homelessness from public systems. Homeward Trust has committed to annual targets that aim to achieve zero discharge into homelessness by 2023, with the aspiration that 100 percent of those entering homeless-serving systems in 2022 will be connected to housing and supports within twenty-one days, effectively ending chronic and episodic homelessness.

Structure for Ongoing Effectiveness

As demonstrated in examples from Edmonton, Houston, Los Angeles and Paris, it takes mayors willing to bring a broad coalition together to have an impact on homelessness during their administration. But, to achieve success in the long term, cities also require the gravitas of lasting coalitions. Systems-level planning among many disparate players can move aspirations across a further horizon. Otherwise, public agencies subject to electoral cycles and political changes can sacrifice longer-term goals for short-term wins.

Working at the systems level does not occur in isolation but occurs simultaneously with project-level planning and dealing with immediate political and program demands. A well-coordinated group that has representation both inside and outside the existing political structure can potentially manage both short- and long-term agendas. One strategy is to leverage quick wins to build momentum, such as small experiments that can be scaled up to obtain long-term buy-in.

To survive over time, this collaborative table must be predictable in its activities and productive. Setting a regular meeting time is key—spaced far enough apart to keep people's contributions fresh and allow things to get done in the interim. Preparing agendas in advance can be a simple and effective organizing task.

An agenda that starts with a review of current data trends can ground partners in progress and alert them to challenges. Standard categories of shelter utilization and housing placements can be supplemented by data on important incentives. For instance, if a new hospital discharge protocol is being advanced, hospital administrators can report updates on their success in achieving stable-housing discharges for medically frail and tenuously housed clients.

The need for a systemic approach to homelessness applies uniformly to all the cities covered in this book, independent of the size of their problems or the resources at their disposal. But each city finds different ways to achieve their intended ends. While working with international partners on their newly formed plans to address homelessness in 2015, Mexico City officials coined the term *tropicalizar* to describe adapting similar techniques to meet the unique needs of their city's context and needs; in other words, customization or localization for a particular culture, government structure, and economy.

For Mexico City, the path to a more rational and long-lasting solution was through legislation. The important first task in Athens was for city officials to build trust between the disparate groups working in the field, which achieved early victories but might not endure. Part of the success in Paris centered on engagement of the imagination and buy-in of citizens, with the quick and colorful unfurling of the visible Boule to address the new wave of immigrants. Los Angeles also invested heavily in coordinated messaging and community development, which laid the groundwork for increased investment in long-term solutions.

Leadership matters and will shift over time. It behooves a mayor's office to draw together a broad coalition and empower it to carry the work forward, anticipating the loss of a passionate mayor in an election by allowing the community to step up, manage the change, and encourage the new mayor to lead. The coalition must function effectively in the meantime. Mayors can create, support, and leverage these coalitions over time for ongoing systems-level action for the good of their cities and the populations they serve.

And as the conveners in Los Angeles learned when first pulling together their broad coalition for Home for Good, don't forget to serve a good meal. Breaking bread is a universal sign of unity, which is what it will take to achieve the goals described in these pages.

8 Engaging the Community

Sustained commitment to overcoming homelessness rests strongly on an engaged community that understands, supports, and constructively contributes to the strategy. An effective communications campaign can inform the public in ways that broaden networks, encourage innovation, and focus attention on alleviating the struggles of the homeless.

Two different but not necessarily separate passions inspire the public's opinions about homelessness. City residents have a deep compassion for those who are homeless and want them to be treated fairly and humanely.[1] Public polling routinely shows residents are willing to support new taxes for programs that will help the homeless, to see investments in long-term and lasting solutions, and to volunteer their time to work toward solutions.[2] A US national poll conducted in 2019 found that 85 percent of the public believe that ensuring people have a safe, decent, and affordable home should be a priority for the government.[3] At the same time, residents value quality of life in their community and places of work. They don't want to navigate their children around people sleeping in the street, avoid parks that have become de facto open-air shelters, or fear for their safety in passing large street encampments known for drug trade. The same people who want to help the homeless may also have an aversion to the actual homeless person asleep on a bench and to the location of a new shelter next door.

Strategies for engaging the public concerning the problem of homelessness should acknowledge both the compassionate desire to help and the self-interested desire to have streets available for public enjoyment. An effective community strategy must design a campaign to guide public participation in a constructive way that respects the fundamental humanity of those on the street. The campaign should be educational, disseminating concrete facts and information that can counteract misperceptions that generate fear and marginalize those who cannot, or will not, listen. And answers must be provided to specifically overcome the cynical public view that this has all been heard before. Leadership always runs the risk that a community will stop trusting in repetitive promises, especially if the deployment of resources never materializes into measurable progress.

SHAPING CLEAR PUBLIC MESSAGES

Leaders need, through their communications, to constantly reinforce the message that living on a cement sidewalk in a cardboard hut is not a choice anyone would truly, willingly make. Tolerating street homelessness as a lifestyle choice, and using that as an excuse against action, is not a humane response to homelessness.

Throughout the world, extensive histories of human rights abuses have often manifested themselves in social purging of marginalized populations who find themselves on the streets. Acts to protect rough sleepers have intervened to resist these purges, with the unintended consequence of consigning the disadvantaged to exercise their *right* to be on the street as a long-term approach for entire communities. This approach interferes with policies that aggressively move people from unsanitary, life-threatening conditions that cause early mortality and into safe, clean, respectful programs.[4] The challenge for leaders is to be open, clear, and committed and to declare that it is not decent, humane, or charitable to help people stay on the street. Efforts should be applied in every regard—professionally and charitably—toward bringing people inside.

THE VALUE OF PUBLIC ENGAGEMENT

Winning the public hearts and minds is critical to the success of systems-level reform. It takes public will to support calls for new investments in resources, especially if this is to be done through public referenda for new taxes dedicated to investments in a homelessness strategy. An effective campaign is also critical in garnering support from local representatives for measures adopted through legislative changes or in annual budget appropriations.

The hardest win is local, especially in gaining community support for opening new shelters or even permanent supportive housing whenever a proposed site is located close to home. A well-structured and -delivered campaign can help overcome resistance but, as many cities can attest, reaching the public with the intended message by no means guarantees its acceptance. In Athens, for example, the city is hindered in its community outreach by the stark reality that nearly half the homeless population suffers from drug addiction. This problem has hijacked communications efforts, as the public is more interested in what's being done to combat drugs.

At a broader civic level, a mission focus is necessary to overcome the collective sense of ennui—believing that nothing can be done and that any attempt will prove futile. Energizing the belief and commitment to action is as much a strategy to end homelessness as are the policy and programs contained in any concerted effort.

Communicating with intentionality and executing the message well can propel, motivate, inspire, and sustain a campaign. A powerful and disciplined communications campaign is needed to clearly and proactively share the values underlying the plan and the scope of its ambitions. The vehicles used to implement the strategy must contain evidence of concrete actions to drive public sentiment toward support for the strategy. It should also invite constructive volunteer participation. In this way, effective communications are both a generator of energy and momentum and a protection against derailment when the inevitable objections are raised by groups organized against reform or by individuals opposed to certain actions.

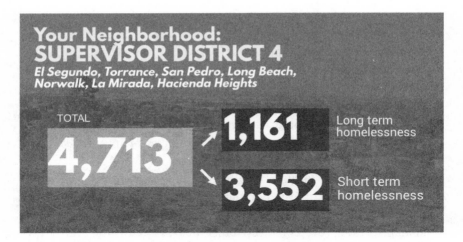

Figure 8. Neighborhood homeless count numbers. United Way of Greater Los Angeles, Everyone In Campaign.

EDUCATE, ENGAGE, ACTIVATE

A communications effort begun in 2016 in the Los Angeles region provides a model for consideration on these fronts. The basic theory of change undergirding the comprehensive communications approach undertaken by the United Way of Greater Los Angeles is the belief that communication shapes discourse, discussions alter thinking, and changed minds generate policy and programs necessary to achieve the solution. This effort has resulted in two referenda (Proposition HHH and Measure H) that will generate significant financial resources to fund the local strategy, and United Way's collaborative work continues to generate local support for specific projects.

Prior to this concerted effort, Los Angeles's public messages regarding homelessness were episodic and unsustained, sent often in reaction to loud opposition against specific actions. Responses were mostly generic—attempting in a single message to reach an enormous county with wildly diverse interests. Without a successful ground campaign, the only voices heard reviled the homeless, opposed service facilities in their neighborhoods, or supported law enforcement policies to clear out the homeless.

The inevitable impression created was of an overwhelming public sentiment in opposition to actions in support of the homeless.

Newly energized by an agenda focused on action, the Los Angeles region's homeless-service advocates and officials decided in 2018 to roll up their sleeves and take on the communications challenge with a proactive campaign. They conducted extensive polling and were surprised to find that public opinion was not what they had assumed. Support and desire for action were present, driven by a strong and widely held belief that the time had come for more effective and humane measures to help those sleeping rough. The opinion research also found that residents were not aware of plans or activities already under way, and were not sufficiently clear on what those programs meant for their community or how they could best help.

In response, the United Way of Greater Los Angeles, a lead community partner in the fight against homelessness, generated a framework for a communications and community-organizing strategy. Taking a long-term vision, the strategy involved sustaining public knowledge and supporting milestone activities consistently over what all the partners recognized would be a long and grueling road ahead for implementation.

Many takeaways emerge from the Los Angeles model. The campaign rolled out in three stages. The first: educate and communicate. A basic lesson learned during the information-gathering stage was that, if the public does not know what the strategy is, they will assume there is no strategy. Dozens of brilliant minds can tackle a challenge. But unless the story is broadcast, who could possibly know the work is under way? Efforts with few short-term wins face a formidable barrier, as interest wanes the longer the public waits for longer-term results. An education component focused on promoting the strategy, laying out the vision and the values that drive that vision, can help each person align their own values with the plan's values and help them identify points of connection where they can contribute and be a part of the momentum for success. Small milestones can be important markers of progress and can refresh the collective memory of the longer-term plan.

Educating the community can be accomplished through high-profile events that generate media coverage. Campaigns can be expensive; any opportunity to generate press coverage will stretch scarce communications dollars farther. Leveraging elected officials and announcing program launches, evaluation results, groundbreakings and ribbon cuttings, can generate news; more importantly, they become opportunities to reinforce the long-term strategy. In this evolving digital-media world, these events can be bolstered with targeted online communications to highlight and reinforce the constant flow of activities.

The second stage of the campaign was engagement. Los Angeles organized a program of in-person events to broaden public participation and make the solutions more real. The partners undertook branding with familiar images and props, including an enormous twelve-foot-tall front door that travels around to community events as an icon for the overall strategy—the symbolic image of arriving at a home of one's own. Holding rallies around key initiatives, such as a bond referendum generating dedicated revenues for homeless programming, created a sense of excitement and momentum and gave residents a concrete way to support the plan. Experience-based community events in every region with structured opportunities to interact, such as open houses in community-based facilities, can also pull in and engage the public.

And the third stage is activation. Without a vehicle for expressing support, the strongest community voice will continue to be one of opposition. If there are no positive messages to share, the oppositional voice remains the only one and the community can slip into the impression that every community member is opposed, even when polling shows otherwise. The objective therefore is to train and activate the quiet majority through community organizing. People who take the opportunity to get out and express their support will move from the presumed opposition column to the compassionate supporter's column.

In Los Angeles, the coalition members cultivated public interest through their education and communications work and engagement events, then members trained and deployed these new community organizers to get involved in passing legislation or approving projects in their neighborhoods. Eventually, after passage of Proposition HHH and Measure H, their 222 campaign, designed to track progress on the implementation of these referenda, also created a way for residents to monitor the progress of adding shelter beds and supportive housing in each community, and to hold each council member accountable to ensuring these targets were achieved.

In a similar move, Paris made a welcome discovery when city officials conducted their first citywide street count in 2018 and found an unexpected source of support in the community. Mayor Anne Hidalgo recruited Deputy Mayor Dominique Versini, a leader in the nonprofit community who had established a street outreach service and developed an aggressive communications campaign to stir more compassion around street homelessness. Deputy Mayor Versini moved forward with a street count despite considerable skepticism as to whether the public would turn out to volunteer. During the weeks leading up to the count, anxiety built over logistical issues compounded by concerns that there would be too few volunteers and teams to adequately cover the territory. Some expressed reservations about the use of untrained volunteers for the task. Contrary to these expectations, Paris officials experienced an outpouring of energetic volunteers who showed up for the midnight count ready and able to assist in a concrete and meaningful way.

The city's subsequent counts have been similarly bolstered by volunteers. Inspired by this success, the city launched La Fabrique de la Solidarité (Factory of Solidarity) in early 2019 after Paris's second count. Volunteers and other residents expressed a desire to do something to tackle homelessness, but were unsure what to do or how to help. The city built a resource center and a mechanism for harnessing the commitment of many residents to contribute to and support the city's mission, including constructive use of cultural programs, education on the issue of homelessness and refuting prejudices, startup and testing of incubator projects, participatory workshops to design city-funded solutions, and even training volunteers to provide direct services.

In fact, by structuring volunteer activities aligned with the values and direction of the community plan, residents can be steered away from actions that, though well meaning, are not conducive to ending homelessness. Such charitable acts as providing meals at feeding stations, distributing blankets, even dispensing vitamins have the unintended effect of keeping people on the street because they are less inclined to accept services inside where it is safe and trained workers can offer more substantive engagement. By offering the community alternative ways to become engaged, these compassionate energies can support the effort to end street homelessness and turn the broad public into an ongoing partner in the effort, even sustaining their support over the long term.

Beyond broad citywide campaigns, city communication plans also require messages microtargeted to specific components. Tailoring a message to each community in Los Angeles is a good example. Broad generic messages can fall flat when activation is focused on the neighborhood level. Different service populations have different housing needs (single adults versus families, for instance). Different neighborhoods have different challenges (a single large encampment in a park versus dispersed individuals hidden in isolated nooks). The activation phase should be customized and segmented to make it manageable. Storytelling events can humanize homelessness for community members by relaying the challenges of people working through struggles and, in many situations, exiting homelessness. Providing clear information on what homelessness looks like, with local solutions pursued at the community level where people reside, helps translate an abstract social problem into a more tangible tragedy facing one's neighbors.

Edmonton has also developed a strong approach to communicating the nature of the city's challenge, strategies to address it, and successes to celebrate. Homeward Trust's webpage is comprehensive, engaging, and up-to-date.[5] Prominently featured on the homepage is Homeward Trust's own logo and icon for all its materials. Notices of events and upcoming initiatives are posted on the site, and it is highly personalized, with stories of individuals served and their successes and challenges, stories that humanize the reality of those suffering the consequences of homelessness. Homeward Trust supplements its website with a blog and a monthly newsletter promoting structured volunteer events to further engage residents.

This communication framework—education, engagement, activation— shifts the prevailing strategy from reactive responses to a proactive campaign that enlivens and clarifies the work. Many obstacles to success remain, however. Leaders need to understand that public patience runs thin. Real, sustained progress takes time, and quick wins are few. And there will always be opposition. A proactive and sustained strategy inoculates the campaign against the negative narrative that can occur over opposition to, for example, the location of a new shelter.

No engagement effort wins unanimous support. Done well, however, the effort will build a solid base of support by mollifying concerns, thus shrinking the base of opposition and generating enough support to proceed. The messaging should never diminish the concerns of skeptics, but rather should validate their feelings and educate them on the facts. Leaders must display the confidence of their convictions and invite objectors to see firsthand what shelters and affordable housing are capable of achieving. Community engagement should not stop once approval has been achieved. Creating an ongoing forum for local engagement diminishes confrontation, provides an outlet for concerns, and enables city officials to know immediately what residents are thinking and, if necessary, to respond.

GOOD RELATIONS WITH THE PRESS

What happens if someone in shelter commits a heinous crime? Or if an angry group of homeless people in a street encampment destroys public property? Situations such as these quickly reach reporters' ears and, chances are, turn into print, radio, and television stories with negative headlines and vivid photographs before anyone from a city agency has the chance to fully investigate the matter and develop solid talking points for explaining the unfortunate set of circumstances to the public. Too quickly, a single isolated event can become a major crisis, often leading to public outcry to close the shelter or immediately remove the encampment. Such a meltdown can be averted through a solid media strategy.

Having access to the press is key to minimizing damage and reassuring the public that the situation is being taken seriously and that appropriate steps are being taken to address any concerns. Laying the groundwork in advance by building media relationships greatly improves the chances of a fair and balanced story. When the family shelter system in New York City was under court supervision in the early 2000s because of long delays in processing applications for shelter, the time spent educating reporters in advance paid off by having news stories explain the complexity of the matter: how many prior court orders had, in fact, created an inefficient and burdensome application process.

A communications point person or group should be integrated in any coalition of city officials, nonprofits, and others involved with ensuring that the city's homeless population is treated humanely and that proper services are delivered. The communications element is core, even when there is no crisis. Decisions being made every day need to be conveyed to the public clearly and coherently. Although press releases serve a function, the most effective communication is person to person. Someone within the coalition should be adept at and comfortable with schmoozing with the press. A phone call, or occasional lunch, goes a long way toward building good media relations and—most important—trust.

Solid trust between media outlets and those working to alleviate the city's homeless situation take time to build and solidify. But the payoff is tremendous, both on proactive and reactive stances. The siting of a new shelter, for instance, involves mass public approval. A communications expert with good skills can get out in front of this project by encouraging members of the press to listen to all the reasons for putting a shelter on that particular street corner. They can anticipate the neighborhood's concerns. And, in advance of any negative publicity, can shape arguments and talking points so that everyone in the coalition offers the same strong reasons for the placement. Los Angeles County's comprehensive shelter development strategy did just that, making clear the regional nature of the problem and the importance of shelters strategically located throughout the entire county. News stories contain both sides of the situation. However, the more articulate and consistent the rationale for the shelter, the higher placed those quotes will likely appear in the story. When stories appeared, Los Angeles officials would follow through with engagement events, deploying community organizers in every region to get involved in approving projects in their neighborhoods, carrying the strategic messages through to the street level and reporting on progress. County officials would also humanize the residents who were to live in proposed new facilities through storytelling events hosted to introduce people to real-life triumphs of those exiting homelessness.

Handling a crisis poses a more complex set of challenges; meeting them is easier when one has the media's trust. Reaction to an explosive event requires advance planning, not unlike a fire drill procedure. Reporters, often the first to know of the blow up, will immediately contact the communications point person, who may or may not have the full details. The emergency plan goes live. Such prearranged procedures may trigger an immediate conference call, a fact-finding mission, a statement sent to all media outlets, and outreach to the public. That would all occur on Day One. In subsequent days, the coalition may develop other statements that explore what went wrong, steps being taken to correct the situation, and, if necessary, an apology.

HARNESSING COMPASSION THROUGH WELL-DIRECTED VOLUNTEERISM

Mobilizing city residents in a comprehensive campaign can unleash energetic volunteerism. In Paris, the outpouring of more than seventeen hundred volunteers for a street count opened Mayor Anne Hidalgo's eyes to the desire of residents to do more for the homeless. In fact, the city's participatory budgeting process for 2016 resulted in a minishelter proposal receiving the most votes, followed by more municipal investment to get the initiative off the ground and to evaluate its effectiveness.

This discovery of compassion proved so validating to the city that the mayor and deputy mayor explored more ways to leverage citizen involvement. Paris officials began to generate ideas about how citizens could identify creative strategies to channel volunteerism. As a result, the city has repurposed several centrally located buildings as centers for civic engagement and innovation on a range of issues.

In closing, a word of caution: A clear and comprehensive engagement strategy must have room for engagement, learning, and evolution. But the strategy must also chart a deliberate and determined path toward an end. Programs should not only incorporate feedback from residents and clients but also be evidence based and accountable to a clear theory of change over time. Leaders and program managers must involve the public and be informed by evidence. An honest conversation allows for both.

9 Understanding the Homeless System

STREET COUNTS, BY-NAME LISTS, AGENCY
DATABASES, AND BASIC RESEARCH

When Bogotá mayor Enrique Peñalosa tackled head-on the human trafficking, drug dealing, and homelessness in the city's seediest district, El Bronx, he was criticized for pushing the homeless problem underground by diffusing criminal and street-living groups into residential neighborhoods—and he had no strategy to counter that belief. In Baltimore and Nashville, officials engaged long-standing nonprofit and religious providers to oversee the needs of the homeless, but had set no common goals, measures, or systems for addressing those needs. Officials in Paris, as well as in Athens, faced growing pressures to address burgeoning homeless populations, but had no basic count of the number of people sleeping on their streets and no way to tell whether their efforts were producing results.

How can data and information help cities attack their accountability problems? Should a city even care about numbers when discussing homeless people? After all, putting a number on individual circumstances is sometimes seen as dehumanizing the homelessness as it risks minimizing its complexity. And collecting data can divert time and money from providing direct services.

Further, counting the number of homeless people is an uncertain science. A variety of methods are used, but none is perfect. To begin with, the homeless population is hard to reach. They are transient and often have no address; they may resist being counted and hide from surveyors; and use of volunteers and safety concerns prohibit access to certain areas, such as abandoned buildings or subway tunnels. Also, the number of homeless people on a given night is vastly different from the number over the course of a year. Even with widespread use of databases, the systems that providers, religious groups, and government rely on are not always compatible or may be proprietary; and the type of data collected may be inconsistent.

Definitions of who is homeless vary geographically and are influenced by vastly different bureaucratic structures, legal interpretations, and cultural contexts. It is no coincidence that localities with more-generous social programs often have a more inclusive definition of homelessness.

Despite difficulties in measuring the number of homeless, understanding the magnitude of homelessness in a community *is* important. Street homelessness is harmful for those who live in public spaces and has negative effects on the communities and areas in which street homelessness proliferates. For humanitarian and quality-of-life reasons, people on the street are helped by public, private, and nonprofit agencies, as well as by citizens, many of them united by the vision that street homelessness, as a condition of urban life, should not simply be accepted (or should be at least rare and short-lived).

Street counts, along with by-name lists and program-level data of homeless individuals, shine a light on stories and struggles that otherwise might go unnoticed. Regularly tracked individual- and program-level data serve as bellwethers, but numbers will not answer questions about program effectiveness, or the causes of homelessness, or the impact of efforts on levels of homelessness in a community. More in-depth evaluations and research address those larger, thornier questions; for those, a city needs studies with systematic selection of subjects and rigorous research designs. Well-designed studies are particularly useful for exploring large questions and understanding programs that affect large populations.

Data collection enables a city to scope out the situation. For over a decade, US and Canadian cities—and, more recently, an increasing number of international cities—use a point-in-time street count or a survey of service users to provide an annual measure of the extent of homelessness. Conducted every year or every other year, these estimates involve a comprehensive survey of how many people are living on the street. These street estimates are simultaneously paired with a summary of the number of people in shelter in order to obtain a complete point-in-time figure. By including basic demographics, such as gender, age, and duration of homelessness, that allow the city to track the size and shape of the problem over time, officials can chart the trajectory of homelessness for the city.

A BRIEF HISTORY OF MODERN STREET COUNTS IN THE TEN CITIES

In the United States, efforts at counting the street homeless have progressed tremendously over the past quarter century, from guesstimates in the 1980s, to unverified estimates by advocates and experts, to more systematic approaches involving surveys of individuals, often involving sampling strategies.[1] Perhaps the earliest estimating method with merit was the Census Bureau's 1980 *casual count* and *mission night,* which enumerated individuals in welfare and food stamp offices, shelters, bus stations, and other locations where homeless individuals were likely to be found during the night.[2] In the early 1980s, a few cities experimented with service-user methods to count the homeless, such as in Nashville and Los Angeles, or the point-in-time street count, such as in Chicago.[3] As part of the 1990 and 2000 US censuses, the federal government attempted to produce a count of persons visible in street locations, through the Shelter and Street Night (S-Night) count, but cautioned that its method was never intended to produce a count of the total population of homeless at the national, state, or local level, and the results were attacked by watchdog organizations.[4] In 2005, inspired by rough-sleeper initiatives in London and modeled on a counting method used earlier in Chicago, New York City developed a rigorous methodology and conducted its first citywide count. In 2007, building on the experience of New York City and other cities, the US Congress mandated biennial street counts from all its local homelessness coordinating (continuum of care) agencies, as a condition for receiving federal funding from the Department of Housing and Urban Development. The federal government provided guidance on how to conduct counts but left it to localities to choose their preferred method.[5]

Houston conducted its first count in 2005, and Baltimore, Los Angeles, and Nashville all conducted their first citywide counts two years later.

Similar developments occurred in Canada, which was an early player in conducting regular street counts.[6] In 1999 and 2000, Edmonton conducted two counts a year, and then every other year from 2002 to 2018. Canada developed guidelines for common methods in its annual counts and, in early 2016, called for a national effort, though many major cities opted out; the 2018 result was more successful, with the number of communities increasing from thirty-two to sixty-one.[7] In 2018, the timing of the Edmonton count was moved from October to April to be in sync with the Canadian standard, and the definition of who was included was slightly changed.[8]

Some Latin America countries have made occasional efforts to count rough sleepers within their borders. As a part of the Colombia national census, Bogotá's estimates of the homeless began in 1997 and repeated every four to seven years, with the most recent count having been conducted, as of this writing, in 2017.[9] Bogotá introduced its own municipal assessment—termed a *georeferenciación de parches y cambuches* (a geographical mapping of where homeless people congregate socially or live in encampment-like structures)—in 2014, repeated in 2017. Mexico City conducted its first count as a municipality in 2015, and, as required in the city's new homeless protocol, it continues to perform counts every other year. The third was done in the winter of 2019, at the start of the new mayoral administration, albeit with a changed methodology.

Aside from perhaps the United Kingdom, no European country has made counts mandatory or even strongly recommended. A number of nations, regions, and cities across Europe have conducted either regular, periodic, or one-off counts, but more have been led by nonprofits or researchers than by local or national officials. By 2020, major cities were conducting point-in-time street counts infrequently or not at all, despite a call to formally do so by the Fédération Européenne des Associations Nationales Travaillant avec les Sans-Abri (European Federation of National Organizations Working with the Homeless, known as FEANTSA) and the 2006 recommendations of the UN Conference on European Statisticians for the 2010/2011 Census.[10] France conducted national estimates of the homeless for cities larger than 20,000 in 2001 and

2012.[11] Paris piloted a count in January 2018, followed by its first full-city point-in-time street count the following month, a procedure now repeated annually. The city of Athens conducted its first pilot street count in December 2017, and in May 2018, the Greek National Ministry piloted a street count in seven cities, including Athens.

Most places conduct counts once a year, as in New York City, or every other year, as in Baltimore. A few cities have more frequent regular counts, twice or more a year, as in Edmonton in the early years. In too many places, counts are done infrequently and irregularly, as in the case of Bogotá, or not at all, as was the case until recently in Mexico City, Paris, and Athens.

CHALLENGES WITH COUNTING THE STREET HOMELESS

If something as basic as counting people on the street is crucial to building a citywide coalition to fight homelessness, why have Athens, Paris, and Mexico City only recently conducted their first estimates? Lack of political will and leadership can explain some of the paucity or absence of homeless counts, but complexities of how to design a street count and how to carry it out are not to be discounted. In some cities and countries, a data-centered culture may be weak or absent in the social services field. The definition of who is homeless, discussed earlier, and the locations where counters should look must be established. To be counted as homeless, does someone have to be legally residing in the country (as in Greece), and should surveys exclude people in makeshift housing in shanty towns or slums (as in parts of Mexico City and Bogotá)?

In Bogotá, for example, a question arose about how to count recyclers who pushed around wooden carts in which they also lived. The carts were their working place, much as a fisherman might stay in a boat, and many had families outside the city where they could stay. The decision was made to ask the recyclers themselves about their housing situation; most replied that they considered themselves homeless, even if they often resisted the notion at first.

One defining difference in homeless counts is whether they are conducted on the streets or in places where homeless people seek services, such as soup kitchens or drop-in centers. To determine the homeless status

STREET COUNTS

Jay Bainbridge

Many lurid tales may be told by volunteers sent out in bands in the dark of night to survey the homeless in El Bronx (Bogotá), Tepito (Mexico City), La Colline (Paris), or in the old days, Tompkins Square Park (New York City). In the pilot count of Manhattan, overeager teams of volunteers of ten or more, all aiming flashlights, intimidated and scared away many potential interviewees who felt their space was being invaded. In advance of the Mexico City street survey, I briefed an armed security team assigned to accompany us, explaining that we would be approaching homeless people—individually or in large groups or encampments—and that it would be OK. The first time we entered an encampment community, you could see the security people stiffen up on alert, ready to react. Soon, they noticed the community members engage and talk with us, even banter and joke. We were with social workers and outreach workers who had over time developed relationships with the people.

Waking people up has risks. Once, on the edge of Central Park, a woman was sleeping on a bench in the middle of winter. The team wondered if she was all right. What to do? An experienced social worker took a step closer while the rest of the team kept a distance, and asked, "How are you doing?" From out of nowhere came a strident screech and the woman bolted upright. As the social worker tried to appease her, and the team took several steps back, the screaming grew louder. Everyone apologized as they moved away slowly and left. Another team of professionals followed up later.

In Bogotá, where food is provided to people who are woken up, the response is more welcoming. Everyone has a unique social sector ID number that they are asked to provide to receive services; most know it by heart and share it freely. However, Bogotá does present dangers. Use of *basuco*—an extremely addictive and cheap derivative of cocaine—is common. Teams in areas where drugs are dealt often witness lines of people coming and going in a somewhat zombie state as they seek to buy or to find a place to use. Areas where shoes are hanging from wires and poles can indicate an invisible warning barrier not to be crossed without consequences. One team that did so was hailed as it retreated, and photos were taken of the volunteers' license plates, presumably by "narcos" or drug dealers to send a warning.

In the six years I oversaw operations of the New York City street count, no volunteer was harmed. Some of that record is due to taking precautions, such as notifying police of the areas where teams would be sent and allowing them to send patrol officers to areas deemed a possible threat, as well as briefing officers about the nature and process of the count. Any area that poses an imminent threat is treated as "special" and assigned professional staff in the early-morning hours. Some areas, such as abandoned buildings, are considered too dangerous to enter and are outside of the sample.

Another precaution is to make teams big enough (but not too big) to provide safety in numbers, and making sure that teams stay together, or at least within eyesight of one another. Teams are instructed to remove themselves from any situation where they feel uncomfortable, and to call into headquarters if they feel they cannot cover a specific area, or to call 911 if in imminent danger.

of people at service centers, one has to construct a list of all the places frequented by homeless people, so they can be visited or at least systematically sampled. Then, users of the centers need to be interviewed about their housing status on a particular night or over a particular period of time.[12]

A challenge with these counts is that those who are homeless, interviewed in a place where they are receiving services, may wish to hide their housing status. Or they may be shelter residents as opposed to street homeless; also possible, their memory may be faulty about where they were on a particular night. Further, constructing a full list of local centers for social services and assistance may not be realistic, and not all homeless people use such services. In contrast, a point-in-time street count has the advantage of face validity, since each person is actually surveyed on the streets the night of the count. Then again, they may have a place to live and could be sleeping off a binge or a fight with their partner. Street counts adopt more limited definitions of who is homeless. Some innovative

Figure 9. Volunteers surveying for the Paris point-in-time street count, Nuit de la Solidarité, 2018. Guillaume Bontemps/Ville de Paris.

approaches have attempted to combine elements of both street counts and surveys of service users.[13]

Given any definition of who is considered homeless in a city, how does a surveyor-volunteer determine the housing status of people encountered on the streets? Are all people who look homeless—for example, anyone sleeping on a train late at night—without housing? Are there homeless people who do not fit the stereotype? To avoid biased assumptions about who is homeless, one approach is to interview every person on the street during the time of the count. The surveyor collects enough information to provide useful knowledge, but not so much as to deter participation or prolong the interview. Eight to ten questions on a single side of a page is ideal. As uncomfortable as it might be for a surveyor to approach someone late at night to ask about their housing situation, the unease wears off quickly and it is well worth the effort. Every year following counts, stories are told of how a distinguished-looking older gentleman dressed in a three-piece suit and bow tie or a young man in a stylish down coat and nice gym shoes self-reported they did not have a place to stay. Also told are stories of a person who looked disheveled and weakened of faculties *did* have a place.

The time of day the counts are done, over what period of time, and at what time of year will also change results. Conducting counts late at night allows the homeless to settle down in their sleeping spots for the night, sorting some into shelters and reducing the number of people the counters have to approach. However, late-night counts hamper the ability to survey thoroughly, as many are sleeping. Doing counts early in the evening or during the day increases foot traffic and makes it more difficult to de-duplicate with shelter dwellers, who may not be in for the night yet. Early-evening or day counts also make it difficult to survey everyone who passes by, leading to bias based on stereotypes about who is or is not homeless as crowds are triaged for interviews. A survey done over a longer period will count more people since the homeless are cycling in and out of precarious situations. Picking a single night creates a well-defined window and reduces duplication. While no street count method is perfect—they all provide only estimates—consistency matters. The count should happen the same day or time of year, during the same time frame, to most effectively compare results across counts.[14]

Duplicate counting is a big concern with street counts. A person who is counted in one part of town but who moves to another area should not be counted again, especially if there are rewards associated with the survey. In Bogotá, surveyors are able to avoid double counting because residents have a municipal ID, like the US Social Security number, which everyone has memorized and is willing to share with their outreach worker. Also, sleeping homeless people in Bogotá are often woken up to receive food so they are more amenable to being surveyed at night, but that is the exception rather than the rule.

A survey is key for asking about housing status, recording basic demographics, and checking against duplication. Including a short needs assessment for better tailoring of services is also an option. Paris officials chose a longer survey, which provided some desired information but also created logistical challenges. Other cities leave needs assessments out of their street counts and conduct separate surveys using trained personnel.

Cities must confront the fact that street counts involve danger. In New York City, for safety reasons, counters are instructed not to go into obscured private places, indoor ATMs, movie theaters, or all-night food joints, even if they are accessible. How to approach spaces whose occupants are to be counted requires clear direction. Whether teams knock on car windows or rattle tent flaps to survey people (late at night) or make assumptions about who is homeless within will also be informed by decisions about respect for privacy and safety of those on the count. In Paris, tents are assumed a priori to have one person in them, unless the number of shoes outside indicate otherwise or unless the tent dwellers willingly engage with the surveyors. The city of Paris favored the assumption of two, but the national government insisted on establishing a one-person tent standard.

Cities also confront significant logistical challenges in managing a count across a vast territory with a large population. The New York City counts cover all areas where the homeless are expected to be found, and a random sample of the rest—a method also adopted by Mexico City. Initially, Mexico City resisted the notion of random sampling, but for a city of its size, there is no possible way to cover all streets in one night with the resources at the city's disposal. Covering only sites where homeless people are known to congregate would miss a good portion of the population, as homeless people do not always live in large, visible groups and they are mobile. In New York City, nearly half of the estimate of the street homeless population comes from places with low concentrations of homeless. Conducting a pilot with a random sample made this clear to Mexico City officials, who were thankful for information on pockets of unmet need.

In Bogotá, María Consuelo Araújo Castro, *la secretaría distrital de integración social* (district secretary of social integration), and her staff divided the sprawling city into three regions and covered them over three nights instead of sampling. Duplicate counting, they reasoned, would be less of a problem given the city's municipal ID, even if some of the people are sleeping and do not share that information. With less ground to cover in Paris, Vanessa Benoit of the Centre d'Action de la Ville de Paris and Deputy Mayor Dominique Versini chose to do a census of their city in one night, similar to the count in Athens, with deployment hubs in each of its twenty arrondissements.

Covering an entire city in one night presents staffing challenges. New York City and Paris rely heavily on volunteers, while other places such as Mexico City and Bogotá mostly enlist municipal workers. Bogotá's practice of spreading the work over three days makes it easier on staff. In general, cities provide staff compensatory time off in exchange for the late-night hours worked.

Whether a city chooses volunteers, professional staff, or a mix of the two to do the counting, the quality of the information collected always needs to be tested. How does the city's plan and approach ensure that the teams cover all the areas assigned to them in the designated time period (not more, not less) and interview everyone they encounter? In New York City, a method of quality-assurance devised by outside researchers deploys decoys—people posing as everyday citizens placed randomly in areas covered by homeless surveyors—so as to encourage adherence to proper surveying by adjusting the estimate based on the number of decoys missed.[15] The decoys take notes in the field while observing whether or not the street count surveyor teams visited the area within the designated times—providing a measure of proper coverage—and whether or not the surveyors interviewed the decoys—a measure of completeness. Many cities, including Athens, Bogotá, Houston (launched in 2019), and New York City (piloted), are developing apps with GPS capability to precisely document where and when surveys are conducted.

In some cities, such as New York City, Mexico City, Bogotá, Paris, and Athens, the first street counts were precursors to, accompaniments of, or parts of a broader strategic plan. Street counts can be the genesis of new service models, motivation to increase housing and outreach resources, or linchpins to forming broader coalitions. The counts not only provide a measuring stick of progress but also help to focus attention on the homelessness issue, coordinate stakeholders, garner needed resources, communicate to the public, and hold the government accountable.

SUCCESSES WITH STREET COUNTS

Even though Athens and Paris had never done a systematic survey of the number of people sleeping on their streets, officials were able to pull together pilots and, shortly thereafter, full-city counts. In 2017, Maria Stratigaki, Athens's vice mayor for social solidarity, welfare, and equality and Théodora Papadimitriou, an advisor to the mayor—partially inspired by visits to other cities where counts took place and partially motivated by what was perceived as an increase in Athens's unsheltered population—initiated a pilot street count over two months despite initial resistance from local service providers and the national Ministry of Labor. Success with the pilot count, which included the development of an app by a private group to ease data collection, rested primarily on strong cooperation among actors, despite their being from different levels of government with competing political party control. This led to a full-city count organized by the national ministry in 2018, advanced when city and other, civil society actors drafted new legislation on social services as part of a national strategy to combat homelessness. In January 2018, Vanessa Benoit and Simon Vackere of the Centre d'Action de la Ville de Paris and Deputy Mayor Dominique Versini, driven by some of the same motivation and inspiration as in Athens and emboldened by Athens' recent success, organized a pilot count within a month's time, and a full-city count within a month later. Even though all publicly accessible areas in Paris are covered on the night of the count, city officials feel the model could be expanded to include additional "gray areas," such as parks, parking lot staircases, and hallways in decrepit buildings. The Paris approach includes data collection from a lengthy survey and an annual public report on the unsheltered. The count has been a popular activity among those wishing to volunteer, and is a focal point for community engagement, as discussed in the previous chapter.

Among the lessons learned from the successes in Paris and Athens is that the challenges of designing street counts, though complex, can be overcome. Officials from both cities turned around counts within very short time horizons. Parisian leaders were able to carry out their Nuit de Solidarité with strong agency support and staff and a league of volunteers. Athens's mayoral agents did their point-in-time street count on a comparative shoestring—without much of a budget or much organizational support from the city, any state or national agency, or volunteers. Yet Athens was the city that innovated by providing an app for surveyors, and it did so using private development services donated by one individual. Bogotá innovated as well with an app, developed by agency staff in a short time frame, while New York City and Paris have lagged in this respect. (After piloting systems for a number of years, New York City's Department of Homeless Services finally implemented an app to collect data in 2020.) Mexico City leaders cleverly used metro stations as training and launching areas so counters had access to the city's farther reaches, and Bogotá used existing community centers. New York City's homeless agency relied on public schools and sites on the City University of New York campus for training space, as well as using thousands of volunteers.

BY-NAME LISTS IMPROVE TRACKING

Street counts are useful tools for providing overall, year-over-year account-ability; however, they are not robust enough to manage the daily street outreach operations or track placements from the street into homes and shelters. In Edmonton in November 2015, for example, a community of providers and activists led by Susan McGee, CEO of Edmonton's Homeward Trust, set the goal, as part of Canada's 20K Home Campaign, of housing 650 homeless people by January 2018. A central strategy in this initiative was to develop a quality by-name list through coordinated entry into the homeless service system, along with a push for Housing First. Through Homeward Trust's database system, sixty-one homeless-service agencies screened and entered individuals in the by-name lists who were then referred to the proper housing intervention program based on community priorities. Eventually, referrals were being made in real time or at regular meetings. The protocol also allowed tracking changes in real time—inflow versus outflow.

The more providers work together to coordinate and prioritize resources to engage and house those who are on the street, the easier it becomes to share rosters of those served. These by-name lists are community resources that enable providers to match needs with available housing opportunities. The rosters also bolster initiatives that focus on particular subpopulations, such as those in encampments or that target veteran homeless individuals for housing subsidies or chronic substance users for low-threshold services in a Safe Haven.

Edmonton's commitment to end chronic homelessness is made concrete by the use of a single citywide by-name list that includes all individuals known to be homeless, including those who are couch surfing and do not expect to stay in one place for very long. Initially, the city aims to prevent anyone who is homeless for the first time from becoming chronically or long-term homeless. The plan then sets forth a number of strategies for focusing on the highest-needs individuals within priority populations such as indigenous youth, matching them to the best opportunities for overcoming their homelessness. The eligibility criteria for these groups varies by the resource being matched, but typically they include length of time homeless, acuity of need as determined by scoring on survey instruments, and the priority given to youth and families.[16]

Edmonton's goal of ending chronic homelessness will be achieved when no one on its list has been homeless for more than a year or has had more than four episodes of homelessness over three years (the city's definition of *chronic*). In the period since the coordinated effort began, the number of homeless has dropped from 3,709 in 2008 to 1,752 in 2016. Of these, only 410 people on the street and 660 in the shelters are chronically homeless. According to the 2018 progress report, more than 900 people had been housed in the preceding year, exceeding the 20K Home Campaign goal of 650.[17]

By-name lists are not the equivalent of a count, in that they do not accurately or completely reflect the current status. However, these lists can reflect some of the flow in and out of homelessness and homeless people's length of stay better than a point-in-time street count.

A city's list also serves to inform participating partners of the limits of their resources, the mismatch of services to needs, and the gaps in strategies not being filled through the current set of actions. Individuals on the list who cannot be served through existing resources can become the focus of new solutions developed to meet unique or emerging needs. The collective work also creates a forum for these gaps to be discussed and solutions to be devised.

USING AGENCY DATABASES

By-name lists are but one way that cities can collect and use easily available data to track service use among their homeless population, particularly those in shelter, and to seek efficiencies and achieve goals, if they can collect data from all their providers. Capacity management databases contain a wealth of information on shelter inhabitants since anyone who stays a night or uses a service is logged in.

Unlike the point-in-time street count, databases allow agencies and cities to accurately count and de-duplicate the number of homeless people on a given night, over the course of a year, or over multiple years. Agency databases collect information important to the running of the program, such as entry and exit dates, number and types of people served or contacted, client characteristics (e.g., personal identifier, age, gender, ethnicity, past experiences with homelessness), services offered (mental health, employment, drug treatment), and processing time (how long it takes to get a referral, file an application for limited housing, or obtain a transfer for a child's schooling). Process metrics help to determine whether programs are working as intended. With these data, social workers and agency heads assess whether programs have vacancies or waiting lists in relation to population demand.

In addition to looking at what the programs are doing, providers and city agencies want to measure client improvements, which is much harder to document. Databases can be used to collect such outcome information in order to track whether the homeless person's situation, knowledge, or behavior is heading in the right direction. Outcomes include placements in permanent or other forms of housing; reductions in the number of chronically homeless or homeless veterans; the percentage placed in housing who returned to homelessness after a year; decreased substance use; and improved health and well-being.

Determining individual or program progress requires constant effort. Setting metrics for service standards and intended outcomes is an important step toward creating an efficient and effective homeless services agency or system. Integrated systems that weave together data from multiple service systems can illuminate the cycles of multiagency involvement and track progress in reducing institutional involvement across agencies as successful interventions are made.

COORDINATED INTAKE AND DATA TRACKING

As discussed in chapter 7, on systems-level thinking, both service providers and the homeless are often frustrated by how fractured and siloed services can be. One client may interact with multiple case managers, each with overlapping or contradictory goals and each unaware of what the others are doing. Each program, agency, or department may have its own intake form and client ID, with background and usage information whose content and format may or may not match those at other places. Consequently, each time a homeless person applies for a service, they are asked the same long set of questions answered many times before.

Regrettably not all cities have coordinated intake and data tracking, which limits the extent to which information about particular programs can be generalized across a city.

Some public shelters, especially those serving domestic violence victims, AIDS patients, alcohol and drug users, or refugees, are not tracked in the broader homeless system. Some shelters are privately run, such as those operated by religious organizations, and do not necessarily share data with public facilities. And those living on the streets frequently refuse to share their real name or identifiers and may go by an alias. As a result, information gathered on the street cannot be cleanly linked to instances when the person sought other services, such as shelter or substance-use treatment, and were required to provide an official identification card. Persuading partners operating outside a coordinated tracking system to share their data, or simply collaborate in reporting to allow a complete count, is necessary to generate accurate information at the city level.[18]

Cities that lack coordinated data tracking have particular difficulty deriving accurate figures for the number of unduplicated homeless over the course of a period and the length of time it takes for homeless to receive services.

For example, Baltimore provides a wide array of services to those experiencing homelessness, including emergency shelter; transitional housing for youth, veterans, and those fleeing domestic violence; Rapid Rehousing; permanent supportive housing; and emergency rental assistance. Service quality varies across programs, but important steps have been taken to unify all providers to adopt Housing First principles and best practices in delivering high-quality homeless services. Even so, the city has been unable to put in place coordinated entry for shelter; as a result, while leaders would like to monitor data carefully to ensure they are meeting goals, they are unable to do so.

In Nashville, the city put in place a new governance structure to unify what had been a bifurcated system, thereby joining city government with relatively strong, independent, religiously affiliated nonprofits, and instituting a coordinated entry into the homeless system. As of 2019, the new system had achieved greater coordination and many successes; however, lack of common goals made it difficult to establish an outcome-based approach. The new governing body did adopt a three-year strategic plan in summer 2019 outlining steps that should be taken to build a common agenda. In Paris, all city social service agencies used a social work case management system, yet it has not been completely extended to NGOs and providers and thus does not cover the entire homeless population being served. The French national government also collects some data that it does not share with the city, providers, NGOs, or the community, either at the individual or the aggregate level. Athens recently initiated a shared case system as well, linking Social Solidarity Department cases with those of KYADA—a municipal government–contracted agency providing outreach and emergency services. However, NGOs are currently not included in the data sharing, even though their clientele overlaps with that of other providers.

Having reams of agency data can be a powerful tool, though they leave many pertinent questions unanswered. Agency databases are used primarily to document usage and to facilitate billing. They are not research files. Workers reliably enter data on when service started and ended, along with important case management notes. There are trade-offs, however, between the quantity of questions asked of a client when service is initiated and the quality of the data, especially if the information requested is not perceived as essential to one's daily work. Academic and policy experts may wish to know extensive background and childhood experiences of clients, but unless the caseworker finds the information helpful in stabilizing the individual and placing them in housing, a lengthy set of research questions is not likely to be filled out.

Cities need to be aware that data may be complete and accurate but not meaningful. In Paris, and across France, a person who is homeless can dial a national telephone number, 115, to request access to a shelter. The hotline is open 24/7, and the call volume is usually quite high around the time that shelters open their doors for the night. The centralized structure allows for a coordinated intake, and the daily call volume data, including requests for accommodation, are carefully tracked. Before Paris began its annual street homelessness count in 2018, the 115 call data were some-times used as a proxy to estimate the needs of people on the street. The Paris street homeless census included a question that asked each individual living on the street if they used the 115 hotline. The 2019 census results showed that 63 percent of street homeless respondents never called the hotline. The call data were a perfectly good measure for hotline utilization, but did not represent the shelter needs of most street homeless in the city as many homeless bypassed the hotline in securing shelter.

DATA MATCHES

Agencies outside homeless services that impact the number of homeless and the nature and duration of their housing permanency or loss constitute another valuable source of information. Child welfare agencies, hospitals, mental health centers, jails and prisons, or housing courts share clientele, even if not their missions. These agencies are not likely to initiate coordinated data sets, though some cities have attempted such projects to rationalize multiple services delivered to one person or family by giving caseworkers access to data across systems so they can see all that is being done for their client. Of course, opening up information on clients to multiple agencies raises issues of confidentiality and accountability.

One way to breach information silos across agencies with differing missions is to negotiate one-time or ongoing data-matching agreements. For instance, if more people seem to be coming into the homeless system from foster care agencies, domestic violence shelters, evictions, prisons, or hospitals, information from any two agencies can be matched on identifiers and combined into one database to analyze the flow of people from one place to the other.

Matching databases across agencies is easier in theory than practice, as unique identifiers may not match and data quality may be inconsistent. Combining databases poses challenges, but new technology can help. In addition, the data matches are often set up as one-time or periodic exercises saved for common agendas or initiatives across agencies.

An example of two distinct organizations collaborating to reach a shared and mutually beneficial goal occurred in New York City when the homeless-services commissioner and the probation commissioner established seemingly disparate goals, but were working with the same people. For homelessness, the goal was to reduce the instability of cycling in and out of shelters. For probation, the cycling occurred in jails. Each agency attended to those who used their services consistently: the chronically homeless and the frequently incarcerated. A data match revealed a huge overlap of individuals engaged in the two cycles: many of the same people were shuffling between the two venues, yet they were not identified in either agency initiative as heavy users of services. The two agencies adopted a new, collaborative approach for doing business by creating new goals and setting up integrated systems coordination and mutual accountability. The new program—FUSE (Frequent User Systems Engagement)—involves the collaboration of nonprofits, a national supportive housing organization, and six city agencies: Correction, Homeless Services, Health and Mental Hygiene, Housing Preservation and Development, the Housing Authority, and the Human Resources Administration. Sharing data allows FUSE to serve the most-frequent users of multiple-service systems, coordinate interventions, and prioritize cases for placement in supportive housing. The program resulted in dramatically lower use of shelter, emergency services, and jail and produced high rates of housing stability (86 percent permanently housed after two years from original placement).[19]

WELL-CRAFTED RESEARCH AND OTHER SOURCES OF INFORMATION

In addition to routinely collecting data on the overall number of people living in shelters or on the street, a city gains from collecting basic knowledge concerning those experiences or experiences in other places. Not all information presents itself as a number or a figure on a chart to be managed, as a list of risk factors, or as an easy-to-read flow chart.

As part of designing its new prevention program, Mexico City's agency for youth that is in charge of homelessness prevention and family homelessness, Sistema para Desarrollo Integral de la Familia (DIF CDMX), not only collected client characteristics from shelter logs but also interviewed homeless people and outreach staff about what risk factors they thought contributed most to their homelessness. Following its homeless street count, New York City Department of Homeless Services staff and contracted nonprofit agencies have periodically conducted needs analyses of the street homeless population using trained outreach workers along with agency policy staff to conduct early-morning surveys in the field using a snowball sampling technique. The teams start at a place where they know homeless people sleep, and ask those they interview if there is anyone like them nearby whom they can also talk to. The needs analysis is used to document whether the street population changes over time in its age, causes of homelessness, substance use, and provenance. Gaps in services can thus be adjusted. Baltimore uses its Lived Experience Committee, consisting of people previously or currently homeless, to provide input into decision making. Other cities have client advocacy offices that collect ideas from those being served, sometimes with committees who meet regularly with leadership. Another worthwhile practice is to visit shelters or walk the streets where homeless people reside to talk to clients and staff, observe who is homeless, and witness what types of services are being provided.

Bogotá's Secretaría Distrital de Integración Social is a model for the use of multiple types of data to understand a city's street homeless population. Working with the national government, the municipal government was an early entrant of street counts in 1997, though these soon became infrequent adjoints of the census, occurring every few years at first, until seven years passed between the two most recent ones, in 2011 and 2017. To fill the gap in the national census taking, Bogotá initiated two *georeferencia* projects (2014 and 2017) that mapped the locations of homeless people. It also collected and mapped data on homicides of homeless people on the streets (2014–2015), surveyed those at risk of homelessness (2014), and conducted a public opinion survey of citizens about their perceptions of homelessness (2015).

Using multiple forms of data, an evaluator can assess whether a program is meeting its clear outcome targets. What percentage of people receiving prevention services are coming into shelters or ending up on the streets? If a lot of people served in prevention programs become homeless, that could indicate a problem. However, if 100 percent of the people being served by prevention services are staying housed, that could point to another problem—namely, that services are not going to those at high risk of homelessness.

Understanding program impacts usually involves some type of comparison or control group to answer the question of what would have happened absent the intervention. If the prevention program is being offered in some communities of high need and not others, the communities receiving prevention can be compared with those that do not, before and after the program has been implemented.

For example, as a way to explain unusually high increases in the New York City shelter population and in Los Angeles street homeless counts from 2010 to 2017, economist Brendan O'Flaherty compared changes in each of those cities to changes in immediately surrounding areas. His research showed that New York City shelter populations grew far more than in surrounding New Jersey communities (which actually decreased) or the rest of New York State (which increased far less). In Los Angeles, the change in the unsheltered population was different from the rest of the county and surrounding areas. Both suggested that city policies played a role in the unusual numbers, as opposed to simply external or economic factors.[20]

Comparison or control groups differ in how rigorously comparable they are, one of the strongest options being a random assignment design, though it is not always practical. For times when random assignment is not possible, as because it is not ethical or because the study is being done retrospectively, researchers can use statistical techniques to fashion comparison groups with advanced multiple regressions, or other strong designs such as natural experiments or regression discontinuity. For example, researchers Robert Collison and Davin Reed have taken the universe of housing court records in New York City from 2007 to 2016 to look at the effect of evictions on homelessness, personal physical and mental health, and income. They took advantage of the fact that housing court cases are generally randomly assigned to courtrooms. Since each courtroom has different tendencies and practices in terms of leniency, this variation can be quantified and used (in economics terms, as an instrumental variable) to identify the causes and effects of evictions, separate from individual characteristics. Collison and Reed found that evictions do increase homelessness and health problems, with long-term lingering effects, but have less effect on income.[21]

A full picture of the potential impact of homeless programs requires comparison groups of both people who are homeless and those at risk of becoming that way. Out of the group of at-risk people, some will have episodes in shelter or on the street over the years. Some of the best impact research is found in time-series studies that start with a base population at risk and follow them for a decade or more.[22]

Without a comparison or control group, it will be impossible for decision makers in a city to know whether any changes following a program are due to the efforts of agencies, the community, and the clients, or due to some other factor, like a change in the economy, or weather, or luck. A highly successful program's effects could be masked by other, co-occurring events.

A program may be successful without having a big (or any) visible impact on overall homelessness. That can happen for a number of reasons, one of them being the tricky dynamics of the shelter and street systems. Shelters where more violence occurs can lower the census as homeless avoid it, for example. Or, if a prevention program keeps someone at risk of homelessness in their apartment, that apartment is not available to someone who is currently homeless. In this musical chairs situation where the number of apartments is limited, programs to solve homelessness can compete with one another.

Given the complexity of the homeless system, it is essential to collect and monitor multiple types of information, from counts, to databases, to interviews, and well-designed evaluations or statistical studies. The studies need not be the city's own. There is tremendous value in sharing research and information across jurisdictions, even across the globe, through informal networks, policy or research conferences, and organizations such as FEANTSA and the European Observatory on Homelessness, the Canadian Homeless Hub, and the National Alliance to End Homelessness. Edmonton supports collection of knowledge through its own community research group and funding program, and Bogotá has organized an international research conference.

10 Managing for Results

PERFORMANCE MANAGEMENT AND MODELING

The setting was the crisis center for the city of Paris, near the elegant Hotel de Ville, that houses the mayor's office and has been municipal headquarters since 1357. Deployed around a large U-shaped table were key deputies (*adjoints,* who are elected officials themselves) and their staff responsible for the city's social services, housing and shelter, health, security, and press. At their ready disposal were significant resources—material, personnel, information, experience, judgment, and influence—to respond to anything that might happen that night—February 15, 2018. On the big screens circling the room flashed images of what was taking place at any town hall in the twenty arrondissements, interspersed with data reports and charts, lists of needs and actions taken. The occasion was the city's first street count, led by Mayor Anne Hidalgo, called La Nuit de la Solidarité.

Homelessness is not frequently managed or dealt with within the walls of a crisis center, but, in principle, it helps to have similar frameworks and resources available to respond to any developing need, cyclical trend, or unexpected failure, even if that crisis "room" is a virtual one. That conceptual image of real-time resources and information at the ready captures the aims of managing for results through performance measures.

Collecting data helps in better understanding homelessness, but it is just as important for responsible parties to use information in real time to address problems as they arise, documenting what works—and what doesn't—with systems, data and accountability, and solid management.

Governments and nonprofits interested in managing for results are increasingly using regularly reported indicators or measures, such as outcomes collected in databases, as a way to enhance performance management systems. Pictures and data might not be projected on live screens, as in the Paris crisis center, but they are reviewed at a designated time by top management to assess progress in meeting goals. The information that constitutes performance measures consists of quantitative and qualitative indicators of various aspects of public or nonprofit programs. The measures are tracked and reported at regular intervals, provide objective information to improve decision making as well as accountability, and prove critical to results-oriented management.[1]

Consider this: in New York City, the 2018 subway point-in-time count was 1,771, down 2 percent from the prior year, which is an insignificant change. Does that mean the outreach and Safe Haven services offered had no impact over the year? In fact, teams encountered and documented nearly 9,000 discrete individuals just in the subways, and assisted over 1,500 into better settings. Therefore, it is important to go beyond the annual street counts to measure the impact, or lack thereof, of the work.

In Edmonton, about 100 new people become homeless every month, and another 10 to 20 reenter the by-name registry. By the same token, Edmonton shows monthly resolutions of 100 to 200 people being housed by the service network, resolving their own problems, or leaving the rolls. Although the overall change in homelessness can seem small, a lot of activity is taking place.

Performance measures show that the services provided by New York City and Edmonton—outreach, Safe Havens, shelter, and housing—contribute to lowering the street population, and that resources are being deployed where and when they are needed. In addition, they track relevant components of effective and efficient service delivery, such as how many contacts are being made with newly homeless individuals, what percentage have case management plans, and their housing goals. They can also include those who are housing service eligible and have completed the required applications and been placed into housing, and the time involved at each stage, and can be used to identify who returns to the streets after a year and after two years.

Performance management measures need to be meaningful and understandable, comprehensive, timely and actionable, practical and cost-effective.[2] In developing them, it is recommended that the measures be tied directly to the mission and that they be results driven.[3] However, doing it right need not be complicated.

Performance results give mayors the information to act quickly to fix an inefficient program. Sudden bottlenecks with apartment inspections become readily apparent. Good performance results allow a mayor to expand a program, such as strengthening links with an enterprising landlord. Regular data on the number of contacts being made, placements into housing, or entries into Safe Havens opens a window on activity at the street level. General trends can also be monitored through by-name lists or interim minicounts.

When Bogotá broke up trafficking houses in its ground zero for homelessness—El Bronx—citizens worried that poor residents residing in those buildings, many of them drug users, would show up on their neighborhood sidewalks. Through policy analysts' regular mapping of the geography of homelessness, city workers were able to document that that wasn't so. Vigilance with tracking allowed city officials to see that the problem resurfaced a few years later in the neighborhood of San Bernardo, which was then targeted for further intervention. Police and social workers cooperated to dismantle pockets of drug and human trafficking feeding off vulnerable street homeless people before the networks could establish deep roots.

There is an important distinction between outcome-level change and program effect. Outcome-level change is the difference of accumulated activities at different points in time—the 2 percent drop in subway homelessness in New York City in 2018, for example. Program effect, by contrast, is that portion of an outcome change that can be attributed to a particular program as opposed to the influence of other factors. In the case of the New York City subway count or the Edmonton by-name list, the outcome-level change was relatively small, but the program effect was likely larger, since many placements were being made. New people coming onto the streets, perhaps as part of a regular flow of people who move to the city to find work without luck or a wave of new migrants, were masking the impact.

Program effects are more difficult to assess and require more careful evaluation or research than performance measures provide; yet identifying them serves a vital purpose in understanding the true impact of program operations, achievement, and efficiency. Evaluations and studies take time and occur after the fact. Leaders need active data to address pressing crises and want to stay on task using performance indicators to measure progress in real time.

Generally, performance measurement data are reviewed in a variety of formats, including trends over time, point-in-time comparisons, actual-versus-targeted performance comparisons, and disaggregation by relevant subunits. Part of what makes performance management successful is tracking and regular review of results.[4] The use of data dashboards—a series of charts or tables with information on key performance measures that is regularly updated and reviewed, whether privately by a provider or in public reports—is an effective tool to keep abreast of developments, to allow mid-course corrections, and to keep staff focused on primary goals.

A Houston example shows how a city can use measures to plan, implement, monitor, and further evaluate performance and hold managers accountable. Starting in 2011, the Mayor's Office, led by Annise Parker, spearheaded an all-hands-on-deck approach to tackling the many dimensions of homelessness across a vast region. Houston's The Way Home coalition (referenced in chapter 6 in conjunction with prevention) includes local government, regional public housing and Veteran's Affairs offices, nonprofit agencies, and other community and private sector leaders. Under that umbrella, the city uses a coordinated, data-driven approach that matches resources to needs for housing and service support, and a shared governance model that brings together more than one hundred service providers.

The public website for Houston's Coalition for the Homeless gives the number of people housed since 2012, the success rate for local housing programs, the number of unique people accessing homeless assistance the previous year, and the amount in public funds expended for homeless solutions. Under the heading "How Are We Doing, Reports and Data" are links to all of the recent street and shelter counts. Through "The Way

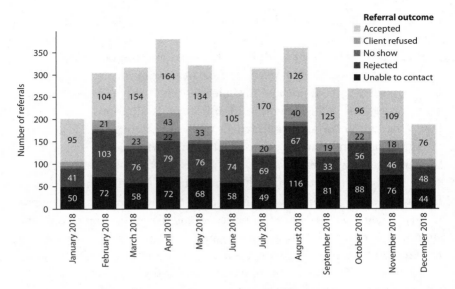

Figure 10. In its online system dashboards, Houston's The Way Home Coalition tracks key indicators for the community, such as the number of people who access services and the outcomes of referrals over the twelve months preceding January 2019.

Home" portal, any interested person can find the most recent performance measurements and system dashboards.

The performance measure modules look at key indicators for the community: change in number of homeless persons from year to year, length of time homeless, the number who exit homelessness to housing, and returns to homelessness within six months, twelve months, or two years. Other charts show changes in employment and income growth, the number of first-time homeless, the number of successful placements from street outreach into housing, and the percent who remain housed after a year.

The coordinated-access dashboard is rich with systems-level data, including a graph of two-year housing placements that tracks how the community is performing with such priority populations as veterans, youth, and chronically homeless individuals. At the homeless-provider level, monthly numbers are charted to demonstrate how successful each provider is in housing those it serves, keeping homeless stays short, increasing income, and preventing returns to homelessness. All the coordinated access dashboard indicators are produced and updated monthly.

A public website with regularly updated performance measures can highlight accomplishments, as well as show unmet needs that require attention, thus engaging a broader audience in the ongoing crisis. Providing real-time information establishes the commitment of the community, communicates what works, and empowers more cities to follow the examples.

Houston was able to achieve a 57 percent reduction in overall homelessness from 2011 through 2016 (from 8,471 to 3,626). The dashboards not only kept providers' focus on reducing homelessness and achieving systemic goals, but also explained the big changes to the public by showing the demands being put on the city's housing and social services, how they were being responded to by whom, and the extent of the unmet or new needs.

Tracking basic indicators can go a long way toward determining progress, such as the number of new people becoming homeless, the number exiting, the number of placements in housing, the median length of a homeless stay, and the percentage who return to homelessness within a year or two, comparing what is happening each month with what happened the previous month, the same time the prior year, and even going back five years or more.

An official visiting New York City from the Paris municipal government asked if he could participate in street homeless outreach in the South Bronx. The government official expected to see a large number of people living on the street, most likely because he had an outdated perception of the borough as a place facing many social challenges, such as crime, addiction, and homelessness. Some of the negative perception was based in reality, since the first city point-in-time street count in 2005 found 587 persons sleeping on the Bronx streets. However, as the outreach team drove around for several hours in the middle of the night, they didn't encounter any people sleeping rough. The Paris visitor questioned whether the street outreach partners were taking a sanitized route. In fact, he was witnessing success. The city and its partners had effectively implemented a Housing First model and created transitional housing options such as drop-in centers, stabilization beds (short-term placements, such as YMCAs, while a person waits for an opening for permanent housing), and Safe Haven shelters. The number of street homeless in the Bronx had declined to a low of 43 in 2016—though it ticked up to 115 in 2019. An observer might not believe such results, even if seen with their own eyes, if the city did not conduct an annual street count and document placements in permanent housing over the years. It is possible to effectively reduce street homelessness, but a city must also have a credible way to demonstrate progress. Absent a regular metric, the good work that had been done on the frontlines of the Bronx might not have been noticed, or believed. The combination of good planning and program design, sound management and skilled staff, and dedicated partnerships focused on a unified goal led to tangible results. The street count (and the Parisian observer) were testimony.

Performance management systems need not be expensive or sophisticated. One of the most famous, complex, and copied performance management tools, the New York Police Department's COMPSTAT system, had humble roots. According to one story, likely apocryphal, working under newly appointed police commissioner William Joseph Bratton, Deputy Police Commissioner Jack Maple asked his deputies what data the precincts uniformly collected. As he was told the seven major crimes—murder, manslaughter, rape, arson, burglary, larceny—Deputy Commissioner Maple instructed a staff member to drive around to each precinct to collect those data points on an Excel spreadsheet every week. In the beginning, crimes were indicated by using pins on a map. The tools and data used mattered less than the principles behind them—timely and accurate information or intelligence, rapid deployment of resources, effective tactics, and relentless follow-up—which revolutionized crime fighting at the time. Both New York City and Los Angeles now have access to sophisticated data systems in homeless services. However, of the ten cities discussed in this book, Bogotá, though having fewer resources, is in many ways a leader in terms of its multiple uses of data, while Paris, which has access to rich services and staffing, is sometimes *limited* because of a lack of coordinated data systems. A great deal of power can come from agreeing on only a few measurable goals, outcomes, or targets and tracking them consistently in real time, such as reducing the number of children on the streets, or eliminating homelessness among veterans of a war, or increasing housing placements and decreasing the average length of time spent homeless for an aging cohort or a newly formed subpopulation sleeping rough.

Good use of data not only helps to identify challenges and opportunities but also can communicate and engage outside stakeholders, spur action, and adjust programs if necessary. The purpose is not to count beans, but to move toward better solutions.

HOW TO MODEL THE END OF HOMELESSNESS

Knowing whether problems with a specific homeless individual or group are being addressed, or whether citywide programs are cost-efficient and meet the needs of those they serve, represents only a portion of the information city officials require to manage homelessness in their jurisdiction.

To achieve the goal of ending homelessness—or of making it only rare, brief, and nonrecurring—officials must agree on a benchmark number that can be tracked to demonstrate the city's progress. In Edmonton, the annual street count and by-name list are used to gauge success, with the latter consisting of both unsheltered and sheltered people known to the system and receiving services. Targets are set for the overall impact of programs and for key process indicators, such as whether an assessment plan is in effect within a designated time, a housing plan is established where necessary, and people are referred to appropriate supportive services.

Many factors influence the journey through a homelessness system: who is homeless and who among those at risk are seeking services; the city's homeless policies and resources; the influence of economic factors; and city housing and regulation policies. Understanding a system's dynamics given complex and multiple determinants requires knowing some of the flow elements: what portion of the population will come and go quickly, how long they stay, how many will likely be long-term stayers, and what the characteristics are of those who will come and go repeatedly. Also critical to predicting flow is knowing how many entrants will appear for services and some of their characteristics. Among discharges or exits from the homeless system, placements will be strong indicators of success, whether it be a return to family or a move to subsidized or public housing, a Safe Haven, or supported housing. Some who leave the homeless system may return quickly, others after a year or more.

Essentially, evolving plans should be viewed as a big math problem: calculating how many people can be served, and for which outcomes, from the full range of initiatives included in the strategy. What level of efficiency will it take to meet the needs of every person on the street and in shelter, such that they can move to permanency? The calculation includes service levels sufficient to address the current population, and takes into account expectations about how many newly homeless people there will be and how many will exit the rolls. From the point when permanency for those currently experiencing homelessness is achieved, the scale going forward need only be enough to meet the expected new onset of homelessness. The more that preventive strategies reduce that onset, the less that needs to be retained in the ongoing homeless service system capacity.

A simple example can clarify the challenge: If 5,000 people are living on the streets, 80 percent of whom are there for more than 90 days, with a priority set to serve the chronically homeless population, then action is needed for 4,000 people. If another 1,000 come to the streets annually, and 50 percent will stay at least 90 days, then solutions are needed for 500 more annually. The same projections must be done for shelter demand and dynamics.

As part of the target-setting process, Edmonton's Homeward Trust initially projected the likely number of homeless in the absence of any change of effort, leading to an expected population increase from 1,642 in April 2018 to 1,825 In January 2020. The coalition next developed a strategy of doubling the number of housing placements annually, generating a drop from the projected 1,825 to an anticipated 471. Finally, by increasing diversions by 23 percent, the Edmonton partners now believe they can reduce the city's homeless population to zero.

To end homelessness as a community, Homeward Trust joined forces with multiple stakeholders to set these targets and monitor progress. A part of that commitment is to summon proper and sufficient resources to achieve the goals. To illustrate the commitment, Homeward Trust has also charted homeless-services capacity changes over time, including the number of units of service by program type, and allows for the reallocation of resources from emergency services to permanent supportive housing.

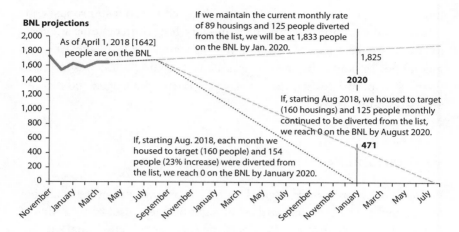

Figure 11. Edmonton Homeward Trust models the expected trajectory of people registered on its by-name list of community members experiencing homelessness, based on current levels of housing placements and diversions, with estimates of efforts needed to reduce the number to zero in two years, 2018. Homeward Trust Edmonton, 2020.

As part of its plan, the city estimated needing 1,000 units of supportive housing; by 2017, there were 201 units available. An update to the plan includes the need for an additional 900 units over six years; as of 2019, the city was aggressively pursuing those units.

Tracking homelessness system-wide also requires coordinated data systems or matching data between systems, or both, so that partners can understand the interrelationships of service systems that affect the homeless outcome and can detect impact from efforts to improve results. What happens to an individual or group of people will not necessarily translate into system-wide patterns. For example, if more people exit jails and prisons into the shelter system, the shelter census should rise. In a New York City case, the opposite occurred; as more people exited jail or prison, the shelter census declined.[5] System dynamics can be complicated and not flow in expected ways, as many factors come into play with offsetting effects. Integrated data will reveal the overlap between the child welfare system and the homelessness system, the movement between jails and prisons and the shelters, and between hospitals and homeless drop-in centers and street outreach. By going beyond simple outcome tracking to fully integrated data for management and analysis, cities can foster robust conversations about improving practices, in everything from defining supports for those facing evictions; to planning discharges from medical health, mental health, and substance programs; to targeting scarce resources to the most-appropriate recipients; to keeping partners engaged and focused on the overarching goals.

MANAGING PERFORMANCE IS NOT ENOUGH

Performance monitoring provides an early warning system for changing trends, but it will not necessarily shed light on the causes or solutions of the newly identified trend. Past performance, as the stock market disclaimer goes, is no guarantee of future results. Rather, identifying underlying causes of any phenomenon requires a more scientific approach.

There are other consequences of relying too heavily on performance measurement systems. Managing by performance can lead to an unbalanced incentive structure that results in goal displacement or gaming— one agency trying to shift harder cases to another one, for instance. Alternatively, an incentive system linked to targets can lead to timid targets or misrepresentation of results, rather than serving as motivation to reach higher.[6] Further, maintenance costs of performance management systems may be significant and staff may resist or feel threatened by the ongoing scrutiny.[7]

Sometimes data are not good enough to be credible, as in early estimates of the number of street homelessness based on expert opinions. Noncomparability of data from different sources can create reliability problems, such as different definitions of who is homeless across agencies; or changes in street count methods, such as shifts in time of year; or the application of new federal definitions and inclusion of some facilities in the category of "provisionally housed" rather than simply "who," as recently occurred in Edmonton.

Because performance measures are limited in terms of evaluating cause and effect, the information can be misleading and produce erroneous impressions about program effectiveness or lack thereof. In New York City, a sudden rise in the number of families coded as coming from out of town elicited great alarm. How should the city respond to a seeming undesirable side-effect of the right to shelter? After further research, two new facts emerged. First, based on interviews at the coordinated-entry point, the code for "out of town"—OT in the database—was being interpreted as "other" and used as a catchall when the clients were not forthcoming with the new requirement to provide an exact latest address. Second, interviews with clients revealed that most who were from out of town had been New York City residents in the prior five years. Families were returning home after housing, work, or relationships failed in another place. The specter of foreign hordes invading the Big Apple soon dissipated, and the focus shifted to prevention services that might mitigate the tenuousness of part-time work among low-income families.

COMPLICATIONS ARE NOT AN EXCUSE FOR INACTION

There is still a considerable amount that practitioners don't know about the problems of homelessness as a whole. They need to further develop special-population best practices, to craft systems-level responses and projection, and to acknowledge that it is sometimes hard to answer *what if* questions. Cities may not know what would have happened had the policies and resources applied been different, or the impact of each contribution. Homelessness is a permeable and dynamic system where practitioners and policy makers know only what they witness. But evidence points to a big unseen buffer area of marginally housed people—including institutions, doubling-up, and hidden homeless—where it is more difficult to assess whether or not needs are imminent and whether policies are hitting pay dirt.

Also, those who set projections should realize that the system does not always behave as expected. Providing a better housing subsidy may counterintuitively increase homelessness, as when more people seek the subsidy or when people stay longer in shelter to access it. A city may need to place four or more (Edmonton officials say as many as eight) homeless people from the street to reduce the annual count by one. These challenges can be frustrating to policy makers, elected officials, and the public, all of whom are engaged in seeking solutions.

Many unanswered questions about homelessness remain. Both at the personal and aggregate level, the field lacks knowledge on both the causes and the solutions. What helps one homeless individual may not leverage big-system changes; for example, prevention may keep one person housed but reduce the supply of units available to those currently homeless, much as in a game of musical chairs. Administering programs with the deepest sense of integrity entails seeking and supporting well-designed studies. Pursuing and broadcasting reliable research can ensure that resources are applied to the best approaches, and helps spread knowledge across systems and cities, allowing cities to learn from one another.

Ending homelessness, at least as a visible and long-lasting element of urban life, requires doing the math: Will the sum of all efforts add to zero. If so, when? In short, all program components must add up to a sufficient effort to get to zero and solve homelessness. While there may always be a modest number of people who do become homeless despite well-designed, -managed, and -resourced programs in a deeply integrated service system, partners can agree that ending homelessness has been achieved when the mass of homeless is no longer a fixture of urban life and homelessness is indeed rare, brief, and nonrecurring.

11 Managing in Emergencies

The global COVID-19 pandemic hit Europe and the Americas suddenly in late February 2020. Across the world, the imperative to "flatten the curve" of the disease's spread led to shuttering of businesses, disruption of schools, and demands that residents stay at home except to deal with essential needs like purchasing food and getting urgent health care. Referred to as sheltering in place, the concept over the many ensuing months was that individuals would stay in their homes, practice social distancing when they had to be out, and remain quarantined if they, or anyone they had direct contact with, became ill.

As cities moved into this emergency mode, managers on the frontline of serving the homeless were faced with the question, What does "shelter in place" mean for people who are without a home?

Street homelessness suddenly became a seemingly unmanageable public health crisis, instilled with fearful questions about how to help people without homes stay safe and concerns about how rapidly infection could spread among this extremely vulnerable population clustered closely in shelters and on streets. City officials confronted the alarming scenario of the homeless infecting one another in large numbers and putting the general public at greater risk.

The pandemic demonstrated once again, however, the incredible resilience, ingenuity, and commitment of those who oversee services for the homeless in cities across the globe. During a range of previous emergency situations, the homeless delivery system proved uniquely adept at using shelter management tools to pivot from dire situations to effective emergency management. Shelter operators can manage bed capacity in challenging moments, and their staff can carry out, without faltering, the provision of daily meals, managing personal hygiene in shared quarters, and establishing routines for supportive services that meet clients' individual needs. Public agencies and their nonprofit partners have established strong working relationships for collaborating across the different organizational structures in order to merge skills and resources and ensure urgent needs are met. In many jurisdictions, shared data systems for supporting individual needs across multiple service venues are already in place. And, in even the hardest-hit cities, these coordinated efforts have led to transitioning the displaced from emergency accommodations to housing when going home was not an option.

When a sudden event creates an urgent new demand for safe shelter, the homeless-services community has the apparatus to respond. The ability to act quickly benefits those without permanent homes, as in Nashville when a tornado tore straight through a women's shelter and the largest street encampment; and helps those hit with a sudden loss of housing, as in Los Angeles during wildfires and New York City during hurricanes. Lessons learned from these earlier disasters were tested to the limit when COVID-19 struck cities around the world.

LESSONS FROM PRIOR EMERGENCIES

The cities profiled in this book have grappled with many different recent emergencies: huge population displacements from North Africa and the Middle East to Athens and Paris; earthquakes in Mexico City and wildfires in Los Angeles; and tornadoes and floods in Nashville and Houston. While international relief organizations and national governments work at the macro level to harness resources and set broad parameters for response, it falls on the states or provinces, regions, and localities to be the frontline responders; or, if national and international systems are slow to activate, the default becomes those closest to the disaster. The reality is that emergencies require quick boots on the ground, worn by those familiar with local needs, resources, and systems. For these reasons, urban leaders are called to emergency response with greater and greater frequency. These experiences have informed local preparedness strategies and equipped local leaders with proven strategies for effectively managing a wide range of circumstances.

Population Displacement and Migration

One type of emergency that has overwhelmed some cities and demanded extraordinary response has been the swell of demand for housing and services from newly arrived migrating populations. In Athens, the challenge during the long, hot "summer of migration" in 2015 was not a long-term demand by newcomers for housing; rather, it was a short-term need of enormous proportion. The refugees fleeing political oppression and war in Syria were leaving the shores of the Aegean Sea in overloaded lifeboats, wave upon wave, with many lives lost in the treacherous process, headed to the nearest Greek islands, which also became quickly overcrowded. A state of emergency demanded the refugees be decanted to safety on the mainland, where they flooded Piraeus, the port outside Athens, by the thousands. The survivors arrived without plans and without accommodation, most seeking other destinations across Europe where families and friends could be found and new lives could be fashioned.

But leaving Athens for other areas became difficult. Increasingly, borders were being closed, even within the open-border European Union. While collective EU-wide solutions were being debated in Brussels, thousands of men, women, youth, and children were left unassisted to establish their right to refugee status and its protections and to find a bed. Thousands disembarked from ships at Piraeus and found their way across the ancient city of Athens to the terminus of the main railway out of Greece to Northern Europe. The small public park outside the station, across the street from the multiservice center tending to those long without homes in Athens, became the gathering place and encampment for many awaiting a train ticket and a ride to their destination. Over the course of weeks, constantly churning crowds of refugees concentrated in this small neighborhood park. Without sanitary facilities or a regular source of food and care, it quickly became a humanitarian disaster.

Athens mayor Giorgos Kaminis pleaded with the national government and European leaders to address this international crisis. When the city could wait no longer, Athens's officials initiated a series of actions, starting with finding property and assigning local social service providers to establish the first refugee camp. Only later did the national government and several international relief organizations join this effort as partners. Mayor Kaminis also called upon all Athenians to open their doors to make room in their homes for as many refugees as each could accommodate. At a time when the Greek economy was in crisis—subject to a punitive austerity plan from the EU with unemployment high and resources stretched thin—Athenians shared the little they had by bringing those in need into their homes. One deputy mayor opened her family's home to as many as nine refugees at one time, including a woman who gave birth during her stay.

This refugee crisis continued for almost a year, greatly taxing a small and overworked City Hall. An important lesson learned here is that the mayor's bully pulpit can be a very powerful tool in calling for responsible parties to do their job. By initiating symbolic acts of proposing properties for refugee camps and opening up citizens' doors, Athens mayor Kaminis was able to stand up and say, "We are doing our part; where are you in doing yours?"

As the crisis subsided in Athens with the slowing of the flight from Syria and the departure of refugees to further destinations as their legal status was determined, urban centers in Northern Europe began to experience the later stages of this crisis in a different form. Paris, as well as Berlin, London, and Amsterdam, received these refugees, not as way stations but as final destinations.

The northern gateway to the city of Paris, the Gare du Nord in the 18th arrondissement, a neighborhood of many immigrant populations, soon became a destination place for newly arriving migrants from places as diverse as Syria and Afghanistan, Egypt and Somalia. Because their legal status was unresolved and Paris was their final stopping place, many people and families were caught in limbo. Inadequate refugee-processing

capacity and a lack of temporary accommodations left thousands in growing encampments around the city, particularly in the Gare du Nord.

Paris mayor Anne Hidalgo called out to the president and to other
European leaders to step up and assist in more quickly resolving the refugee status, which would allow individuals to secure housing, receive benefits, and seek employment. Again, a lethargic response left thousands
stranded, and, once again, it fell to the mayor to restructure a solution.
Mayor Hidalgo charged her staff with identifying locations for service
sites that could provide advocacy for the thousands going through the asylum process, and a decent bed, food, and sanitation in shelters for the
many sleeping in tents throughout the city's refugee encampments.

La Boule (the Bubble) was an artful and innovative solution conceived
and constructed in just two months in the summer of 2016. Located in an
empty lot adjacent to an abandoned and gutted four-story warehouse on
a desolate rail terminal just below the massive encampments, La Boule
was designed as a temporary pop-up facility. A tent structure standing
three stories high and colored bright white and yellow in the pattern of the
Fleur de Lis when seen from above, the facility housed asylum application
services and health and legal screening and benefits. A medical services
trailer was also located in the lot. The area transformed into a minicity of
community clusters of wooden cabins housing four individuals each,
stacked side by side and accompanied by community dining facilities and
congregate bathrooms. Housing more than a thousand individuals, the
entire facility was codesigned with local artists, faith leaders, and community members. Playful murals and game tables interspersed among the
clustered communities, and a volunteer-staffed distribution point for
donations, allowed local Parisians to lend a hand in supporting those
being served.

La Boule stood as a symbol of hope and respite to thousands who fled
violence and persecution for a better life but too often faced xenophobic
discrimination and callous disregard. Mayor Hidalgo responded with
immediacy, humanity, and compassion to counteract the prior indiffer-
ence. The mayor's leadership eventually provoked the national government to act: national officials opened service sites and expanded shelter
capacity, allowing the city to step back. These city actions also provided a
forum within which Mayor Hidalgo could make a more progressive case

for caring for the refugees, pushing her national counterparts to offer further support.

In both Athens and Paris, the actions of these capital cities clearly fell in the categories of national and international responsibilities. But national and international leaders, removed from the sense of urgency regarding the conditions being suffered (but not distant geographically in these capital cities), needed to be prodded into action by highly public and swift municipal action. These acts provided immediate relief but also created focal services for the mayors to demonstrate what could be done quickly; as such, they became tools in their continued advocacy for increased national and international responses.

These experiences can be contrasted with that in Bogotá, where Colombia's national government took a proactive and early stance when demographics changed. During the time the city was conducting its first municipal count of rough sleepers, a historic peace agreement was reached with the Revolutionary Armed Forces of Colombia (FARC), which had run its own paramilitary government in isolation deep in the forests of Colombia. Originally a deeply political movement, FARC's organization survived over time underground, funded in part by organized drug operations, and mounted a reign of terror among its own members that spilled into neighboring communities. Trapped in its own history, the community tried for many years to pull itself out if its illicit operations and into mainstream legitimacy. But in 2016, in a historic agreement that won him the Nobel Peace Prize, President Juan Manuel Santos brokered the final details and secured national approval to reconstitute FARC as a legitimate political party and to reintegrate the population into mainstream society.

The immediate concern raised whether the cities, especially the capital of Bogotá, could absorb this new population. Fears arose of an influx of FARC newcomers with no family or social ties into the cities like refugees, putting too great a demand on shelters and ultimately winding up on the streets. In fact, the national government made adequate provision for housing the anticipated population surge, and no crisis came to pass. Thousands of units of new social housing were planned, built, and set aside for members of the returning community. Organized across multiple sites and jurisdictions, the effort successfully relocated thousands of FARC members in mainstream society. While the ongoing implementation of the peace agreement faced many disruptions, the avoidance of a home-lessness crisis in Colombia demonstrated how a planned, proactive national strategy can anticipate and provide for housing needs when a city is faced with rapidly changing demographics.

Yet, two years later, Bogotá had a different experience with an international crisis that afflicted all of Latin America. In 2018, when the grossly mismanaged, oil-dependent Venezuelan economy collapsed, almost half the working population was without a job, and an incapacitated national government offered no relief measures to ensure its population could survive the crisis. Over 4 million individuals packed their families and necessities and began to trek by car, bus, and train and on foot across Latin America to seek new homes.

Again, the international community failed. Enormous human need was disregarded as local governments were confronted with swelling ranks of new arrivals. Camps built along paths of exit were bypassed as refugees preferred the opportunities they hoped to find in urban centers. Many found family and friends to take them into already overcrowded housing. But many others wound up on the streets, joining the ranks of local homeless and seeking out safe places where they could have a place to sleep, daily sanitation, and food while seeking employment. These refugees would remain among those rough sleeping when the COVID-19 pandemic descended.

Environmental Displacement

Great migrations of people demonstrate the inadequacy of international planning bodies to anticipate, manage, and respond to the humanitarian needs that are the consequence of economic and political displacement. Where there is a lack of planning and response from those legally responsible, local governments and residents are left with treating people with a modicum of human dignity. Mayors stand on the frontline, even of global political crises.

Mayors are often the first to act in the fallout from another global crisis—climate change. Many of the great cities were built on the coast, where deep and protected harbors were critical to national defense; eventually these ports became keys to national and international economic viability as global trade emerged and developed. Now, these world cities sit in massive flood zones prone to environmental displacement during unprecedented storm surges, and exposed along the paths of massive weather systems building up in oceans and slamming shores with a force no planning effort can withstand. The human toll is enormous and home-less-serving systems are an integral part of the emergency response.

Thanks to its experiences responding to the 9/11 terrorist attacks and to the displacement caused by and recovery from Hurricanes Irene and Sandy, the New York City municipal government is no stranger to step-ping up during emergencies.

In 2012, Hurricane Sandy hit the coastal areas of southern Brooklyn and Queens, along Staten Island and New Jersey, and even through lower Manhattan, wiping out power on Wall Street and in City Hall. When the flood subsided, more than fifty people were dead, primarily from drown-ing in their own homes. Power systems—both at the building and regional-substation levels—were permanently damaged, tens of thousands were without light and heat, and hundreds of homes were uninhabitable.

In anticipation of the storm, municipal leaders turned to the city's emergency playbook, which included plans for the opening of emergency mass sheltering operations in schools on three days' notice, placing the responsibility for operationalizing the plan with the city's Department of Homeless Services. Stockpiles of cots, linens, and personal hygiene pack-ages, along with pop-up feeding operations and water, were deployed to schools adjacent to the anticipated impact area beginning on Friday, so that people fleeing their homes on Sunday into Monday had a safe place to ride out the storm.

But, as with many emergencies, it was the unanticipated that stressed the system and tested the endurance of public and private partners to respond. The emergency shelters were designed to be very short-term facilities—three-to-five days at the most. While the majority who came in were able to return home or go to the home of another family or friend within days, a large cohort had no other options and quickly tired of the prepackaged meals and the high-density congregate settings offering no privacy or personal space. Intensifying the frustration, hundreds of vulner-able elderly were in this category, having been shuttled by ambulance to an armory drill floor configured overnight especially for their care in Park

Slope, Brooklyn. They had been transported from their flooded nursing homes on the shores of Coney Island during the storm after having decided, disastrously as it turned out, to *shelter in place*. When the power went off and there was no question that they would have to leave, the state of New York had no accommodations for them, leaving it on the city to fashion a response overnight. When it became clear many could not return to their former nursing homes and the congregate setting was medically unviable, it took weeks to identify relocation opportunities across the region. The Department of Homeless Services (DHS) continued to deliver support and coordination on site, eventually aided by an outpouring of generosity from the community that brought in home-cooked meals, provided chamber music concerts, and offered massage and healing to the residents.

For those who lacked a place to return, DHS had to devise a longer-term sheltering solution. The status and needs of those displaced by Hurricane Sandy were much different from those of people in the traditional shelter system, which was not designed to handle a huge surge of long-term homeless. Their eligibility for disaster relief assistance did, however, put these displaced people at a strategic advantage over the chronically homeless: they could get access to hotel rooms while permanent options were set up. DHS managed a displaced system within a homeless system for two full years until the needs of all the individuals were resolved. The lessons from Sandy regarding the relocation of clients from long-term hotels with rental assistance would prove particularly useful in the COVID-19 fight.

During Hurricane Harvey in 2017, the vigilance of Houston's homeless providers in monitoring popular gathering spots for the rough-sleeping population saved lives through prevention and through quick deployment on the eve of the storm to make every effort to coax them inside. Houston's bayous in dry times are large vacant spaces offering privacy and shade to the homeless; however, these flood-capture basins fill on a moment's notice when flash storms dump rain on parched, hard soil.

Through the city's coordinated strategy involving multiple outreach teams of public agencies such as the police department and private entities such as nonprofits serving the region, an all-hands-on-deck approach saturated the known encampments with workers when Harvey's trajectory became clear to warn of record storms and rainfall. Because such events had become more and more regular, it was harder to convince these rough sleepers to seek shelter in advance of the storm. Outreach workers would be withdrawn from the streets when the shutdown order was given in advance of the deluge, ensuring their lives were protected; therefore, convincing the rough sleepers in advance that this was no ordinary storm became imperative.

When Harvey hit, the rainfall was so sudden and great that these massive canyon-like bayous became raging rivers that eventually spilled over and filled surrounding streets and neighborhoods. No one left would have survived.

While this outreach was being conducted, the city worked with county and private partners to open emergency shelters for the anticipated surge in demand by displaced people, housed and unhoused. A dedicated 500-bed facility was established for the homeless to serve their unique needs and to isolate them from the general population. A massive operation that was to house 12,000 displaced residents was opened in the George R. Brown Convention Center, eventually spilling over into the adjoining Toyota Center.

Staffed largely by volunteers shuttled in through an emergency dispatch system, the convention center operated for weeks until all but 2,500 people remained with nowhere else to go. At this point, the homeless services' infrastructure was engaged to assess the situation and plan its redress. As expected, about half of this remaining population was determined to have been formerly homeless. An initial effort brought the remaining number down to 1,600. Without further options, these individuals had nowhere else to go. In response, an extraordinary collaboration of public and private partners created, through fund-raising and coordination, the Housing for Harvey program, a Rapid Rehousing initiative that coordinated landlord access to 2,000 rental units through a six-month rental assistance voucher. This effort housed the remaining population and allowed the convention center and emergency shelter to close. Such a collaborative process would become the model for the city's COVID-19 response.

Earthquakes are an ominous perpetual threat throughout the world. California cities like Los Angeles have elaborate disaster-preparedness plans that include provision of sheltering operations after seismic waves lead to devastating destruction. As earthquakes are chronic in California, state officials permanently designated every public employee as an emergency worker capable of being deployed during these dire circumstances.

Earthquake plans have also been activated with greater frequency in the past two decades in response to displacement caused by wildfires originating to the northwest, burning south into Los Angeles neighborhoods, and displacing many from their homes. In Los Angeles, the city's response plan includes an emergency-sheltering protocol that employs the facilities and staff of the city's Department of Parks and Recreation to convert forty-two community recreation centers into shelters within thirty-six hours. Wildfires in the summer of 2019 activated these emergency shelters on a limited basis, providing staff with the experience of setting up these locations on short notice. Such experience proved useful six months later when the COVID-19 response would require activating the shelters once again.

Public Health Emergencies

There has been no global public health challenge like COVID-19 in a century, and during that time the world has vastly changed through trade and travel, shrinking distances and putting people from across the globe into more immediate contact with one another. On a smaller scale, regional or population-based communicable disease epidemics such as SARS, Ebola, and H1N1 have been managed as public health crises. While none had the breadth and magnitude of COVID-19, important lessons were learned, and tried-and-true strategies have been developed that have informed responses to subsequent epidemics. The outbreak of highly contagious tuberculosis, in particular, has tested homeless providers because of the risk posed to the vulnerable in congregate settings.

Tuberculosis is a disease caused by an infection, typically of the lungs, and spreads through droplets passed person to person in close proximity through coughs and sneezes. While curable with treatment, it can be fatal to people with underlying health conditions. While public health officials believed the disease to have largely been conquered in nations with advanced economies, the United States saw a resurgence of cases in the 1980s and 1990s among the poorest neighborhoods and most vulnerable residents, particularly those diagnosed with HIV/AIDS. Cases tripled in

New York City from 1978 through 1992, leading to an influx of resources and rapid deployment of strategies in places where outbreaks were observed, such as the close quarters of jails and shelters.[1] Comprehensive public health responses were put in place to detect, respond to, and contain these outbreaks. These strategies were crucial in New York City when a new outbreak occurred in a men's shelter as recently as 2004. With the city's public health agency in the lead, the homeless agency hosted and managed the resources necessary to ensure appropriate health services and protection to clients.

The routines became familiar to the world years later with the outbreak of Ebola in Africa, MERS and SARS in Asia, and worldwide with COVID-19: aggressive testing to identify infected individuals; contact tracing to locate every person who had contact with them; and isolation in designated housing for those infected or who have come into contact with the infected, with monitoring and enforcement of restrictions. This containment has successfully protected shelter residents and prevented a wider community spread. These public health protocols were therefore adopted as standard best practices and deployed in containing communicable disease outbreak, providing guidance for the pandemic.

HOW CITIES HAVE RESPONDED TO COVID-19

When countries globally imposed restrictions on human contact as the primary protective strategy against transmission of the COVID-19 virus pending a proven treatment or vaccine, businesses and schools closed and residents were directed to stay at home, traveling out only for necessary shopping and urgent medical care. Once the magnitude of the threat was realized, city streets everywhere became devoid of traffic and, overnight, were turned into ghost towns.

Sheltering in place to maintain a safe social distance, however, doesn't apply if your cot is just inches away from another person in a congregate shelter, or if your sleeping bag on the street is your bed. It became immediately apparent to homeless service providers that they had an enormous responsibility to protect vulnerable clients and, in doing so, to protect the population at large.

After confirming the nation's first COVID-19 cases, state and local governments developed strategies for protecting and isolating both sheltered and unsheltered homeless populations. The magnitude of the new bed requirements to accommodate these people was enormous. Leading homeless-services researcher Dennis Culhane, with colleagues from the University of Pennsylvania, the University of California–Los Angeles, and Boston University created a modeling tool that would allow US jurisdictions to estimate the need for beds within their jurisdictions to accommodate both shelter and isolation units.[2] The researchers used data on the known number of homeless, sheltered and unsheltered, and the virus's expected rate of transmission. Adding considerations about the degree of health vulnerability of the homeless population, they estimated that 300,000 new beds would be required to appropriately shelter people from the streets, and 200,000 new beds would be required to dedensify existing shelters and provide adequate social distance between existing beds and private units for isolation. They estimated the national cost for this response at $11.5 billion.

The magnitude of that effort alone exceeded a decade's worth of US national investment in homeless services, and depended on thousands of local governments acting independently to implement the plan successfully. The consequences of a failure to do so could pose extraordinary danger to those without homes, and an ongoing public health risk of transmission to the general population.

Building on lessons learned from prior emergencies, cities mounted major efforts to protect the safety of those who were homeless during the COVID-19 epidemic. They drew on lessons from emergency shelter operations during natural disasters, public health interventions to manage high-risk populations and places, and permanent housing strategies used in a crisis. Some cities aspired to enlarge shelter capacity sufficiently to give every person on the street a bed. The range of expansion reached from constructing new congregate facilities to using private units in hotels and motels vacated during the pandemic.

City officials understood the need to isolate three distinct groups from the general homeless population: those who were ill with the virus; those having had contact with others who had tested positive, but were not yet known to be ill or potential carriers; and those vulnerable to and at higher risk of severe illness or death were they to get sick. At the same time, social distancing norms had to be applied across every shelter, and even on the streets between rough sleepers, to reduce the risk of transmission in general.

To meet this need, three levels of care were developed: Tier 1, or the sick shelter, for those who had contact; Tier 2, or the Person Under Investigation shelter; and Tier 3, with capacity for those who were vulnerable. How cities responded to these needs varied tremendously and evolved over time as outbreaks and standards shifted locally.

Houston had made tremendous progress in overcoming street homelessness in the 2010s, only to see it surge again with a change in mayors and a shift in City Hall priorities. Rather than being daunted by the reemergence, however, the homeless coordinating team muscled forward with efforts to tackle the ever-shifting encampments that would pop up around the downtown area. A growing awareness that homelessness tackled once does not mean it is tackled forever brought City Hall's attention back to the issue. When the virus began its spread across the United States, Houston relied on the strong network of partners who had previously worked together in the region to fashion a COVID-19 response strategy.

Knowing the health status of homeless individuals became key to each city's efforts to safely provide shelter as the virus raged. Insufficient testing capacity with slow results hindered early efforts, and providers came to depend on referring people based on symptoms only, a dangerous default as many positive cases were asymptomatic and contagious. Rather than relying on referrals to the citywide testing infrastructure, which was overwhelmed by multiple priorities, the Houston homeless network developed its own testing capacity to support shelter and outreach workers needing to refer clients.

The first stage of Houston's work included setting aside testing capacity to be accessed through a hotline number for outreach and shelter workers and for the homeless. This endeavor progressed to adding a safe-transport system for those screened by the hotline and directed to testing sites. In a single trip, the system provided transport, in–taxi cab testing, and a return to a quarantine facility until results were known, followed by a deep cleaning of the cabs. This innovative collaboration with the taxi industry ensured that the ill could be tested without infecting others and was arranged through a public transportation contract, reimbursable through the

Federal Emergency Management Agency (FEMA). The final stage of the effort added mobile-testing capacity: taking tests to the clients, starting with the largest homeless shelters and encampments. This iterative and comprehensive effort blanketed the homeless population with priority-to-testing access, treating the ill and protecting others from infection. Such a massive and coordinated effort went a long way in protecting many people in the homeless system from the virus's worst effects.

With the United States' largest rough-sleeping homeless population, the city of Los Angeles knew that it would be challenging to provide beds to its 14,000 unsheltered homeless during this crisis. In an impressive commitment to do just that, the city undertook a comprehensive effort to locate as many of those 14,000 beds as possible to give these people a safe place to sleep.

Many hotels and motels vacated as a result of the drop in business travel and tourism, creating a silver-lining opportunity to provide individual units for those who were sick or had been in contact with an infected person. This use of hotel and motel rooms took time to negotiate with many individual owners, but was fast-tracked across California by Governor Gavin Newsom's creation of Project RoomKey—a specific pre-approval that funneled emergency funding reimbursements from the federal government to the states would be made available to California localities that entered into contracts with hotels for this purpose. Los Angeles, primarily through the county government, acted quickly to use Project RoomKey. For the symptomatic or confirmed positive COVID cases, as well as for those persons under investigation, private units allowed clients to be isolated from contact with others.

These private units were also made available to those with underlying health conditions who are most vulnerable to becoming severely ill if exposed. While virtually all homeless are vulnerable due to generally poor health and multiple underlying conditions, priority for separate units was given to the elderly and those with underlying conditions that would make them more susceptible to potentially fatal consequences.

Given that even the younger and healthier clients are vulnerable, Los Angeles's goal was to bring every homeless person inside in some way, reducing their risk and general public exposure. Other cities achieved this through new congregate settings established in convention centers, public auditoriums, community centers, and other large facilities devoid of the public gatherings now prohibited by most states and localities. The Los Angeles Homeless Services Authority, with help from the American Red Cross, activated once again the forty-two recreation centers across the city to serve as short-term shelters. The use of new congregate shelters differed from guidance issued by the Centers for Disease Control and Prevention (CDC) that recommended leaving people on the street undisrupted if a private unit was unavailable and if safe distancing on the street could be maintained.[3] Following these guidelines, in the CDC's estimation, would ensure a certain stability in the population and create some chance that their movements might be more easily tracked should any outbreak occur.

Believing that rough sleepers' health would be better protected inside, many cities preferred an approach that at least offered a bed indoors and an improved ability to monitor and provide safety through triaged bed assignments, case work supervision, and better access to safe sanitation and food. Federal reimbursement for new shelter was at 100 percent for congregate settings and 75 percent for individual units, presumably to discourage a too-generous local approach.

Los Angeles's ambitious goal to house all 14,000 street homeless individuals was based initially on a mixed model of congregate and individual unit expansion, calculating new capacity on top of the underlying system in place. These goals were considerably tempered when a reexamination of these facilities in cooperation with public health officials made clear that the anticipated capacity could not be achieved when accommodating safe distance between cots within the facilities. The process of dedensification across existing shelters and in new facilities reduced the expected capacity by half. While many thousands were ultimately provided shelter, many other thousands remained on the streets through the outbreak.

For those waiting for a bed inside or destined to stay on the street, the city turned its attention to maximizing safety. Officials deployed more than a thousand outreach workers and medical teams to test and monitor those on the street, distributed thirty thousand masks, and communicated social-distancing and hygienic recommendations. Homeless agencies began managing safe distancing on the streets, often in sanctioned encampments that could provide increased levels of personal hygiene support and food access within designated street-sleeping areas. Many homeless administrators who had worked for years to fend off encampments became, in this crisis, the effective landlords of open-air sleeping arrangements. Enforcing safe camping rules and prescribing minimal distance between tents dragged the homeless agencies into the business of sanctioning and regulating behaviors on the streets they had worked assiduously over the years to squelch.

With an already robust and diverse network of congregate shelters for single adults operated by contracted service providers, New York City encouraged social distancing, isolation, and lockdown within its shelters. Symptomatic shelter residents, whether they had been tested or not, were isolated in private rooms within the shelter, if possible; and, in time, the city created hotel space for residents who tested positive or needed extra precautions. Eventually, the city developed a triage system to start referring clients at greatest health risk from congregate shelters to hotels, as well as those discharged from the hospital in recovery. Families experiencing homelessness in New York City already have private living spaces, making it easier for them to shelter in place. Infected family members could be sent to isolate in a city-operated hotel.

The city also moved to depopulate large congregate shelters to hotels, along with the service providers' staff, to manage the operations and provide better supportive services and client supervision. An even bigger challenge was caring for clients with a serious mental illness or substance-use problems in hotels, where often no meals are provided, no onsite health care is offered, and no staff monitor whether residents comply with isolation or quarantine orders. This experience was shared across cities, and many, including New York City, found that working with nonprofit providers—who could provide services in the hotels—was a more effective way of recruiting the right skilled staff, rather than deploying repurposed municipal employees from other disciplines as essential emergency workers.

Providers quickly adopted advances in telehealth, equipped their clients with smartphones, and ensured facilities had Wi-Fi so as to open barrier-free channels of communication between providers and clients. Telehealth does not substitute for the direct human connections that are often required for mental health support, nor does it help clients overcome the stress of social isolation, but the critical new tools could support clients' basic needs.

A new challenge emerged when New York State officials declared the increased concentration of homeless people sleeping in the city's subways a public health problem. Although ridership had dropped by 90 percent at the peak of the virus, making the subways clean and safe for commuting essential workers had become increasingly hindered by the regular presence of homeless in the otherwise deserted subways. Sanitation staff were reluctant, for safety reasons, to ask the sleeping homeless to move for cleaning to occur, yet deep cleaning was required to instill the public's confidence in the subway to return gradually to work.

To address this challenge, Governor Andrew Cuomo imposed a daily shutdown of the subways from 1 to 5 A.M., effectively creating an eviction from the subway cars of every person, including the homeless. Approximately two thousand individuals (the number found to be on the subway during the most recent point-in-time count) were thus added to the rough sleepers who might be out in the open at a time when people were expected to stay inside. Treating this as an opportunity for engagement, the Metropolitan Transportation Authority (MTA), working with its outreach providers and sheltering partners, put together a strategy to conduct coordinated outreach at the twenty-nine end-of-line stations across the city's five boroughs. Police officers would canvass the subway cars to alert people that it was closing time and they had to leave. The officers would inquire if anyone would like services; those indicating an interest would be referred to outreach teams waiting in the stations. Trained outreach staff engaged the interested individuals and offered a variety of shelter options, from traditional city shelter and Safe Haven accommodations to stabilization beds or a drop-in center. For those accepting, safe transport was arranged.

Six hundred people accepted placement in the first seven days of operation, greatly surpassing the city's expectations. To many involved, this coordinated effort to ensure hygienic subways and protect the homeless demonstrated the dual dynamics in overcoming street homelessness. First, if there are rules and those rules are enforced, people will comply. When told the subways were to be closed, rough sleepers accepted that without a struggle. Second, when offered services, many rough sleepers

Figure 12. Homeless outreach workers from BRC have been assigned to New York City's subways for over a decade. They played a critical and effective role during the COVID-19 pandemic in assisting hundreds to safety as the subway system closed each night for the first time in its history. Photo by Matthew Lapiska, courtesy of BRC Transit Outreach.

accepted a bed over sleeping outside. Bottom line: when offered choices and quick transport, hundreds of homeless who had been deemed "service resistant" did, in fact, accept a safe place to sleep during the pandemic.

COVID-19 hit Nashville in mid-March at a particularly difficult time. The annual winter shelter program was shutting its doors, emptying dozens of beds made available by faith-based organizations for the cold months and discharging many people back to rough sleeping. In fact, program officials informed the city that, as a volunteer-driven operation staffed largely by the elderly, it would end two weeks ahead of its March 30 date so as to protect the vulnerable volunteers who were asked to stay at home during the pandemic. At the same time, a tornado had hit Nashville on March 2, running directly over a women's shelter and through the city's largest encampment of rough sleepers. Emergency shelters opened by the Red Cross to house those displaced by the tornado were occupied largely by those from the shelter and encampment, complicating service delivery needs. But when the COVID-19 virus started to sweep across the United States, national organizations like the Red Cross had to galvanize resources for deployment to pandemic responses elsewhere, causing an abrupt closing of the Nashville tornado shelter operations.

Through this coincidence of bad timing and natural disaster, Nashville experienced a large jump in encampments and in the population sleeping in them on the eve of COVID-19. Like many cities, Nashville was strapped for resources and faced growing budget gaps. Acquiring individual hotel and motel units was largely off the table. To manage the expected COVID-related need, the city's Office of Emergency Management, coordinating with its Social Services Agency, opened two new congregate sheltering facilities in a public fairground. The first was run by the Social Services Agency for individuals in the shelter system or on the street, equipped with only two hundred beds to allow adequate space for social distancing. The second, a 250-bed operation run by the Office of Emergency Management, staffed by temporarily hired health care staff, and provided guidance from the city's Department of Health, was reserved for the homeless who tested positive but did not need hospitalization, and those who had contact with a person who was COVID-positive. The remaining homeless response during the pandemic focused on an encampment strategy to communicate the message about safe distancing and personal protection among those who remained on the streets.

MANAGING FOR THE LONG TERM

Many months into the global pandemic shutdown, updated public health information clarified that the situation was indeterminate. When officials and providers realized that it could be up to a year before vaccines and treatments would be widely available, a longer period of isolation and protection became the norm for vulnerable populations like the homeless who suffer many underlying health risks, even as some portions of society returned to work and limited social activity. Spaces secured for the short term began to transition into longer-term solutions.

Cities had to start shifting attention from emergency response to assessing whether their temporary facilities could be maintained beyond the sixty-to-ninety-day time frame originally envisioned. Resources had to be devoted to the social and emotional needs of clients, particularly those in isolation. Budget officials grappling with the hemorrhaging of resources resulting from economic meltdown also faced the ongoing costs of sheltering many more homeless.

Not long into this dawning of a chilling new reality, innovative minds turned to converting the pandemic emergency into an opportunity. Fashioned using resources made available through public and private emergency funding, efforts were made to reconfigure temporary solutions into a permanent trajectory toward ending homelessness.

Nashville's Homeless Management Impact Team was not at the center of the initial emergency operations; gradually, however, it was brought in more fully to focus attention on client needs and to pose the question of what the longer term held. Realizing the potential duration of the shelter-in-place restrictions and the benefits of ongoing close contact with clients, the team reached out to a local philanthropy with which it had collaborated before, the Frist Foundation, and posed the question, What if we created a pathway to housing for our clients and made this crisis an opportunity for the unhoused?

This daring leap forward on homeless policy caught on in cities across the globe. Conversations explored what it would take to move people onward to housing rather than back to shelter or street. Cities, faced with the moral dilemma of what it means to send people back to the streets without a home during an indeterminate public health crisis, began shaping strategies to convert the crisis into a permanent opportunity for overcoming homelessness.

Nashville secured a small grant to intervene with the most vulnerable rough sleepers and do a COVID Rapid Rehousing pilot. The city used grant funds to place the highest-risk population in specially secured hotel space and work intensively with them for one month on a transition to permanent housing. A typical "move-on" case management approach would have taken 120 days of engagement before the person successfully secured housing. In this pilot effort, Nashville aspired to do that within 30 days, triaging the client through the coordinated Homeless Management Information System to access placement in preferred housing.

In Houston, the aspirations went further still. There, the team of partners who had been working assiduously to tackle the city's peripatetic
encampments expanded their partnership network from a planning body
to an action body. Spurred on by new guidance from the CDC that urged
local continuums of care to be more action oriented, staff shifted their
focus into a *do* rather than *tell* mode. Hurricane Harvey had taught the
city a lot about coordinating public and private efforts to integrate funds
and management to achieve permanency for homeless clients.[4] Building
on that experience, the city's homeless services agency pulled partners
together behind the collective challenge that every person housed in a
temporary COVID shelter would receive a pathway to housing. Drawing
on case management and rental assistance shaped partially out of
resources from the pandemic and supplemented by private fund-raising
from local philanthropic partners, work began.

This initiative established a $50 million fund to provide 500 bridge
units to house people temporarily, while efforts were under way to move
5,000 people through Rapid Rehousing to scatter-site units with light
ongoing case management or to permanent supportive housing for those
with the greatest need. If successful, this initiative could end chronic
homelessness in Houston.

Across cities, it is the homeless service systems often at the helm of emergency sheltering operations that, during a crisis, frequently expand in size
to many times that of the chronically homeless population managed on a
daily basis. Care in a time of crisis demands not just beds and food but the
skilled interventions of social service providers to support and engage
traumatized individuals. Cities that were more successful in quickly meeting needs in the emergent COVID-19 pandemic were those that relied on
experts in engagement and management from the start, leveraged strong
local collaborations to plan and act, and took a long view of permanency
to pivot from emergency to opportunity for the homeless.

No emergency is like any other, a lesson many cities learned from
observation, through mass migrations, environmental disasters, and a
public health crisis like nothing in living memory. Emergency preparedness plans need to be in place to respond to as many circumstances as can
be imagined, but inevitably there will be circumstances no one anticipates.

The frontline emergency response must adapt moment-by-moment in order to swiftly identify emerging needs while considering what might come next. Out of these iterations, transformation can occur, solving the crisis of the moment and altering the system for the longer term and the public good.

Conclusion

Overcoming street homelessness has all the traits of an impossible-to-solve social problem: entrenched poverty and inequality, poor access to needed supports, and difficult-to-navigate processes at the client level. Teams of people work day in, day out with clients struggling with many medical and mental health challenges; and these dedicated individuals are working within flawed service systems with limited time to do the critical work across multiple organizations and levels of government. No one owns the issue. Homelessness as an issue is itself homeless.

So why would the conclusion to this book be that ending homelessness can be done? No better reason than the proven successes—despite remarkable challenges and some failed efforts—in the ten cities reviewed here, and in many other cities. The lessons may be found throughout this book, and are summarized below.

Major challenges fall outside the control of street outreach and shelter services. Anyone who looks to the sheltering agency as the responsible entity for solving homelessness misses the point. They may as well look to a hospital emergency room to prevent disease and provide cures. Shelter is just that, an emergency intervention. This problem cannot be addressed fundamentally by asking shelter or outreach workers to try harder at

Figure 13. A formerly homeless woman in Mexico City receiving keys to her new home, January 31, 2017. Bloomberg Associates.

solving their clients' misfortunes. True, lasting solutions require reform of health and social supports, and access to affordable housing resources.

Effective outcomes require sustained cross-system collaboration. Imagine the biggest cross-system matrix. That is what is necessary for change. Every opportunity should be leveraged. Athens, Paris, and Bogotá each pulled their national counterparts to the table in establishing local processes for estimating the number of people on their streets. That involved putting organizations, often at odds with one another, in a room to hash out solutions to an issue in which they share an interest and desire for a mutual outcome.

Solutions require the input of systems that produce the problem: hospitals, jails, prisons, behavioral health facilities, child welfare systems, domestic violence systems, housing providers, housing courts, and others.

But solutions also require the participation of those who can contribute to the solution, often the *same* entities. In New York City, a collaboration that started between the city's probation agency and its homeless agency grew to include the hospital system, welfare system, and housing agency. Only the combined efforts of these organizations could conquer the flaws that generate homelessness, which boils down to a common imperative: to avoid discharging any person from a service into homelessness or into a situation that places them at high risk of homelessness. The original collaboration in New York City gave rise to a successful discharge-planning program that has been replicated nationally.[1]

Solutions also require input from people who have experienced homelessness. Their voices regarding the real challenges, and the usefulness of what is being offered to help meet those challenges, brings a necessary dose of reality to any ongoing effort to tackle barriers and structure solid solutions.

Only partners working together can tailor services to effectively serve the complex needs of the homeless individual in their current condition. An exciting example of this occurred in Baltimore, where the health services team and homeless team collaborated to identify how health service revenues could be used for housing development. Together, the teams realized the beneficial health effects and savings that can result from housing a medically frail individual otherwise inclined to a life on the street.

The frustration when efforts fail can be great, such as occurred with Bogotá's repeated attempts to draw the local health authority into a comprehensive approach to addressing homelessness. Key strategies for identifying people and enrolling people in critically needed services fell on the cutting-room floor. A committed junior health analyst who shared the homeless-services team's passion for reform was never able to garner the sustained commitment of the city's health agency leaders, who failed to move past lip service.

Not every success requires every partner at the table. Some efforts may start small and build over time. Others may congregate within a big collective tent from the start. Some may be forced to shed dead weight to restore productive energy in the room. The bottom line is that success requires the shared conviction that no human being should be left to live destitute on the streets without dignity and care. Any partner who comes to the table with that conviction has the ability to put aside ego and organizational issues and wholeheartedly collaborate in iterative problem solving.

This type of cross-system collaboration works best under the guidance of a trusted convener and strong leader supported by a well-organized governance process. Because homelessness is not centrally owned by any one entity, it is up to the local partners to figure out who to get behind or who to push to the fore. As is certainly true in the ten cities described here, that person is often the mayor. The annual meeting of the US National Alliance to End Homelessness is dominated by staff from mayors' offices and municipal agencies seeking a venue in which to share ideas.

But mayors can have short tenures, and political cycles eventually remove the mayor who has been dedicated to the issue, creating a potential gap. An dynamic local collaboration is one where the community can hold the coalition together during political transitions and recruit the new mayor to take the lead. If that doesn't happen, the coalition must maintain the lead. Nashville's successful reorganization of the regional homeless planning groups into a single entity placed the city in a much stronger position to weather a stormy series of short-termed mayors. Edmonton empowered Homeward Trust—a nonprofit agency committed to ending homelessness—to be its trusted community partner. While the provincial and federal governments have taken responsibility for housing and homelessness policy, the city of Edmonton defined local leadership roles through Homeward Trust to create the infrastructure for collaborative action on the ground.

The sustaining force of many of these effective collaborations is the committed devotion of frontline managers who have dedicated themselves to the work, often without public attention or fanfare. Behind a committed mayor is the staff who bring their passion to the issue, frame the partnerships, develop action plans, and propel the work forward. Almost every collaboration is fueled by individuals who persevere to raise the alarm about need, withstand disruptive leadership transitions, and do the hard work between meetings, such as listening to frontline service providers and those experiencing homelessness. Each of the ten cities described in this book have that driven manager, or managers, without whom the work would never have gotten done.

Putting solid partners in place ensures that a prime set of best and emerging practices are followed across jurisdictions in order to effectively reduce homelessness. At the core of those best practices are solid data, the glue that holds the collaborative partners together, informing service systems with a better understanding of the people they serve. Street counts effectively measure change over time and can be energizing points of civic engagement. Paris has taken this to a whole new level, building on lessons from the street count to develop an entire practice of civic engagement in addressing public issues across a wide range of disciplines.

The emergence of by-name lists has demonstrated the ability to galvanize partners around the very concrete lives of those in need. Integrated service-system data help to illuminate the complex interrelationships among systems and track how clients cycle through their doors, revealing systemic reforms that can alter outcomes for the better. Los Angeles has been developing sophisticated tools that help to prioritize among its masses of homeless to ensure the highest and best use of the increasing flow of resources coming online.

Considerable evidence is building around best practices, as researchers and providers come to know what strategies work to engage clients and support their needs at all stages throughout the process from street to stability. No longer can the homeless-services system refer to any person as a "service-resistant" client. Instead, providers are challenged to offer services that the clients will accept in a manner that offers them the dignity every human deserves. Unless systems' reforms recognize the power of the client to drive the process forward, and the ability not to, the best-conceived strategies will fail. Seeing the client as the primary stakeholder among many key stakeholders is not only critical; it is essential. Simply asking, and listening, informs design—listening to what homeless people's actions are saying about what works and what does not, without blame, stigmatization, or dehumanization. This theme permeates best practices emerging in prevention, street outreach, shelter services, and housing permanency. "Meeting the client where they are" is no longer just a social work philosophy; it is a program design element that is crucial for success. Curbside counseling, low-threshold shelters, and Housing First strategies are all adaptations that adjust the strategy to the needs of clients, rather than expect clients to meet the needs of the services. These practices are skipping across borders and continents, with Athens replicating the BRC's Safe Haven model, and Bogotá and Mexico City installing HomeBase prevention.

Finally, the work can be done, but it is never over. If you take your eye off the fast-moving dynamics for a minute, something will pop back up. Because the sources of the problem are so diverse and can emanate from any quarter at any time, pencils never get put down. The solution requires ongoing vigilance and constant scanning of the horizon for future events that might contribute to the cause. Houston was the poster child of success in the United States until a change in leadership disrupted the powerful effects of its local collaboration. The city had to work hard to address this interruption and restore the energy of the collaboration. In August 2017, Hurricane Harvey displaced thousands of residents and contributed to a slight increase in homelessness. Ongoing success may mean reactivating existing partners or bringing in new partners. No one can view ending homelessness as a time-limited exercise. The commitment must be permanent.

It can be done, and these ten cities are proving just that.

APPENDIX   Definitions of Homelessness

There is no global definition for this universal problem. Some countries call it street homeless; others call it sleeping rough. Definitions vary, making cross-border comparisons of the magnitude of the problem a challenge.

UNITED STATES

There are two national definitions of homelessness in the United States. The most widely used is from the Department of Housing and Urban Development (HUD), which distinguishes between literal homelessness and being at risk.

In the literal category are those living unsheltered—in places not meant for human habitation such as cars, parks, abandoned buildings, public spaces, or train or subway stations—and those living sheltered in emergency or temporary accommodations. At-risk individuals, including those staying temporarily with family or friends, are not counted as homeless.

The second US definition of homelessness applies to children and youth. The McKinney-Vento Homeless Assistance Act of 1987 provides this broader categorization of who is homeless, adding children and youth who are sharing the housing of other persons due to loss of housing, economic hardship, or a similar reason; and those who are living in motels, hotels, trailer parks, or camping grounds due to the lack of alternative adequate accommodations. Under the act's broader definition for schoolchildren, families living doubled-up would be counted as homeless.

CANADA

The Canadian definition of homelessness (as spelled out by the Canadian Observatory on Homelessness) encompasses the unsheltered and those in emergency shelters (including domestic violence and disaster shelters), as well as those who are technically homeless in provisional accommodations, such as temporary housing, couch-surfing, short-term temporary rental accommodations, care institutions without housing options, and reception centers for migrants. This is a relatively broad definition of homelessness.

GREECE

Each member state in the European Union has its own definition of homelessness. Some countries, such as France, have no national definition. Others employ expansive standards that mix the literal definition of homelessness with those at-risk or those formerly homeless.

Most European countries tie their definition to a typology of homelessness developed by the Fédération Européenne des Associations Nationales Travaillant avec les Sans-Abri (European Federation of National Organizations Working with the Homeless, or FEANTSA). The methodology instructs countries to choose which of the following subcategories are included in their official definition:

- Rooflessness—without a shelter of any kind, sleeping rough
- Houselessness—with a place to sleep, albeit temporary; in an institution or shelter
- Living in insecure housing—threatened with severe exclusion due to insecure tenancies, eviction, or domestic violence
- Living in inadequate housing—in caravans on illegal campsites, in unfit housing, or in extreme overcrowding.[1]

Greece recently adopted an official definition based on the FEANTSA typology. As of 2012, homeless persons are defined as all persons legally residing in the country who lack access to safe and adequate accommodation, whether owned, rented or freely released, that would meet the habitation requirements, required by law or building codes, for water and electricity. The homeless include particularly those living in the streets or shelters and those who are hosted, out of need, in institutions or other enclosed forms of care (Law 4052). Thus, the official count excludes the substantial number of migrant refugees flowing into the country. While many continue on to other destinations in Europe, many stay. The absence of their numbers in the homeless count highlights the struggle many European countries continue to have in managing the demands of this migration crisis.

FRANCE

There is no official definition of homelessness in France, but its people have a right to housing, recently reinforced under the DALO law (Droit au Logement Opposable; Enforceable right to housing), adopted in 2007. Citizens excluded from housing can make an appeal to an independent committee, demanding their housing rights.

MEXICO

Mexico has no official definition of homelessness. It does have a General Law of Social Development, which states that housing is a social right, and that people or social groups in situations of vulnerability have the right to receive service and support that contribute to diminishing their discrimination and disadvantage.

Like many global megacities, Mexico City has a history of mass migration resulting in people living in informal housing that does not meet local building codes. Historically, squatters have built homes in the outskirts of town where they could find space on vacant underdeveloped lands. Over time, the government has formalized these areas and services have been brought into the neighborhoods. Residents of these areas are not typically considered homeless despite living in often significantly substandard housing.

COLOMBIA

Colombia defines as homeless a person who makes the street their dwelling place, either permanently or temporarily, and has broken ties with their family. Furthermore, the definition clarifies that "the street" falls short of the totality of elements that meet basic human needs.

Both Mexico and Colombia place homelessness within the realm of human rights, defining homelessness both as serious deprivation of access to housing and as an extreme form of social exclusion, discrimination, and loss of dignity. Defining homelessness as a human rights issue has implications for both how people are identified and how they are served.

Notes

INTRODUCTION

1. Mayoral Workgroup on Homelessness, "Executive Summary," City of Baltimore, June 30, 2017, https://human-services.baltimorecity.gov/sites/default/files/MayoralWorkgroupReport-FINAL.pdf.

2. "Key Strategies," *The Journey Home,* accessed June 30, 2020, https://journeyhomebaltimore.org/key-strategies/.

3. Bernard C. "Jack" Young, "Mayor Young to Launch Independent Office of Homeless Services," press release, City of Baltimore, Maryland, June 6, 2019, https://content.govdelivery.com/accounts/MDBALT/bulletins/24946a7.

4. "Baltimore City Continuum of Care 2019 Point in Time Count Report," *The Journey Home,* accessed June 30, 2020, https://homeless.baltimorecity.gov/sites/default/files/PIT%20Report%20Draft%202019_Update%208.30.19_Update.pdf.

5. "Homeless Count," Homeward Trust, accessed June 30, 2020, http://homewardtrust.ca/wp-content/uploads/2018/01/Homeless-Count-Graph-White.jpg.

6. Rice Kinder Institute for Urban Research, "The 2019 Kinder Houston Area Survey: Tracking Responses to the Economic and Demographic Transformations through 38 Years of Houston Surveys" (May 2019), 7, https://kinder.rice.edu/sites/default/files/documents/KI%202019%20Houston%20Area%20Survey%20Report.pdf.

7. Mariana Alexander, "A $3 Billion Problem: Homeless Services in NYC," Citizen Budget Commission, May 24, 2018, blog post, https://cbcny.org /research/3-billion-problem.

8. Matthew Desmond, *Evicted: Poverty and Profit in the American City* (New York: Crown, 2016).

9. *Shelby County v. Holder,* 570 U.S. 529 (2013).

10. Audrey Smedley and Brian Smedley define institutional or structural discrimination as "the uneven access by group membership to resources, status, and power that stems from facially neutral policies and practice". "Race as Biology Is Fiction, Racism as a Social Problem Is Real: Anthropological and Historical Perspectives on the Social Construction of Race," *American Psychologist* 60(1) (January 2005): 16–26.

11. National Alliance to End Homelessness, "State of Homelessness: 2020 Edition," accessed June 30, 2020, https://endhomelessness.org/homelessness-in-america/homelessness-statistics/state-of-homelessness-2020/; United States Census, ACS Demographic and Housing Estimates, ACS 1 Year estimates (2019), https://data.census.gov/cedsci/table?q=race&tid=ACSDP1Y2019. DP05&hidePreview=false (race alone or in combination).

12. Employment and Social Development Canada, "Everyone Counts 2018: Highlights; Preliminary Results from the Second Nationally Coordinated Point-in-Time Count of Homelessness in Canadian Communities" (2019), accessed June 30, 2020, https://www.canada.ca/en/employment-social-development/programs /homelessness/reports/highlights-2018-point-in-time-count.html#3.4.

13. US Department of Housing and Urban Development, "HUD 2019 Continuum of Care Homeless Assistance Programs Homeless Populations and Subpopulations: NY-600 New York City CoC, Point in Time Date," January 28, 2019, https://files.hudexchange.info/reports/published/CoC_PopSub_CoC_NY-600-2019_NY_2019.pdf. US Census Bureau, "2018 American Community Survey 1-Year Estimates Population Division—New York City Department of City Planning," November 2019, https://www1.nyc.gov/assets/planning/download/pdf /planning-level/nyc-population/acs/dem_2018acs1yr_nyc.pdf.

14. Los Angeles Homeless Services Authority (LAHSA), "Report and Recommendations of the Ad Hoc Committee on Black People Experiencing Homelessness," December 2018, https://www.lahsa.org/item.ashx?id=2823-report-and-recommendations-of-the-ad-hoc-committee-on-black-people-experiencing-homelessness.pdf&dl=true.

15. LAHSA, "Report and Recommendations." US Census Bureau, "QuickFacts: Los Angeles City, California," accessed June 30, 2020, https://www .census.gov/quickfacts/fact/table/losangelescitycalifornia/RHI125218.

16. United Nations, "We Can End Poverty: Millennium Development Goals and beyond 2015," accessed June 30, 2020, https://www.un.org/millenniumgoals /poverty.shtml.

17. While long discussed by economists, income inequality became popularly acknowledged with the publication of French economist Thomas Piketty's tome *Capital in the Twenty-First Century*, trans. Arthur Goldhammer (Cambridge, MA: Harvard University Press, 2014).

18. Wendell Cox and Hugh Pavelitch, "16th Annual Demographia International Housing Affordability Survey: 2020 Rating Middle-Income Housing Affordability," *Demographia* (3rd quarter, 2019): 8–10, http://www.demographia.com /dhi.pdf.

19. Harvard Graduate School of Design and Harvard Kennedy School, *The State of the Nation's Housing, 2018*, Joint Center for Housing Studies of Harvard University (2018): 7–12, http://www.jchs.harvard.edu/sites/default/files /Harvard_JCHS_State_of_the_Nations_Housing_2018.pdf.

20. Ligia Teixeira and James Cartwright, eds., *Using Evidence to End Homelessness* (Bristol, UK: Bristol University Press, 2020).

21. "Opening Doors: Federal Strategic Plan to Prevent and End Homelessness," United States Interagency Council on Homelessness, updated 2015, accessed June 30, 2020, https://www.usich.gov/resources/uploads/asset_ library/USICH_OpeningDoors_Amendment2015_FINAL.pdf.

1. THE TRANSFORMATION OF HOMELESS SERVICES

1. Alex S. Vitale, *City of Disorder: How the Quality of Life Campaign Transformed New York Politics* (New York: New York University Press, 2008). Amy M. Donley and James D. Wright, "Cleaning Up the Streets: Community Efforts to Combat Homelessness by Criminalizing Homeless Behaviors," *Homelessness in America* 3 (2008): 75–92.

2. Best-known examples include Toynbee Hall in London and Hull House in Chicago.

3. Dennis P. Culhane et al., "The Age Structure of Contemporary Homelessness: Evidence and Implications for Public Policy," *Analyses of Social Issues and Public Policy* 13, no. 1 (2013): 2.

4. Luisa Fernanda and Zamudio Rocha, "Homelessness Policies in Bogotá, Colombia, towards Integral Human Development," *Campos Magazine in Social Sciences* 6, no.1 (2018): 48–49. Edmonton Task Force on Homelessness, "Homelessness in Edmonton: A Call to Action," Homeward Trust, May 14, 1999, http:// homewardtrust.ca/wp-content/uploads/2016/12/May-1999-Edmonton-Homeless-Count.pdf.

5. Cécile Brousse, Jean-Marie Firdion, and Maryse Marpsat, *Les Sans-Domicile* (Paris: La Découverte, coll. Repères Sociologie, 2008): 118; Aristides Sapounakis, "Homelessness in a Mediterranean Country: The Case of Greece," *Contributions in Sociology* 135 (2001): 119–20.

6. Dragana Avramov, "The Changing Face of Homelessness in Europe," *Contributions in Sociology* (2001): 4–17.

7. Volker Busch-Geertsema, William Edgar, Eoin O'Sullivan, and Nicholas Pleace, "Homelessness and Homeless Policies in Europe: Lessons from Research," *Conference on Homelessness* 9 (2010): 53–57.

8. "LAHSA-Administered Safe Parking Sites in Los Angeles," Los Angeles Homeless Services Authority, updated July 7, 2020, https://www.lahsa.org/news?article=592-safe-parking.

9. Avramov, "The Changing Face of Homelessness in Europe," 24.

10. "Health and Homelessness," American Psychological Association, 2011, https://www.apa.org/pi/ses/resources/publications/homelessness-health.

11. Nicholas Pleace et al., "The Finnish Homelessness Strategy: An International Review," Ministry of the Environment, Helsinki (2015), 50–51, https://helda.helsinki.fi/bitstream/handle/10138/153258/YMra_3en_2015.pdf.

12. Volker Busch-Geertsema et al., "Homelessness and Homeless Policies in Europe," 71–73.

13. Jeffrey Olivet et al., "Outreach and Engagement in Homeless Services: A Review of the Literature," *Open Health Services and Policy Journal* 3, no. 1 (2010): 53–70; Julie A. Lam and Robert Rosenheck, "Street Outreach for Homeless Persons with Serious Mental Illness: Is It Effective?" *Medical Care* (1999): 894–907; Sally Erickson and Jamie Page, "To Dance with Grace: Outreach and Engagement to Persons on the Street; 1998 National Symposium on Homelessness Research," *US Dept. of Health and Human Services and US Dept. of Housing and Urban Development* (1999): 1–24.

14. Sam Tsemberis et al., "Consumer Preference Programs for Individuals Who Are Homeless and Have Psychiatric Disabilities: A Drop-In Center and a Supported Housing Program," *American Journal of Community Psychology* 32, nos. 3–4 (2003): 305–17.

15. "Controlled Clinical Trials Involving Motivational Interviewing" (a bibliography), Motivational Interviewing Resources, updated January 30, 2020, https://motivationalinterviewing.org/sites/default/files/mi_controlled_trials_0.pdf; Jennifer Hettema, Julie Steele, and William R. Miller, "Motivational Interviewing," *Annual Review of Clinical Psychology* 1 (April 2005): 91–111.

16. "Key Considerations for Implementing Emergency Shelter within an Effective Crisis Response System," United States Interagency Council on Homelessness, August 2017, https://www.usich.gov/resources/uploads/asset_library/emergency-shelter-key-considerations.pdf; "Are All Shelters the Same?" BRC, September 1, 2016, https://www.brc.org/are-all-shelters-same; "Emergency Shelter Learning Series," National Alliance to End Homelessness, April 25, 2017, https://endhomelessness.org/resource/emergency-shelter/; "Comparative Analysis of Homeless Facilities and Programs in Selected U.S. Cities and Counties," City of Virginia Beach Department of Housing and Neighborhood Preservation,

September 19, 2011, https://www.vbgov.com/government/departments
/housing-neighborhood-preservation/Documents/homeless-families-individuals
/Homeless%20Shelters%20Comparison%20Report%209.19.11.pdf.

17. Deborah K. Padgett, Benjamin F. Henwood, and Sam J. Tsemberis, *Housing First: Ending Homelessness, Transforming Cities, Changing Lives* (Oxford: Oxford University Press, 2016), 50–61; "National Final Report: Cross-Site At Home/Chez Soi Project," Mental Health Commission of Canada, 2014, https://www.mentalhealthcommission.ca/sites/default/files/mhcc_at_home_report_national_cross-site_eng_2_0.pdf; Finkel et al., "Rapid Re-housing for Homeless Families Demonstration Programs Evaluation Report, Part 2: Demonstration Findings—Outcomes Evaluation," huduser.gov (Office of Policy Development and Research, US Department of Housing and Urban Development), April 2016, https://www.huduser.gov/portal/sites/default/files/pdf/RRHD-PartII-Outcomes.pdf;Debora Rog, "Permanent Supportive Housing: Assessing the Evidence," *Psychiatric Services* 65, no. 3 (March 2014): 287–94, https://ps.psychiatryonline.org/doi/pdfplus/10.1176/appi.ps.201300261.

18. Dan Herman et al., "Randomized Trial of Critical Time Intervention to Prevent Homelessness after Hospital Discharge," National Center for Biotechnology Intervention, July 2011, https://pubmed.ncbi.nlm.nih.gov/21724782/.

19. Daniel Gubits et al., "Family Options Study: 3-Year Impacts of Housing and Services Interventions for Homeless Families," *Abt Associates* (October 2016).

20. Howard Rolston, Judy Geyer, and Gretchen Locke, "Evaluation of the Homebase Community Prevention Program: Final Report," *Abt Associates* (June 2013): 1-D-10; Sarena Goodman, Peter Messeri, and Brendan O'Flaherty, "Homelessness Prevention in New York City: On Average, It Works," *Journal of Housing Economics* 31 (2016): 14–34, http://www.law.nyu.edu/sites/default/files/ECM_PRO_074707.pdf; Marybeth Shinn et al., "Efficient Targeting of Homelessness Prevention Services for Families," *American Journal of Public Health* 103 (2013): S324–S330, https://doi.org/10.2105/AJPH.2013.301468.

21. Martha R. Burt, "Strategies for Preventing Homelessness," US Department of Housing and Urban Development and the Office of Policy Development and Research (May 2005), xix–xxv, http://webarchive.urban.org/Uploaded PDF/1000874_preventing_homelessness.pdf.

2. ENGAGING PEOPLE ON THE STREETS

1. Tyler Blint-Welsh, "Federal Data Shows Nearly 80,000 Homeless in NYC, *Wall Street Journal,* October 24, 2019, https://www.wsj.com/articles/federal-data-show-nearly-80-000-homeless-in-new-york-city-11571922000?mod=searchresults&page=1&pos=1; Department of Homeless Services, "NYC HOPE

2019 Results," New York City, accessed June 30, 2020, https://www1.nyc.gov /assets/dhs/downloads/pdf/hope-2019-results.pdf.

2. "The Police Response to Homelessness," Police Executive Research Forum, June 2018, https://www.policeforum.org/assets/PoliceResponsetoHomelessness.pdf.

3. "Core Elements of Effective Street Outreach to People Experiencing Homelessness," United States Interagency Council on Homelessness, May 24, 2019, https://www.usich.gov/tools-for-action/core-elements-of-effective-street-outreach-to-people-experiencing-homelessness.

4. NYU Silver Communications Office, "NYU Silver Study Counters Narrative That Street Homeless Are Service Resistant," Silver School of Social Work, New York University, June 4, 2019, https://socialwork.nyu.edu/news/2019 /nyu-silver-studycountersnarrativethatstreethomelessareserviceres.html.

5. Hettema, Steele, and Miller, "Motivational Interviewing."

6. "Chronically Homeless," National Alliance to End Homelessness, updated January 2020, https://endhomelessness.org/homelessness-in-america/who-experiences-homelessness/chronically-homeless/.

7. Elizabeth K. Hopper, Ellen L. Bassuk, and Jeffrey Olivet, "Shelter from the Storm: Trauma-Informed Care in Homelessness Services Settings," *Open Health Services and Policy Journal* 2 (2009): 131–51, http://www.traumacenter.org /products/pdf_files/shelter_from_storm.pdf.

8. "No Safe Place: The Criminalization of Homelessness in U.S. Cities," National Law Center on Homelessness and Poverty, accessed June 30, 2020, https://nlchp.org/wp-content/uploads/2019/02/No_Safe_Place.pdf.

9. Legal Action Center, "Helping Moms, Dads, and Kids to Come Home: Eliminating Barriers to Housing for People with Criminal Records," December 2016, available via Publish Online, https://indd.adobe.com/view/04243d7e-5a9a-4bd8-9d97-1bb1ce77b9c5.

10. Panagiota Fitsiou and Nikos Kourachanis, "Social Policy Challenges for Homeless People with Mental Illness: Views of Greek Mental Health Professionals," *European Journal of Homelessness* 13, no. 2 (2019): 47–62, https://www .feantsa.org/public/user/Observatory/2019/EJH/EJH_13_2/RN1-Feantsa-2019_13-2_v02.pdf.

11. Benjamin Oreskes, "Homeless People Could Lose the Right to Sleep on the Sidewalks If Western Cities Have Their Way," *Los Angeles Times*, September 25, 2019, https://www.latimes.com/california/story/2019-09-25/boise-homeless-encampment-amicus-brief-supreme-court-appeal-cities.

12. Marianne B. M. van den Bree et al., "A Longitudinal Population-Based Study of Factors in Adolescence Predicting Homelessness in Young Adulthood," *Journal of Adolescent Health* 45, no. 6 (December 2009): 571–78, https://www .jahonline.org/article/S1054-139X(09)00144-X/fulltext.

13. Scott O. Lilienfeld, "Why 'Just Say No' Doesn't Work," *Scientific American*, January 1, 2014, https://www.scientificamerican.com/article/why-just-say-no-doesnt-work/.

14. "Schizophrenia," National Institute of Mental Health, updated May 2018, https://www.nimh.nih.gov/health/statistics/schizophrenia.shtml.

15. "Liz Murray," No Barriers, accessed June 30, 2020, https://nobarriersusa .org/about/people/liz-murray/.

16. Muzzy Rozenblatt, "The Needs of the So-Called 'Service-Resistant,'" Bowery Residents' Committee, April 1, 2016, https://www.brc.org/needs-so-called-service-resistant.

17. Sarah Johnsen, Suzanne Fitzpatrick, and Beth Watts, "Homelessness and Social Control: A Typology," *Housing Studies* 33, no. 7 (2018): 1106–26, https:// www.tandfonline.com/doi/full/10.1080/02673037.2017.1421912.

18. Bill de Blasio, Dean Fuleihan, and Jeff Thamkittikasem, "Mayor's Management Report," City of New York (September 2019), 199, https://www1.nyc .gov/assets/operations/downloads/pdf/mmr2019/2019_mmr.pdf.

19. "Core Elements of Effective Street Outreach to People Experiencing Homelessness," United States Interagency Council on Homelessness, June 2019,https://www.usich.gov/resources/uploads/asset_library/Core-Components-of-Outreach-2019.pdf.

20. Jeffrey Olivet et al., "Outreach and Engagement in Homeless Services."

21. "Core Elements," June 2019.

22. "Home-Stat Reaches New Milestone: Nearly 1,500 Unsheltered Homeless New Yorkers Helped Off Streets," press release, City of New York, January 17, 2018, https://www1.nyc.gov/office-of-the-mayor/news/041-18/home-stat-reaches-new-milestone-nearly-1-500-unsheltered-homeless-new-yorkers-helped-off-streets.

23. Graham Rayman and Ginger Adams Otis, "NYPD Top Cop Defends Homeless Outreach amid Series of Crimes Related to Shelter Residents," *New York Daily News*, December 21, 2016, https://www.nydailynews.com/new-york /nypd-top-defends-homeless-outreach-crime-uptick-article-1.2919333?gclid=Cjw KCAjwusrtBRBmEiwAGBPgE1RCB7szydC3VR5ZO942z71PGyv2jom6FB5E-MaW-ONJiPK0h_yMouhoC3KoQAvD_BwE. In June 2020, as part of New York City's effort to reform policing, the unit was disbanded.

24. "Public Safety," Downtown Alliance, accessed June 30, 2020, https:// www.downtownny.com/public-safety.

25. "Response to Encampments on Public Land," City of Edmonton, accessed June 30, 2020, https://www.edmonton.ca/city_government/documents/PDF /EncampmentResponseFlowCharts.pdf.

26. Olivet et al., "Outreach and Engagement in Homeless Services."

27. "Core Elements," June 2019.

28. Olivet et al., "Outreach and Engagement in Homeless Services."

29. Benedict Carey, "Nakesha Williams Died Homeless on a Manhattan Street: Should She Have Been Forced into Treatment?" *New York Times,* March 6, 2018, https://www.nytimes.com/2018/03/06/health/nakesha-williams-involuntary-commitment.html.

30. "No Safe Place."

31. In the United States, policies in regard to involuntary commitment are most often enacted by states, and few states allow involuntary commitment for treatment and rehabilitation, usually only in cases where the person is at risk to themselves or others. In New York State, a person can be civilly committed to inpatient treatment if they demonstrate a need that rises to the level of being a danger to self or others, but a medical professional must decide that the service is medically necessary, and a court is needed only if the patient challenges the commitment. Another New York state program involves the removal of a person from the street, or even from their home, for assessment in a hospital emergency room. Such removal is temporary, often limited to seventy-two hours at most, the key distinction being removal for assessment and not treatment. In 2006, the Netherlands implemented a policy in its four largest cities to get all homeless people off the streets. The law barred any person from sleeping outside, but also required individual treatment plans for all homeless persons and mandated that the municipalities find the necessary housing and services. Generally, any policy that forces treatment or services for homeless people is decried by advocates and human rights groups as abuse of human rights or criminalization of homelessness. The Netherlands' policy was eventually struck down.

32. "Section 9.58: Transport for evaluation; powers of approved mobile crisis outreach teams," New York State Senate, accessed June 30, 2020, https://www.nysenate.gov/legislation/laws/MHY/9.58.

33. "Housing Not Handcuffs: Ending the Criminalization of Homelessness in the U.S. Cities," National Law Center on Homelessness and Poverty, October 2018, accessed June 30, 2020, https://nlchp.org//wp-content/uploads/2018/10/Housing-Not-Handcuffs.pdf.

34. "The Police Response."

35. Kevin M. Fitzpatrick, Mark E. La Gory, and Ferris J. Ritchey, "Criminal Victimization among the Homeless," *Justice Quarterly* 10, no.3 (1993): 353–68, https://www.tandfonline.com/doi/abs/10.1080/07418829300091881?journalCode=rjqy20.

36. Kevin Stiff and Joe Polzak, "Law Enforcement Strategies to Address Homelessness," PowerPoint of presentation, CIT International Crisis Intervention Team conference, Kansas City, MO, August 15, 2018, http://www.citinternational.org/resources/Documents/H.O.T.%20Cops%20-%2021st%20Century%20Policing%20of%20the%20Homeless.pdf.

37. "Tent City, USA: The Growth of America's Homeless Encampments and How Communities Are Responding," National Law Center on Homelessness and Poverty, 2017, https://nlchp.org/wp-content/uploads/2018/10/Tent_City_USA_2017.pdf.

38. Richard Emblin, "El Bronx: The Living Hell at the Heart of Bogotá," *(Bogotá) City Paper*, July 11, 2016, https://thecitypaperbogota.com/bogota/el-bronx-the-living-hell-at-the-heart-of-bogota/13666.

3. SHELTERING OPTIONS THAT WORK

1. Joseph Chamie, "As Cities Grow, So Do the Numbers of Homeless, *Yale Global Online,* July 13, 2017, https://yaleglobal.yale.edu/content/cities-grow-so-do-numbers-homeless.

2. DeBlasio, Fuleihan, and Thamkittikasem, "Mayor's Management Report."

3. Substance Abuse and Mental Health Services Administration, *A Treatment Improvement Protocol: Behavioral Health Services for People Who Are Homeless* (Rockville, MD, 2013), 25–30, https://www.ncbi.nlm.nih.gov/books/NBK138725/pdf/Bookshelf_NBK138725.pdf.

4. Katy Miller, "Using Shelter Strategically to End Homelessness," United States Interagency Council on Homelessness, April 1, 2016, https://www.usich.gov/news/using-shelter-strategically-to-end-homelessness.

5. San Francisco Department of Homelessness and Supportive Housing, "Navigation Centers Presentation," accessed October 2, 2020, https://hsh.sfgov.org/wp-content/uploads/2019/03/HSH-Nav-Slideshow-FINAL.pdf.

6. Martha R. Burt et al., "Strategies for Improving Homeless People's Access to Mainstream Benefits and Services," Office of Policy Development and Research, US Department of Housing and Urban Development, March 2010, https://www.urban.org/sites/default/files/publication/28626/412089-Strategies-for-Improving-Homeless-People-s-Access-to-Mainstream-Benefits-and-Services.PDF.

7. Matthew J. To, Thomas D. Brothers, and Colin Van Zoost, "Foot Conditions among Homeless Persons: A Systematic Review," *Plos One* 11, no 12 (December 9, 2010), https://journals.plos.org/plosone/article?id=10.1371/journal.pone.0167463.

8. The term *safe haven* was used in the United States in the early 1990s to refer to a federally funded supportive housing program and has since been adopted to describe the model in this book.

9. "Housing First," National Alliance to End Homelessness, April 20, 2016, https://endhomelessness.org/resource/housing-first/.

10. The actual Safe Haven census in New York City on the night of September 6, 2019, was 1,040.

11. Michael J. Berens, "A Review of Research: Designing the Built Environment for Recovery from Homelessness," Design Resources for Homelessness, http://designresourcesforhomelessness.org/wp-content/uploads/2015/11/OrientationReport.pdf.

12. The Stages of Change model operates on the assumption that people do not change behaviors quickly and decisively but rather through a cyclical process, moving through six stages: pre-contemplation, contemplation, preparation, action, maintenance, and termination. "Motivational interviewing" is a clinical approach that helps people with chronic health, mental health, and substance use disorders make positive behavioral changes to support better health. The approach upholds four principles—expressing empathy and avoiding arguing, developing discrepancy, rolling with resistance, and supporting self-efficacy, thus empowering a client's belief in their ability to make a successful change. "Critical time intervention" is an evidence-based practice that mobilizes support for society's most vulnerable individuals during periods of transition. It facilitates community integration and continuity of care by ensuring that a person has enduring ties to their community and support systems during these critical periods. For more details, see Wayne W. LaMorte, "The Transtheoretical Model (Stages of Change)," Boston University School of Public Health, updated September 9, 2019, https://sphweb.bumc.bu.edu/otlt/mph-modules/sb/behavioralchangetheories/behavioralchangetheories6.html#:~:text=The%20TTM%20posits%20that%20individuals,change%20for%20health%2Drelated%20behaviors; "Spotlight on PATH [Projects for Assistance in Transition from Homelessness] Practices and Programs: Motivational Interviewing," SAMHSA (Substance Abuse and Mental Health Services Administration), US Department of Health and Human Services, accessed November 1, 2020, https://www.samhsa.gov/sites/default/files/programs_campaigns/homelessness_programs_resources/path-spotlight-motivational-interviewing.pdf; "CTI Model," Center for the Advancement of Critical Time Intervention, accessed October 3, 2020, https://www.criticaltime.org/cti-model.

13. Stephen Eide, "Benchmarking Homeless Shelter Performance: A Proposal for Easing America's Homeless Crisis," Manhattan Institute, October 4, 2018, https://www.manhattan-institute.org/html/urban-policy-2018-benchmarking-homeless-shelter-performance-proposal-easing-americas-homeless-crisis-11522.html.

14. Stephen Zacks, "Design for Dignity," *Oculus* (Winter 2018), AIA New York, https://www.aiany.org/membership/oculus-magazine/article/winter-2018/design-for-dignity/.

4. DEVELOPING AN AFFORDABLE HOUSING STRATEGY

1. "Bogota Population 2020," *World Population Review,* accessed June 30, 2020, https://worldpopulationreview.com/world-cities/bogota-population/.

2. Gregory Suttor, *Still Renovating: a History of Canadian Social Housing Policy* (Montreal: McGill-Queens University Press, 2016), 7–8.

3. Benjamin S. Carson Sr. to Gavin Newsom et al., September 18, 2019, HUD. gov, accessed October 5, 2020, https://www.hud.gov/sites/dfiles/Main/documents /SOHUD_Response_POTUS.pdf.

4. Mary Schwartz and Ellen Wilson, "Who Can Afford to Live in a Home? A Look at Data from the 2006 American Community Survey," US Census Bureau, accessed November 16, 2020, https://www.census.gov/housing/census/publications /who-can-afford.pdf.

5. Susan K. Urahn, "American Families Face a Growing Rent Burden," Pew Charitable Trusts, April 2018, 4, https://www.pewtrusts.org/-/media/assets /2018/04/rent-burden_report_v2.pdf.

6. "America's Rental Housing, 2020," Joint Center for Housing Studies of Harvard University (2020), 28, https://www.jchs.harvard.edu/sites/default /files/Harvard_JCHS_Americas_Rental_Housing_2020.pdf.

7. Philip M. E. Garboden, "The Double Crisis: A Statistical Report on Rental Housing Costs and Affordability in Baltimore City, 2000–2013," *Abell Foundation* 29, no. 1 (May 2016): 1, https://www.abell.org/sites/default/files/files/cd-doublecrisis516.pdf.

8. Foundation Abbé Pierre and FEANTSA, "Second Overview of Housing Exclusion in Europe, 2017," FEANTSA, accessed October 5, 2020, https://www.feantsa.org/download/gb_housing-exclusion-report_ complete_20178613899107250251219.pdf.

9. BC Non-Profit Housing Association, "Welcome to the Canadian Rental Housing Index," Canadian Rental Housing Index, accessed June 30, 2020, http://rentalhousingindex.ca/en/#intro. Canadian Rental Housing Index was compiled using data from the 2016 long-form census.

10. BC Non-Profit Housing Association, "Welcome to Canadian Rental Housing Index."

11. Nicole Elsasser Watson et al., "Worst Case Housing Needs: 2017 Report to Congress," (Washington, DC: Office of Policy Development and Research, US Department of Housing and Urban Development, August 2017).

12. "Selected Initial Findings of the 2017 New York City Housing and Vacancy Survey," NYC (February 9, 2018), 2-3, https://www1.nyc.gov/assets /hpd/downloads/pdfs/about/2017-hvs-initial-findings.pdf.

13. "Rental Assistance: I Am a Landlord or Broker," NYC Human Resources Administration, accessed June 30, 2020, https://www1.nyc.gov/site/hra/help/landlords.page.

14. Organisation for Economic Co-operation and Development, *Working Together for Local Integration of Migrants and Refugees in Paris* (Paris: OECD Publishing, 2018), 81, https://doi.org/10.1787/9789264305861-en.

15. "New Pilot Helps Landlords Be Part of the Solution to Homelessness," Enterprise, accessed June 30, 2020, https://www.enterprisecommunity.org/sites/default/files/media-library/where-we-work/new-york/come-home-nyc-2-pager-4-2-15.pdf.

16. Alexander, "A $3 Billion Problem."

17. "How Is Your File Evaluated?" Listing of Housing Demand, City of Paris, accessed June 30, 2020, https://teleservices.paris.fr/cotation/les-criteres.html.

18. Janny Scott, "Homeless Given Apartments in Buildings Called Unsafe," *New York Times*, February 2, 2007.

19. Diana Scholl, "Critics of Homeless Program Fight to Save It," *City Limits*, March 11, 2011, https://citylimits.org/2011/03/11/critics-of-homeless-program-fight-to-save-it/.

20. "Directory of New York City Housing Programs: Advantage," CoreData.nyc, NYU Furman Center, accessed June 30, 2020, https://furmancenter.org/coredata/directory/entry/advantage. Mosi Secret, "Clock Ticks for a Key Homeless Program," *New York Times*, May 31, 2011, https://www.nytimes.com/2011/06/01/nyregion/new-york-city-close-to-ending-key-housing-program.html.

21. Matt Flegenheimer, Nikita Stewart, and Mireya Navarro, "After Playing Down a Homeless Crisis, Mayor de Blasio Changes His Tone," *New York Times*, September 1, 2015, https://www.nytimes.com/2015/09/02/nyregion/de-blasio-tackling-the-perception-and-reality-of-a-homeless-crisis.html.

22. Department of Homeless Services, "DHS Data Dashboard Charts FY 2015-2020," NYC, updated October 31, 2020, https://www1.nyc.gov/site/dhs/about/stats-and-reports.page.

23. Finkel et al., "Rapid Re-housing for Homeless Families Demonstration Programs Evaluation Report, Part II: Demonstration Findings – Outcome Evaluation," *Abt Associates* (April 2016). https://www.huduser.gov/portal/sites/default/files/pdf/RRHD-PartII-Outcomes.pdf.

24. Finkel et al., "Rapid Re-housing for Homeless Families Demonstration Programs Evaluation Report, Part II."

25. Mary Cunningham, Sarah Gillespie, and Jacqueline Anderson, "Rapid Re-housing What the Research Says" (Washington, DC: Urban Institute, 2015).

26. Metropolitan Development and Housing Agency, "Envision Nashville," presentation to Urban Land Institute, Nashville, TN, June 14, 2019, https://

ulidigitalmarketing.blob.core.windows.net/ulidcnc/2019/07/ULI-bfast-vjeh-Part-1
.pdf.

27. Metropolitan Development and Housing Agency, "Envision Nashville."

28. Metropolitan Government of Nashville and Davidson County, "Recommended Operating Budget for Fiscal Year 2020–2021," May 2020, https://www.nashville.gov/Portals/0/SiteContent/Finance/docs/OMB/fy21_budget/Recommended/FY21RecommendedBudgetBook.pdf.

29. Juan Pablo Garnham, "Why Homelessness Is Going Down in Houston but Up in Dallas," *Texas Tribune*, July 2, 2019.

30. Garnham, "Why Homelessness Is Going Down."

31. "About Us," Paris Habitat, accessed June 30, 2020, https://www.parishabitat.fr/Pages/Anglais-About-us.aspx.

32. "Abbe Pierre, 94; Helped Homeless and Served as France's Conscience," *Los Angeles Times*, January 23, 2007.

33. Feargus O'Sullivan, "Paris Declares War on 'Ghettos for the Rich,'" *Citylab*, May 17, 2016, https://www.citylab.com/equity/2016/05/paris-declares-war-on-ghettoes-for-the-rich/483072/.

34. "Key Strategies," *The Journey Home.*

35. Casey Dawkins, Mark Miller, and Lisa Sturtevant, *The Timing of Inclusionary Zoning Adoption in U.S. Cities and Counties* (College Park: University of Maryland, 2015).

36. Department of City Planning, "Mandatory Inclusionary Housing," NYC, accessed June 30, 2020, https://www1.nyc.gov/site/planning/plans/mih/mandatory-inclusionary-housing.page.

37. "Baltimore City Council Legislation," Baltimore City Council, accessed June 30, 2020, https://baltimore.legistar.com/LegislationDetail.aspx?ID=2813514&GUID=645B2F5E-8772-4BF8-BE44-7E4573691BCE&Options=&Search=.

38. Michael Braverman, "Professional Services Request for Proposals: Inclusionary Housing Requirements," Baltimore City Department of Housing and Community Development, updated May 22, 2020, https://dhcd.baltimorecity.gov/sites/default/files/INCLUSIONARY%20HOUSING%20RFP%20Revised%20052220.pdf.

39. Department of Regional Planning, "Second Dwelling Unit (Accessory Dwelling Unit) Pilot Program," Los Angeles County, accessed June 18, 2010, http://planning.lacounty.gov/secondunitpilot.

40. Office of Governor Gavin Newsom, "Governor Gavin Newsom Signs 18 Bills to Boost Housing Production" news release, October 9, 2019, https://www.gov.ca.gov/2019/10/09/governor-gavin-newsom-signs-18-bills-to-boost-housing-production/.

41. "National Housing Co-investment Fund," Canada Mortgage and Housing Corporation, accessed June 30, 2020, https://www.cmhc-schl.gc.ca/en/nhs/co-investment-fund.

5. SUPPORTIVE HOUSING TO TARGET COMPLEX NEEDS

1. Brenda Rosen and Jamie Rubin, "How New York is Ending Homelessness," *Apolitico*, June 25, 2019, https://apolitical.co/solution_article/how-new-york-is-ending-homelessness/.

2. Brian Sullivan, "HUD Marks 20 Years of McKinney-Vento Homeless Assistance Act: Landmark Legislation Credited with Saving Hundreds of Thousands of Lives," news release no. 07-109, July 18, 2007, HUD Archives: News Releases, https://archives.hud.gov/news/2007/pr07-109.cfm. "McKinney-Vento Act Fact Sheet," National Coalition for the Homeless, June 2006, https://www.nationalhomeless.org/publications/facts/McKinney.pdf.

3. Ted Houghton, "A Description and History of the New York/New York Agreement to House Homeless and Mentally Ill Individuals." Corporation for Supportive Housing, May 2001, https://shnny.org/uploads/NY-NY_Agreement_History.pdf.

4. Dennis P. Culhane, Stephen Metraux, and Trevor Hadley, "Public Service Reductions Associated with Placement of Homeless Persons with Severe Mental Illness in Supportive Housing," *Housing Policy Debate* 13, no. 1 (2002): 107, https://shnny.org/uploads/The_Culhane_Report.pdf.

5. Sandy Mazza and Joey Garrison, "$24M Housing, 'Service Center' for Homeless Planned in Downtown Nashville," *(Nashville) Tennessean,* April 25, 2018, https://www.tennessean.com/story/money/2018/04/25/housing-service-center-homeless-planned-downtown-nashville/550199002/.

6. Chris Song, "Mayor Cooper Releases Statement on Metro Emergency Shelters and Announces New Permanent Supportive Housing Center," news release, October 17, 2019, Nashville.gov, https://www.nashville.gov/News-Media/News-Article/ID/8985/Mayor-Cooper-Releases-Statement-on-Metro-Emergency-Shelters-and-Announces-New-Permanent-Supportive-Housing-Center.aspx.

7. Doug Smith, "Desperate to Build More Homeless Housing, L.A. County Seeks Help from the Private Sector," *Los Angeles Times,* December 6, 2019,https://www.latimes.com/california/story/2019-12-06/homeless-housing-county-supervisors-private-sector-help.

8. "Supportive Housing Funding Sources Now Available for NY City & State," Corporation for Supportive Housing, updated June 2017, https://www.csh.org/2017/06/supportive-housing-funding-sources-in-now-available-for-ny-city-state/.

9. Corporation for Supportive Housing, "Dimensions of Quality Supportive Housing Guidebook," 2nd ed., 1–2, accessed June 30, 2020, https://d155kunxf1aozz.cloudfront.net/wp-content/uploads/2013/07/CSH_Dimensions_of_Quality_Supportive_Housing_guidebook.pdf.

10. "Supportive Housing," US Interagency Council on Homelessness, updated August 15, 2018, https://www.usich.gov/solutions/housing/supportive-housing/.

11. US Department of Housing and Urban Development, "HUD 2019 Continuum of Care Homeless Assistance Programs Housing Inventory Count Report," Mayor's Office of Homeless Services (Baltimore), updated October 16, 2019, https://homeless.baltimorecity.gov/sites/default/files/CoC_HIC_State_MD_2019 .pdf.

12. "Housing Authority Launches New Program to Provide Homes for Baltimore's Homeless," Housing Authority of Baltimore, updated February 14, 2019, https://www.habc.org/habc-information/about-us/news/housing-authority-launches-new-program-to-provide-homes-for-baltimore-s-homeless/.

13. Padgett, Henwood, and Tsemberis, *Housing First*, 13.

14. Padgett, Henwood, and Tsemberis, *Housing First*, 12.

15. Sam Tsemberis, Leyla Gulcur, and Maria Nakae, "Housing First, Consumer Choice, and Harm Reduction for Homeless Individuals with Dual Diagnosis," *American Journal of Public Health* 94 (April 2004): 654. Padgett, Henwood and Tsemberis, *Housing First*, 54.

16. Concern arose over the model's viability when, in 2014, Pathways to Housing was facing bankruptcy and owed money to landlords on behalf of their tenants. The New York City government scrambled to reassign clients to other nonprofits and to prevent evictions for the affected tenants. Later analysis showed the financial problems stemmed from mismanagement and not a fatal program flaw. Meanwhile, the organization created a national arm that continues to share lessons and spread the Housing First model across the globe.

17. Pearson et al., "The Applicability of Housing First Models to Homeless Persons with Serious Mental Illness," 61.

18. "National Final Report: Cross-Site At Home/Chez Soi Project," Mental Health Commission of Canada (accessed June 30, 2020), 17, https://www.mentalhealthcommission.ca/sites/default/files/mhcc_at_home_report_national_cross-site_eng_2_0.pdf.

19. Laura S. Sadowski, Romina A. Kee, and Tyler J. VanderWeele, "Effect of a Housing and Case Management Program on Emergency Department Visits and Hospitalizations among Chronically Ill Homeless Adults: A Randomized Trial," *Journal of the American Medical Association* 301, no. 17 (May 2009): 1771–78.

20. Sarah B. Hunter et al., "Evaluation of Housing for Health Permanent Supportive Housing Program," *RAND Corporation* (2017), https://www.rand.org /pubs/research_reports/RR1694.html.

21. Jarrett Murphy, "Housing for NYC's Most Vulnerable under Scrutiny for Screening," *City Limits*, July 5, 2018, https://citylimits.org/2018/07/05/debate-about-whether-nyc-housing-for-the-most-vulnerable-rebuffs-some-who-need-help/.

22. Edmonton Joint Committee on Housing, "Edmonton Community Plan on Housing and Support Services 2005–2009," Homeward Trust Edmonton, January 2005, http://www.homewardtrust.ca/wp-content/uploads/2016/12/CP-2005-2009.pdf.

23. "Community Update," Homeward Trust (November 28, 2018), 2, http://homewardtrust.ca/wp-content/uploads/2018/12/2018-Community-Update-Booklet.pdf.

24. "The Impact of Supportive Housing on Surrounding Neighborhoods: Evidence from New York City," Furman Center for Real Estate and Public Policy (November 2008), 6, https://furmancenter.org/files/FurmanCenterPolicyBriefon SupportiveHousing_LowRes.pdf.

25. "Protocolo Interinstitucional de Atención Integral a Personas en Riesgo de Vivir en Calle e Integrantes de Poblaciones Callejeras en la Ciudad de México," *Gaceta Oficial de Ciudad de Mexico* 95 (2016): 5–58, http://www.data.educacion .cdmx.gob.mx/oip/2016b/A121/FI/148_LinmeamientosINFOMEX2016.pdf. "Pone en marcha Mancera el primer 'Hogar CDMX,'" Cronica.com.mx, January 31, 2017, http://www.cronica.com.mx/notas/2017/1007813.html.

26. "State of Homelessness: 2020 Edition."

27. US Department of Health and Human Services, "The Evidence: Permanent Supportive Housing," Substance Abuse and Mental Health Services Administration, 2010, https://store.samhsa.gov/sites/default/files/d7/priv/theevidence-psh.pdf.

28. National Academies of Sciences, Engineering, and Medicine, *Permanent Supportive Housing: Evaluating the Evidence for Improving Health Outcomes among People Experiencing Chronic Homelessness* (Washington, DC: National Academies Press, 2018), 136, https://doi.org/10.17226/25133.

29. Hunter et al., "Evaluation of Housing for Health," viii. Larimer et al., "Health Care and Public Service Use and Costs."

30. Jocelyn Fontaine, "Supportive Housing for Returning Prisoners: Outcomes and Impacts of the Returning Home-Ohio Pilot Project," *Urban Institute* (August 2012): vii–viii.

31. Hunter et al., "Evaluation of Housing for Health," viii.

32. Thomas Byrne et al., "The Relationship between Community Investment in Permanent Supportive Housing and Chronic Homelessness," *Social Service Review* 88, no. 2 (June 2014): 256.

6. PREVENTION THAT WORKS

1. Dennis Culhane, Stephen Metraux, and Thomas Byrne, "A Prevention-Centered Approach to Homelessness Assistance: A Paradigm Shift?" *Housing Policy Debate* 21, no. 2 (2011): 295–315. Burt, Pearson, and Montgomery,

"Community-Wide Strategies for Preventing Homelessness." Marybeth Shinn, "Homelessness, Poverty, and Social Exclusion in the United States and Europe," *European Journal of Homelessness* 4 (December 2010): 19–44. Jack Tsai, "Lifetime and 1-Year Prevalence of Homelessness in the US Population: Results from the National Epidemiologic Survey on Alcohol and Related Conditions–III," *Journal of Public Health* 40, no. 1 (2018): 65–74.

2. Bruce Link et al., "Lifetime and Five-Year Prevalence of Homelessness in the United States," *American Journal of Public Health* 84, no. 12 (1994): 1907–12.

3. Link, "Lifetime and Five-Year Prevalence of Homelessness."

4. Karen L. Hobden et al., "Comparing Public Opinion and Prevalence of Homelessness in Canada to the United States," *Canadian Journal of Urban Research* 16, no. 1 (2007): 76–92.

5. Brendan O'Flaherty, "Wrong Person or Wrong Place: For Homelessness, the Conjunction Is What Matters," *Journal of Housing Economics* 13 (2004): 1–15.

6. Busch-Geertsema et al., "Homelessness and Homeless Policies in Europe," 51.

7. Shinn, "Homelessness, Poverty, and Social Exclusion." Busch-Geertsema et al., "Homelessness and Homeless Policies in Europe," 53. Martha R. Burt, "What Will It Take to End Homelessness?" *Urban Institute,* October 1 2001, http://webarchive.urban.org/publications/310305.html.

8. Mexico City, Sistema para el Desarrollo Integral de la Familia de la Ciudad de México (City System for the Integral Development of the Family of Mexico City), internal data, October 2018.

9. "Fight Against Poverty and Social Marginalization" (Mayor Kaminis press conference and slide deck), City of Athens, May 30, 2016, https://www.cityofathens.gr/node/28429.

10. Jung Min Park et al., "Public Shelter Admission among Young Adults with Child Welfare Histories by Type of Service and Type of Exit," *Social Service Review* 78, no. 2 (2004): 284–303.

11. Stephen Metraux and Dennis P. Culhane, "Homeless Shelter Use and Reincarceration following Prison Release," *Criminology and Public Policy* 3, no. 2 (2004): 139–60.

12. Michelle Wood, Jennifer Turnham, and Gregory Mills, "Housing Affordability and Family Well-Being: Results from the Housing Voucher Evaluation," *Housing Policy Debate* 19, no. 2 (2008): 367–412.

13. Burt and Pearson, "Strategies for Preventing Homelessness."

14. Culhane, Metraux, and Byrne, "A Prevention-Centered Approach."

15. Tsemberis, Gulcur, and Nakae, "Housing First, Consumer Choice, and Harm Reduction." Richard Cho, "Four Clarifications about Housing First," United States Interagency Council on Homelessness, June 8, 2014, https://www.usich.gov/news/four-clarifications-about-housing-first/.

16. "What Are the Value Based Programs?" Centers for Medicare and Medicaid Services, updated January 6, 2020, https://www.cms.gov/Medicare/Quality-

Initiatives-Patient-Assessment-Instruments/Value-Based-Programs/Value-Based-Programs.

17. Patient Protection and Affordable Care Act, 42 U.S.C. § 18001, Section 3025 (2010). "Hospital Readmissions Reduction Program (HRRP)," Centers for Medicare and Medicaid Services, updated August 11, 2020, https://www.cms.gov/Medicare/Quality-Initiatives-Patient-Assessment-Instruments/Value-Based-Programs/HRRP/Hospital-Readmission-Reduction-Program.

18. Peter Messeri, Brendan O'Flaherty, and Serena Goodman, "Can Homelessness Be Prevented? Evidence from New York City's HomeBase Program," unpublished paper, Columbia University, June 8, 2011, https://a860-gpp.nyc.gov/downloads/08612p80q?locale=en.

19. Rolston et al., "Evaluation of the HomeBase Community Prevention Program."

20. Marybeth Shinn et. al., "Efficient Targeting of Homelessness Prevention Services for Families," *American Journal of Public Health* 103 (December 1, 2013): S324–S330.

21. Messeri, O'Flaherty, and Goodman, "Can Homelessness Be Prevented?"

22. Till Von Wachter et al., "Predicting and Preventing Homelessness in Los Angeles," California Policy Lab and the University of Chicago Poverty Lab, September 2019.

23. Marybeth Shinn, Jim Baumohl, and Kim Hopper, "The Prevention of Homelessness Revisited," *Analyses of Social Issues and Public Policy* 1, no. 1 (2001): 95–127.

24. Von Wachter et al., "Predicting and Preventing Homelessness in Los Angeles."

25. Culhane, Metraux, and Byrne, "A Prevention-Centered Approach."

26. Culhane, Metraux, and Byrne, "A Prevention-Centered Approach."

27. Mary Cunningham and Samantha Batko, "Rapid Re-housing's Role in Responding to Homelessness: What the Evidence Says," *Urban Institute* (October 2018): 1–12, https://www.urban.org/research/publication/rapid-re-housings-role-responding-homelessness.

28. "Two-Generation Playbook," Ascend: The Aspen Institute, September. 2016), https://ascend.aspeninstitute.org/resources/two-generation-playbook/.

29. Data obtained from the Nashville Metro Homeless Impact Division, updated as of June 5, 2020.

7. SYSTEMS-LEVEL THINKING

1. New York City Office of Civil Justice, "2018 Annual Report," Human Resources Administration, 19, https://www1.nyc.gov/assets/hra/downloads/pdf/final_2018_ojc_report_march_19_2019.pdf.

2. Christin Durham and Martha Johnson, "Homelessness Prevention, Intake, and Shelter for Single Adults and Families," *Urban Institute* (2014).

3. A "chronically homeless" individual is defined as a homeless individual with a disability who lives either in a place not meant for human habitation, a safe haven, or an emergency shelter, or in an institutional care facility if the individual has been living in the facility for fewer than ninety days and had been living in a place not meant for human habitation, a safe haven, or an emergency shelter immediately before entering the institutional care facility. To meet the "chronically homeless" definition, the individual also must have been living as described above continuously for at least twelve months, or on at least four separate occasions in the past three years that, combined, total a period of at least twelve months. Each period separating the occasions must include at least seven nights of living in a situation other than a place not meant for human habitation, an emergency shelter, or a safe haven. *Federal Register* 80, no. 233 (December 4, 2015): 75791–75805.

4. "Houston Effectively Ends Veteran Homelessness," Coalition for the Homeless, June 1, 2015, https://www.homelesshouston.org/houston-effectively-ends-veteran-homelessness/.

5. "Program Data," Homeward Trust Edmonton, accessed June 30, 2020, http://homewardtrust.ca/what-weve-learned/performance-evaluation/.

8. ENGAGING THE COMMUNITY

1. Ana Maria Arumi and Andrew L. Yarrow, "Compassion, Concern, and Conflicted Feelings: New Yorkers on Homelessness and Housing," *Public Agenda* (February 2007): 15–18.

2. Office of the Controller, "Homelessness Gross Receipts Tax: Economic Impact Report," Office of the Controller, City and County of San Francisco, November 2018, 7–11, https://sfcontroller.org/sites/default/files/Documents /Economic%20Analysis/hgrt_economic_impact_final.pdf.

3. "Poll: The Public Overwhelmingly Believes Housing Affordability Should Be a Top National Priority; Expects Congress and President to Take Major Action," Opportunity Starts at Home, March 28, 2019, https://www.opportunityhome.org/pollpressrelease/.

4. "The Unhealthy State of Homelessness: Health Audit Results 2014," *Homeless Link,* 2014, https://www.homeless.org.uk/sites/default/files/site-attachments/The%20unhealthy%20state%20of%20homelessness%20FINAL .pdf.

5. Homeward Trust Edmonton, accessed June 30, 2020, http://homewardtrust.ca/.

9. UNDERSTANDING THE HOMELESS SYSTEM

1. US Department of Housing and Urban Development, "A Report on the 1988 National Survey of Shelters for the Homeless," March 1989, HUD User, https://www.huduser.gov/portal/publications/other/survey_homeless.html. James D. Wright and Joel A. Devine, "Counting the Homeless: The Census Bureau's 'S-Night' in Five U.S. Cities," *Evaluation Review* 16, no. 4 (August 1992), https://doi.org/10.1177/0193841X9201600401. Martha R. Burt et al., "Homelessness: Programs and the People They Serve," Integrated Council on the Homeless, December 1999.

2. Carol Caton, "The Epidemiology of Homelessness," in *Homeless in America* (New York: Oxford University Press, 1990).

3. Barrett A. Lee, "Stability and Change in an Urban Homeless Population," *Demography* 26, no. 2 (1989): 323–34. M. Audrey Burnam and Paul Koegel, "Methodology for Obtaining a Representative Sample of Homeless Persons: The Los Angeles Skid Row Study," *Evaluation Review* 12, no. 2 (1988): 117–52. Peter H. Rossi, *Down and Out in America: The Origins of Homelessness* (Chicago: University of Chicago Press, 1991).

4. "Fact Sheet for 1990 Decennial Census Count of Persons in Emergency Shelters for the Homeless and Visible in Street Locations," originally published as a Census Bureau press release, April 12, 1991, reprinted in *Joint Hearing on Quality and Limitations of the S-Night Homeless Count: Joint hearing before the Subcommittee on Government Information and Regulation of the Committee on Governmental Affairs, United States Senate, and the Subcommittee on Census and Population of the Committee on Post Office and Civil Service, House of Representatives*, 102nd Cong. (May 1991). Wright and Devine, "Counting the Homeless."

5. US Department of Housing and Urban Development (HUD), "A Guide to Counting Unsheltered Homeless People," 2nd revision, January 15, 2008, https://files.hudexchange.info/resources/documents/counting_unsheltered.pdf.

6. "Homeless Count," Homeward Trust Edmonton, April 2018, http://homewardtrust.ca/planning-research/homeless-count/.

7. Alina Turner, "Everyone Counts: A Guide to Point-in-Time Counts in Canada," 2nd ed., Employment and Social Development Canada (January 2015), 7–9.

8. "Homeless Count," Homeward Trust Edmonton, April 2018.

9. "Censo habitantes de la calle Bogotá," DANE, 2017, accessed June 30, 2020, https://www.dane.gov.co/index.php/estadisticas-por-tema/demografia-y-poblacion/censo-habitantes-de-la-calle-bogota.

10. United Nations Economic Commission for Europe, "Conference of European Statisticians Recommendations for the 2010 Censuses of Population and Housing" (2006).

11. "The Homeless in France," INED, accessed June 30, 2020, https://www
.ined.fr/en/everything_about_population/demographic-facts-sheets/focus-on/the-
homeless-in-france/.

12. Burt et al., "Homelessness."

13. Kim Hopper et al., "Estimating Numbers of Unsheltered Homeless People
through Plant-Capture and Postcount Survey Methods," *American Journal of
Public Health* 98, no. 8 (2008): 1438–42.

14. HUD, "A Guide to Counting Unsheltered Homeless People."

15. Elizabeth Martin et al., "Issues in the Use of a Plant-Capture Method for
Estimating the Size of the Street Dwelling Population," *Journal of Official Statistics* 13, no. 1 (1997): 59–73. Hopper et al., "Estimating Numbers."

16. In Edmonton's case, the Vulnerability Index–Service Prioritization Decision Assistance Tool (VI-SPDAT), now in its second version, has been widely
adopted for coordinated assessment. It can, with minimal training, be applied to
large populations but has some limitations in terms of reliability and validity.
See Molly Brown and Camilla Cummings, "New Research on the Reliability and
Validity of the VI-SPDAT: Implications for Coordinated Assessment," *homeless
hub,* July 5, 2018, https://www.homelesshub.ca/blog/new-research-reliability-
and-validity-vi-spdat-implications-coordinated-assessment.

17. "2018 Progress Report: Edmonton's Plan to Prevent and End
Homelessness, Homeward Trust Edmonton, accessed June 30, 2020,
http://homewardtrust.ca/wp-content/uploads/2018/12/2018-Goals-and-Targets
.pdf.

18. And even if partner service providers want to share, they often are legally
obligated to have first obtained the client's consent.

19. Angela A. Aidala et al., *Frequent Users Service Enhancement "FUSE" Initiative: NYC FUSE II Evaluation Report* (New York: Mailman School of Public
Health, Columbia University, 2013), https://doi.org/10.7916/D8XH038D.

20. Brendan O'Flaherty, "Homelessness Research: A Guide for Economists
(and Friends)," *Journal of Housing Economics* (2019).

21. Robert Collinson and Davin Reed, "The Effects of Evictions on Low-
Income Households," working paper, New York University, Wagner School
(2018).

22. The Fragile Families and Child Wellbeing Study. The Fragile Families
study follows a cohort of nearly five thousand children born in large US cities
between 1998 and 2000 (roughly three-quarters of whom were born to unmar-
ried parents) See https://fragilefamilies.princeton.edu/. "Journeys Home: A Longitudinal Study of Factors Affecting Housing Stability" (a national survey
of Australians who were homeless or at-risk of homelessness), Melbourne Institute, accessed June 30, 2020, https://melbourneinstitute.unimelb.edu.au
/journeys-home.

10. MANAGING FOR RESULTS

1. Robert D. Behn, *Performance Leadership: 11 Better Practices That Can Ratchet Up Performance* (Washington, DC: IBM Center for the Business of Government, 2004), http://www.businessofgovernment.org/report/performance-leadership-11-better-practices-can-ratchet-performance.

2. Government Accounting Standards Board (GASB), "Performance Reporting for Government: Characteristics Performance Information Should Possess" (2008), adapted from Paul Epstein, James Fountain, Wilson Campbell, Terry Patton, and Kimberly Keaton, *Government Service Efforts and Accomplishments Performance Reports: A Guide to Understanding* (Norwalk, CT: Governmental Accounting Standards Board, 2005).

3. Behn, *Performance Leadership*, 8–10.

4. Shelley H. Metzenbaum, *Performance Accountability: The Five Building Blocks and Six Essential Practices* (Washington, DC: IBM Center for the Business of Government, 2006), http://www.businessofgovernment.org/sites/default/files/Performance%20Accountability.pdf.

5. Brendan O'Flaherty and Ting Wu, "Homeless shelters for single adults: Why does their population change?" *Social Service Review* 82, no. 3 (2008): 511–50. Furthermore, dynamics of shelter systems are not always consistent. While this might have been true in 2008, in 2014–18, the intentional implementation of a changed criminal justice policy as a backlash to the period of mass incarceration, which resulted in dramatic drops in arrests and incarcerations, coincided with a major increase in single adults in shelter and sleeping rough.

6. Metzenbaum, *Performance Accountability*, 39–51.

7. Arie Halachmi, "Performance Measurement: Test the Water before You Dive In," *International Review of Administrative Sciences* 71, no. 2 (2005): 255–66.

11. MANAGING IN EMERGENCIES

1. Thomas R. Frieden et al., "Tuberculosis in New York City—Turning the Tide," *New England Journal of Medicine* 333 (July 27, 1995): 229–33, https://www.nejm.org/doi/full/10.1056/NEJM199507273330406.

2. Dennis Culhane, Dan Treglia, and Ken Steif, "Estimated Emergency and Observational/Quarantine Capacity Need for the US Homeless Population Related to COVID-19 Exposure by Country: Projected Hospitalizations, Intensive Care Units, and Mortality," unpublished Paper, University of Pennsylvania, Scholarly Commons Library, updated: March 27, 2020, https://works.bepress.com/dennis_culhane/237/.

3. "People Experiencing Homelessness and COVID 19 Interim Guidance," US Centers for Disease Control and Prevention, March 22, 2020, https://

www.cdc.gov/coronavirus/2019-ncov/community/homeless-shelters/unsheltered-homelessness.html.

4. "State of Texas Plan for Disaster Recovery: Amendment 5, Hurricane Harvey—Round 1," Texas General Land Office Community Development and Revitalization Program, accessed June 30, 2020, https://recovery.texas.gov/files/hud-requirements-reports/hurricane-harvey/5b-apa5-nonsubstantial.pdf.

CONCLUSION

1. Aidala et al., *Frequent Users Service Enhancement 'FUSE' Initiative.*

APPENDIX

1. FEANTSA, "ETHOS Typology on Homelessness and Housing Exclusion" (Brussels, Belgium, 2005).

Bibliography

"Abbé Pierre, 94; Helped Homeless and Served as France's Conscience." *Los Angeles Times*, January 23, 2007. https://www.latimes.com/archives/la-xpm-2007-jan-23-me-pierre23-story.html.

Abbé Pierre Foundation and FEANTSA. "Second Overview of Housing Exclusion in Europe, 2017." FEANTSA. Accessed October 5, 2020. https://www.feantsa.org/download/gb_housing-exclusion-report_complete_20178613899107250251219.pdf.

"About Us." Paris Habitat. Accessed June 30, 2020. https://www.parishabitat.fr/Pages/Anglais-About-us.aspx.

Affordable Housing Fact Sheet. US Department of Housing and Urban Development. Accessed June 30, 2020. https://www.hud.gov/program_offices/comm_planning/affordablehousing/.

Aidala, Angela A., William McAllister, Maiko Yomogida, and Virginia Shubert. *Frequent Users Service Enhancement 'FUSE' Initiative: New York City FUSE II Evaluation Report*. New York: Mailman School of Public Health, Columbia University, 2013. https://doi.org/10.7916/D8XH038D.

Alexander, Mariana. "A $3 Billion Problem: Homeless Services in New York City." Citizens Budget Commission. May 24, 2018, blog post. https://cbcny.org/research/3-billion-problem.

"America's Rental Housing, 2020" Joint Center for Housing Studies of Harvard University. 2020. https://www.jchs.harvard.edu/sites/default/files/Harvard_JCHS_Americas_Rental_Housing_2020.pdf.

"Are All Shelters the Same?" BRC. September 1, 2016. https://www.brc.org/are-all-shelters-same.

Arumi, Ana Maria, and Andrew L. Yarrow. "Compassion, Concern, and Conflicted Feelings: New Yorkers on Homelessness and Housing." *Public Agenda* (February 2007): 1–35.

Athens, City of. Internal Athens Mayor's Office White Paper to explore housing and work supports to the persons who were formerly homeless. June 2018.

Avramov, Dragana. "The Changing Face of Homelessness in Europe." *Contributions in Sociology* 135 (2001): 3–38.

"Baltimore City Continuum of Care 2019 Point in Time Count Report." *The Journey Home.* Accessed June 30, 2020. https://homeless.baltimorecity.gov/sites/default/files/PIT%20Report%20Draft%202019_Update%208.30.19_Update.pdf.

"Baltimore City Council Legislation." Baltimore City Council. Accessed June 30, 2020, https://baltimore.legistar.com/LegislationDetail.aspx?ID=2813514&GUID=645B2F5E-8772-4BF8-BE44-7E4573691BCE&Options=&Search=.

BC Non-Profit Housing Association. "Welcome to the Canadian Rental Housing Index." Canadian Rental Housing Index. Accessed June 30, 2020. http://rentalhousingindex.ca/en/#intro.

Behn, Robert D. *Performance Leadership: 11 Better Practices That Can Ratchet Up Performance.* Washington, DC: IBM Center for the Business of Government, May 2004). http://www.businessofgovernment.org/report/performance-leadership-11-better-practices-can-ratchet-performance.

Berens, Michael J. "A Review of Research: Designing the Built Environment for Recovery from Homelessness." Design Resources for Homelessness. http://designresourcesforhomelessness.org/wp-content/uploads/2015/11/OrientationReport.pdf.

Blint-Welsh, Tyler. "Federal Data Shows Nearly 80,000 Homeless in NYC." *Wall Street Journal,* October 24, 2019. https://www.wsj.com/articles/federal-data-show-nearly-80-000-homeless-in-new-york-city-11571922000?mod=searchresults&page=1&pos=1.

"Bogota Population 2020." *World Population Review.* Accessed June 30, 2020. http://worldpopulationreview.com/world-cities/bogota/.

Braverman, Michael. "Professional Services Request for Proposals: Inclusionary Housing Requirements," Baltimore City Department of Housing and Community Development. Updated May 22, 2020. https://dhcd.baltimorecity.gov/sites/default/files/INCLUSIONARY%20HOUSING%20RFP%20Revised%20052220.pdf.

Brousse, Cécile, Jean-Marie Firdion, Maryse Marpsat. *Les sans-domicile.* Paris: La Découverte, coll. Repères Sociologie, 2008.

Brown, Molly, and Camilla Cummings. "New Research on the Reliability and Validity of the VI-SPDAT: Implications for Coordinated Assessment." *homeless hub.* July 5, 2018. https://www.homelesshub.ca/blog/new-research-reliability-and-validity-vi-spdat-implications-coordinated-assessment.

Burnam, M. Audrey, and Paul Koegel. "Methodology for Obtaining a Representative Sample of Homeless Persons: The Los Angeles Skid Row Study." *Evaluation Review* 12, no. 2 (1988): 117–52.

Burt, Martha R. "What Will It Take to End Homelessness?" *Urban Institute,* October 1, 2001. http://webarchive.urban.org/publications/310305.html.

Burt, Martha R., and Carol Pearson. "Strategies for Preventing Homelessness." US Department of Housing and Urban Development, Office of Policy Development and Research (May 2005): xix–xxv.

Burt, Martha R., Carol Wilkinson, Brooke E. Spellman, Tracy D'Alanno, Matt White, Meghan Henry, and Natalie Matthews. "Rapid Re-housing for Homeless Families Demonstration Programs Evaluation Report, Part 1: How They Worked—Process Evaluation." *Abt Associates* (April 2016): ii–13.

Burt, Martha R., Jenneth Carpenter, Samuel G. Hall, Kathryn A. Henderson, Debra J. Rog, John A. Hornik, Ann V. Denton, and Garrett E. Moran "Strategies for Improving Homeless People's Access to Mainstream Benefits and Services." Office of Policy Development and Research, US Department of Housing and Urban Development. March 2010.

Burt, Martha R., Laudan Y. Aron, Toby Douglas, Jesse Valente, Edgar Lee, and Britta Iwen. "Homelessness: Programs and the People they Serve." Integrated Council on the Homeless December 1999.

Busch-Geertsema, Volker, William Edgar, Eoin O'Sullivan, and Nicholas Pleace. "Homelessness and Homeless Policies in Europe: Lessons From Research." In *Conference on Homelessness* 9 (2010): 1–88.

Byrne, Thomas, Jamison D. Fargo, Ann Elizabeth Montgomery, Ellen Munley, and Dennis P. Culhane. "The Relationship between Community Investment in Permanent Supportive Housing and Chronic Homelessness." *Social Service Review* 88, no. 2 (June 2014): 234–63.

Carey, Benedict. "Nakesha Williams Died Homeless on a Manhattan Street: Should She Have Been Forced into Treatment?" *New York Times,* March 6, 2018.

Carson, Benjamin S., to Gavin Newsom, Darrell Steinberg, Virginia Bass, and Janet Arbuckle. September 18, 2019. HUD.gov. Accessed October 5, 2020. https://www.hud.gov/sites/dfiles/Main/documents/SOHUD_Response_POTUS.pdf.

Caton, Carol. "The Epidemiology of Homelessness." In *Homeless in America.* New York: Oxford University Press, 1990.

"Censo habitantes de la calle Bogotá." DANE (Departamento Administrativo Nacional de Estadistica). 2017. Accessed June 30, 2020. https://www.dane .gov.co/index.php/estadisticas-por-tema/demografia-y-poblacion/censo-habitantes-de-la-calle-bogota.

Chamie, Joseph. "As Cities Grow, So Do the Numbers of Homeless." *Yale Global Online,* July 13, 2017. https://yaleglobal.yale.edu/content/cities-grow-so-do-numbers-homeless.

Cho, Richard. "Four Clarifications about Housing First." US Interagency Council on Homelessness. June 8, 2014. https://www.usich.gov/news/four-clarifications-about-housing-first/.

"Chronically Homeless." National Alliance to End Homelessness. Updated January 2020. https://endhomelessness.org/homelessness-in-america/who-experiences-homelessness/chronically-homeless/.

Collinson, Robert, and Davin Reed. "The Effects of Evictions on Low-Income Households." Working paper, New York University, Wagner School. (2018).

"Community Update." Homeward Trust Edmonton. November 28, 2018. http://homewardtrust.ca/wp-content/uploads/2018/12/2018-Community-Update-Booklet.pdf.

"Comparative Analysis of Homeless Facilities and Programs in Selected U.S. Cities and Counties." Virginia Beach Department of Housing and Neighborhood Preservation. September 19, 2011. https://www.vbgov.com/government /departments/housing-neighborhood-preservation/Documents/homeless-families-individuals/Homeless%20Shelters%20Comparison%20Report%20 9.19.11.pdf.

"Controlled Clinical Trials Involving Motivational Interviewing." Motivational Interviewing Resources. Updated January 30, 2020. https:// motivationalinterviewing.org/sites/default/files/mi_controlled_trials_0 .pdf.

"Core Elements of Effective Street Outreach to People Experiencing Homelessness." US Interagency Council on Homelessness. May 24, 2019. https:// www.usich.gov/tools-for-action/core-elements-of-effective-street-outreach-to-people-experiencing-homelessness.

Corporation for Supportive Housing. "Dimensions of Quality Supportive Housing Guidebook." 2nd edition. Accessed June 30, 2020. https:// d155kunxf1aozz.cloudfront.net/wp-content/uploads/2013/07/CSH_Dimensions_of_Quality_Supportive_Housing_guidebook.pdf.

Cox, Wendell, and Hugh Pavelitch. "16th Annual Demographia International Housing Affordability Survey: 2020 Rating Middle-Income Housing Affordability." *Demographia* (3rd quarter, 2019). http://www.demographia .com/dhi.pdf.

Culhane, Dennis P., Dan Treglia, and Ken Steif. "Estimated Emergency and Observational/Quarantine Capacity Need for the US Homeless Population

Related to COVID-19 Exposure by County: Projected Hospitalizations, Intensive Care Units and Mortality." Unpublished paper, University of Pennsylvania, Scholarly Commons Library, updated March 27, 2020. https://works.bepress.com/dennis_culhane/237/.

Culhane, Dennis P., Stephen Metraux, and Thomas Byrne. "A Prevention-Centered Approach to Homelessness Assistance: A Paradigm Shift?" *Housing Policy Debate* 21, no. 2 (2011): 295–315.

Culhane, Dennis P., Stephen Metraux, and Trevor Hadley. "Public Service Reductions Associated with Placement of Homeless Persons with Severe Mental Illness in Supportive Housing," *Housing Policy Debate* 13, no. 1 (2002). https://shnny.org/uploads/The_Culhane_Report.pdf.

Culhane, Dennis P., Stephen Metraux, Thomas Byrne, Magdi Stino, Jay Bainbridge, and National Center on Homelessness among Veterans. "The Age Structure of Contemporary Homelessness: Evidence and Implications for Public Policy." *Analyses of Social Issues and Public Policy* 13, no. 1 (2013): 228–44.

Cunningham, Mary, and Samantha Batko. "Rapid Re-housing's Role in Responding to Homelessness: What the Evidence Says." *Urban Institute* (October 2018): 1–12. https://www.urban.org/research/publication/rapid-re-housings-role-responding-homelessness.

Cunningham, Mary, Sarah Gillespie, and Jacqueline Anderson. "Rapid Rehousing: What the Research Says." Washington, DC: Urban Institute, 2015.

Davis, Julie Hirschfeld. "A Senior Republican Admonishes Trump." *New York Times,* January 12, 2018.

Dawkins, Casey, Mark Miller and Lisa Sturtevant. *The Timing of Inclusionary Zoning Adoption in U.S. Cities and Counties.* College Park, MD: University of Maryland, 2015.

De Blasio, Bill, Dean Fuleihan, and Jeff Thamkittikasem. "Mayor's Management Report." City of New York. September 2019. https://www1.nyc.gov/assets/operations/downloads/pdf/mmr2019/2019_mmr.pdf.

Department of City Planning. "Mandatory Inclusionary Housing." NYC. Accessed June 30, 2020, https://www1.nyc.gov/site/planning/plans/mih/mandatory-inclusionary-housing.page.

Department of City Planning, Population Division. "U.S. Census Bureau, 2018 American Community Survey 1-Year Estimates" New York City (November 2019). https://www1.nyc.gov/assets/planning/download/pdf/planning-level/nyc-population/acs/dem_2018acs1yr_nyc.pdf.

Department of Homeless Services. "DHS Data Dashboard Charts FY 2015–2020." NYC. Updated October 31, 2020. https://www1.nyc.gov/site/dhs/about/stats-and-reports.page.

Department of Homeless Services. "NYC HOPE 2019 Results." New York City. Accessed June 30, 2020. https://www1.nyc.gov/assets/dhs/downloads/pdf/hope-2019-results.pdf.

Department of Regional Planning. "Second Dwelling Unit (Accessory Dwelling Unit) Pilot Program." Los Angeles County. Accessed October 6, 2020. http://planning.lacounty.gov/secondunitpilot.

Desmond, Matthew. *Evicted: Poverty and Profit in the American City.* New York: Crown, 2016.

"Dimensions of Quality Supportive Housing Guidebook." Corporation for Supportive Housing. Accessed June 30, 2020. https://d155kunxf1aozz.cloudfront.net/wp-content/uploads/2013/07/CSH_Dimensions_of_Quality_Supportive_Housing_guidebook.pdf.

"Directory of New York City Housing Programs: Advantage." CoreData.nyc. NYU Furman Center. Accessed June 30, 2020 https://furmancenter.org/coredata/directory/entry/advantage.

Donley, Amy M., and James D. Wright. "Cleaning Up the Streets: Community Efforts to Combat Homelessness by Criminalizing Homeless Behaviors." *Homelessness in America* 3 (2008): 75–92.

Durham, Christin, and Martha Johnson. "Homelessness Prevention, Intake, and Shelter for Single Adults and Families." *Urban Institute* (2014).

Eberle Planning and Research, Jim Woodward and Associates, and Matt Thomson. "Homeless Outreach Practises in BC Communities, Volume 1: Summary Report. November 2011.

Edmonton Joint Committee on Housing. "Edmonton Community Plan on Housing and Support Services 2005–2009." Homeward Trust Edmonton. January 2005. http://www.homewardtrust.ca/wp-content/uploads/2016/12/CP-2005-2009.pdf.

Edmonton Task Force on Homelessness. "Homelessness in Edmonton: A Call to Action." City of Edmonton. May 14, 1999. https://www.edmonton.ca/programs_services/documents/PDF/HomelessnessReportMay99.pdf.

Eide, Stephen. "Benchmarking Homeless Shelter Performance: A Proposal for Easing America's Homeless Crisis." Manhattan Institute. October 4, 2018. https://www.manhattan-institute.org/html/urban-policy-2018-benchmarking-homeless-shelter-performance-proposal-easing-americas-homeless-crisis-11522.html.

Emblin, Richard. "El Bronx: The Living Hell at the Heart of Bogota." *City Paper*, July 11, 2016.

"Emergency Shelter Learning Series." National Alliance to End Homelessness. April 25, 2017. https://endhomelessness.org/resource/emergency-shelter/.

Employment and Social Development Canada. "Everyone Counts 2018: Highlights; Preliminary Results from the Second Nationally Coordinated Point-in-Time Count of Homelessness in Canadian Communities." 2019. https://www.canada.ca/en/employment-social-development/programs/homelessness/reports/highlights-2018-point-in-time-count.html#3.4.

Erickson, S., and J. Page. "To Dance with Grace: Outreach and Engagement to Persons on the Street in Practical Lessons; 1998 National Symposium on Homelessness Research." *US Dept. of Health and Human Services and US Dept. of Housing and Urban Development* (1999): 1–24.

"FAQs about Supportive Housing Research: Is Supportive Housing Cost Effective." Corporation for Supportive Housing. Accessed June 30, 2020, https://d155kunxf1aozz.cloudfront.net/wp-content/uploads/2018/06/Cost-Effectiveness-FAQ.pdf.

FEANTSA (Fédération Européenne des Associations Nationales Travaillant avec les Sans-Abri). "ETHOS Typology on Homelessness and Housing Exclusion." Brussels, Belgium, 2005.

Fernanda, Luisa, and Zamudio Rocha. "Homelessness Policies in Bogotá, Colombia, towards Integral Human Development." *Campos Magazine in Social Sciences* 6, no.1 (2018): 48–49.

Finkel, Meryl, Meghan Henry, Natalie Matthews, Brooke Spellman, and Abt Associates, Inc. "Rapid Re-housing for Homeless Families Demonstration Programs Evaluation Report, Part 2: Demonstration Findings—Outcome Evaluation." huduser.gov (Office of Policy Development and Research, US Department of Housing and Urban Development). April 2016. https://www.huduser.gov/portal/sites/default/files/pdf/RRHD-PartII-Outcomes.pdf.

Fitsiou, Panagiota, and Nikos Kourachanis. "Social Policy Challenges for Homeless People with Mental Illness: Views of Greek Mental Health Professionals." *European Journal of Homelessness* 13, no. 2 (2019): 47–62.

Fitzpatrick, Kevin M., Mark E. La Gory, and Ferris J. Ritchey. "Criminal Victimization among the Homeless." *Justice Quarterly* 10, no.3 (1993): 353–68. https://www.tandfonline.com/doi/abs/10.1080/07418829300091881?journalCode=rjqy20.

Fitzpatrick, Suzanne, Nicholas Pleace, and Mark Bevan. *Final Evaluation of the Rough Sleepers Initiative.* Edinburgh: Scottish Executive Social Research, 2005.

Flegenheimer, Matt, Nikita Stewart, and Mireya Navarro. "After Playing Down a Homeless Crisis, Mayor de Blasio Changes His Tone," *New York Times.* September 1, 2015.

Fontaine, Jocelyn. "Supportive Housing for Returning Prisoners: Outcomes and Impacts of the Returning Home–Ohio Pilot Project." *Urban Institute* (August 2012).

Fragile Families and Child Wellbeing Study. Accessed June 30, 2020. https://fragilefamilies.princeton.edu/.

Frieden, Thomas R., Paula I. Fujiwara, Rita M. Washko, and Margaret A. Hamburg. "Tuberculosis in New York City—Turning the Tide." *New England Journal of Medicine* 333 (July 27, 1995): 229–23. https://www.nejm.org/doi/full/10.1056/NEJM199507273330406.

Garboden, Philip M. E. "The Double Crisis: A Statistical Report on Rental Housing Costs and Affordability in Baltimore City, 2000–2013." *Abell Foundation* 29, no. 1 (May 2016). https://www.abell.org/sites/default/files/files/cd-doublecrisis516.pdf.

Garnham, Juan Pablo. "Why Homelessness Is Going Down in Houston but Up in Dallas." *Texas Tribune*, July 2, 2019.

Goodman, Sarena, Peter Messeri, and Brendan O'Flaherty. "Homelessness Prevention in New York City: On Average, It Works." *Journal of Housing Economics* 31 (2016): 14–34.

Government Accounting Standards Board (GASB). "Performance Reporting for Government, Characteristics Performance Information Should Possess." 2008.

Gubits, Daniel, Marybeth Shinn, Michelle Wood, Stephen Bell, Samuel Dastrup, Claudia Solari, Scott Brown, Debi McInnis, Tom McCall, and Utsav Kattel. "Family Options Study: 3-Year Impacts of Housing and Services Interventions for Homeless Families." *Abt Associates* (October 2016).

Halachmi, Arie. "Performance Measurement: Test the Water Before You Dive In." *International Review of Administrative Sciences* 71, no. 2 (2005): 255–66.

Harvard Graduate School of Design and Harvard Kennedy School. *The State of the Nation's Housing 2018.* Joint Center for Housing Studies of Harvard University, 2018. http://www.jchs.harvard.edu/sites/default/files/Harvard_JCHS_State_of_the_Nations_Housing_2018.pdf.

"Health and Homelessness." American Psychological Association. 2011. https://www.apa.org/pi/ses/resources/publications/homelessness-health.

Herman, Daniel B., Sarah Conover, Prakash Gorroochurn, Kinjia Hinterland, Lori Hoepner, and Ezra S. Susser. "Randomized Trial of Critical Time Intervention to Prevent Homelessness after Hospital Discharge." *Psychiatric Services* 62, no. 7 (2011): 713–19.

Hettema, Jennifer, Julie Steele, and William R. Miller. "Motivational Interviewing." *Annual Review of Clinical Psychology* 1 (April 2005): 91–111.

Hobden, Karen L., Carolyn J. Tompsett, Amanda K. Fales, and Paul A. Toro. "Comparing Public Opinion and Prevalence of Homelessness in Canada to the United States." *Canadian Journal of Urban Research* 16, no. 1 (2007): 76–92.

"Homeless Count." Homeward Trust Edmonton. Accessed June 30, 2020. http://homewardtrust.ca/wp-content/uploads/2018/01/Homeless-Count-Graph-White.jpg.

"Homeless Count." Homeward Trust Edmonton. April 2018. http://homewardtrust.ca/planning-research/homeless-count/

"Homelessness Gross Receipts Tax: Economic Impact Report." City and County of San Francisco. November 2018.

"Home-Stat Reaches New Milestone: Nearly 1,500 Unsheltered Homeless New Yorkers Helped Off Streets" (press release). City of New York. January 17, 2018. https://www1.nyc.gov/office-of-the-mayor/news/041-18/home-stat-reaches-new-milestone-nearly-1-500-unsheltered-homeless-new-yorkers-helped-off-streets.

Hopper, Elizabeth K., Ellen L. Bassu, and Jeffrey Olivet. "Shelter from the Storm: Trauma-Informed Care in Homelessness Services Settings." *Open Health Services and Policy Journal* 2 (2009): 131–51.

Hopper, Kim, Marybeth Shinn, Eugene Laska, Morris Meisner, and Joseph Wanderling. "Estimating Numbers of Unsheltered Homeless People through Plant-Capture and Postcount Survey Methods." *American Journal of Public Health* 98, no. 8 (2008): 1438–42.

"Hospital Readmissions Reduction Program (HRRP)." Centers for Medicare and Medicaid Services. Updated August 11, 2020. https://www.cms.gov/Medicare/Quality-Initiatives-Patient-Assessment-Instruments/Value-Based-Programs/HRRP/Hospital-Readmission-Reduction-Program.

Houghton, Ted. "A Description and History of the New York–New York Agreement to House Homeless and Mentally Ill Individuals." Corporation for Supportive Housing. May 2001. https://shnny.org/uploads/NY-NY_Agreement_History.pdf.

"Housing Authority Launches New Program to Provide Homes for Baltimore's Homeless." Baltimore Housing Authority. Updated February 14, 2019. https://www.habc.org/habc-information/about-us/news/housing-authority-launches-new-program-to-provide-homes-for-baltimore-s-homeless/.

"Housing First." National Alliance to End Homelessness. April 20, 2016. https://endhomelessness.org/resource/housing-first/.

Housing Preservation and Development. "Inclusionary Housing Program." NYC.gov. Accessed June 30, 2020. https://www1.nyc.gov/site/hpd/developers/inclusionary-housing.page.

"Houston Effectively Ends Veteran Homelessness." Coalition for the Homeless, June 1, 2015. https://www.homelesshouston.org/houston-effectively-ends-veteran-homelessness/.

"How Is Your File Evaluated?" Listing of Housing Demand. City of Paris. Accessed October 29, 2019 (in French). https://teleservices.paris.fr/cotation/les-criteres.html.

Hunter, Sara B., Melody Harvey, Brian Briscombe, and Matthew Cefalu, "Evaluation of Housing for Health Permanent Supportive Housing Program." *RAND Corporation* (2017): iii-66. https://www.rand.org/pubs/research_reports/RR1694.html.

"The Impact of Supportive Housing on Surrounding Neighborhoods: Evidence from New York City." Furman Center for Real Estate and Public Policy.

November 2008. https://furmancenter.org/files/FurmanCenterPolicyBrie-fonSupportiveHousing_LowRes.pdf.

Johnsen, Sarah, Suzanne Fitzpatrick, and Beth Watts. "Homelessness and Social Control: A Typology." *Housing Studies* 33, no. 7 (2018): 1106–26. https://www.tandfonline.com/doi/full/10.1080/02673037.2017.1421912.

Jolliffe, Dean, and Maria Anna Lugo. "Poverty and Shared Prosperity 2018: Piecing Together the Poverty Puzzle." World Bank Group. 2018. https://openknowledge.worldbank.org/bitstream/handle/10986/30418/9781464813306.pdf.

"Journeys Home: A Longitudinal Study of Factors Affecting Housing Stability." Melbourne Institute. Accessed June 23, 2020. https://melbourneinstitute.unimelb.edu.au/journeys-home.

"Key Considerations for Implementing Emergency Shelter Within an Effective Crisis Response System." US Interagency Council on Homelessness. August 2017. https://www.usich.gov/resources/uploads/asset_library/emergency-shelter-key-considerations.pdf.

"Key Strategies." *The Journey Home.* Accessed June 30, 2020. https://journey-homebaltimore.org/key-strategies/.

"LAHSA-Administered Safe Parking Sites in Los Angeles." Los Angeles Homeless Services Authority. Accessed June 30, 2020. https://www.lahsa.org/news?article=592-safe-parking.

Lam, Julie A., and Robert Rosenheck. "Street Outreach for Homeless Persons with Serious Mental Illness Is It Effective?" *Medical Care* (1999): 894–907.

LaMorte, Wayne W. "The Transtheoretical Model (Stages of Change)." Boston University School of Public Health. Updated September 9, 2019. https://sphweb.bumc.bu.edu/otlt/mph-modules/sb/behavioralchangetheories/behavioralchangetheories6.html#:~:text=The%20TTM%20posits%20that%20individuals,change%20for%20health%2Drelated%20behaviors.

Larimer, Mary E., Daniel K. Malone, Michelle D. Garner, David C. Atkins, Bonnie Burlingham, Heather S. Lonczak, Kenneth Tanzer, Joshua Ginzler, Seema L. Clifasefi, William G. Hobson, and Alan Marlatt. "Health Care and Public Service Use and Costs before and after Provision of Housing for Chronically Homeless Persons with Severe Alcohol Problems." *Journal of the American Medical Association* 301, no. 13 (April 1, 2009): 1349–57.

Lee, Barrett A. "Stability and Change in an Urban Homeless Population." *Demography* 26, no. 2 (1989): 323–34.

Legal Action Center. "Helping Moms, Dads and Kids to Come Home: Eliminating Barriers to Housing for People with Criminal Records." December 2016. Available via Publish Online, https://indd.adobe.com/view/04243d7e-5a9a-4bd8-9d97-1bb1ce77b9c5.

Lilienfeld, Scott O. "Why 'Just Say No' Doesn't Work." *Scientific American,* January 1, 2014. https://www.scientificamerican.com/article/why-just-say-no-doesnt-work/.

Link, Bruce, Ezra Susser, Ann Stueve, Joe Phelan, Robert E. Moore, and Elmer Struening. "Lifetime and Five-Year Prevalence of Homelessness in the United States." *American Journal of Public Health* 84, no. 12 (1994): 1907–12.

"Liz Murray." No Barriers. Accessed June 30, 2020. https://nobarriersusa.org/about/people/liz-murray/.

Martin, Elizabeth, Eugene Laska, Kim Hopper, Morris Meisner, and Joe Wanderling. 1997. "Issues in the Use of a Plant-Capture Method for Estimating the Size of the Street Dwelling Population." *Journal of Official Statistics* 13, no. 1 (1997): 59–73.

Mayoral Workgroup on Homelessness. "Executive Summary." City of Baltimore. June 30, 2017. https://human-services.baltimorecity.gov/sites/default/files/MayoralWorkgroupReport-FINAL.pdf.

Mazza, Sandy and Joey Garrison, "$24M Housing, 'Service Center' for Homeless Planned in Downtown Nashville." *(Nashville) Tennessean,* April 25, 2018.

"McKinney-Vento Act Fact Sheet." National Coalition for the Homeless. June 2006. https://www.nationalhomeless.org/publications/facts/McKinney.pdf.

Messeri, Peter, Brendan O'Flaherty, and Serena Goodman. "Can Homelessness Be Prevented? Evidence from New York City's HomeBase Program." Unpublished paper. Columbia University, June 8, 2011. https://a860-gpp.nyc.gov/downloads/08612p80q?locale=en.

Metraux, Stephen, and Dennis P. Culhane. "Homeless Shelter Use and Reincarceration following Prison Release." *Criminology and Public Policy* 3, no. 2 (2004): 139–60.

Metropolitan Development and Housing Agency. "Envision Nashville." Presentation to Urban Land Institute, Nashville, TN, June 14, 2019. https://ulidigitalmarketing.blob.core.windows.net/ulidcnc/2019/07/ULI-bfast-vjeh-Part-1.pdf.

Metropolitan Government of Nashville and Davidson County. "Recommended Operating Budget for Fiscal Year 2020–2021." May 2020. https://www.nashville.gov/Portals/0/SiteContent/Finance/docs/OMB/fy21_budget/Recommended/FY21RecommendedBudgetBook.pdf.

Metzenbaum, Shelley H. *Performance Accountability: The Five Building Blocks and Six Essential Practices.* Washington, DC: IBM Center for the Business of Government, 2006.

Mexico City. "Sistema para el Desarrollo Integral de la Familia de la Ciudad de México" (City System for the Integral Development of the Family of Mexico City). Internal data. October 2018.

Miller, Katy. "Using Shelter Strategically to End Homelessness." US Interagency Council on Homelessness. April 1, 2016. https://www.usich.gov/news/using-shelter-strategically-to-end-homelessness.

Murphy, Jarrett. "Housing for NYC's Most Vulnerable under Scrutiny for Screening." *City Limits,* July 5, 2018. https://citylimits.org/2018/07/05/debate-about-whether-nyc-housing-for-the-most-vulnerable-rebuffs-some-who-need-help/.

National Academies of Sciences, Engineering, and Medicine. *Permanent Supportive Housing: Evaluating the Evidence for Improving Health Outcomes among People Experiencing Chronic Homelessness.* Washington, DC: National Academies Press, 2018.

National Alliance to End Homelessness. "State of Homelessness: 2020 Edition." Accessed June 23, 2020. https://endhomelessness.org/homelessness-in-america/homelessness-statistics/state-of-homelessness-2020/.

"National Final Report: Cross-Site At Home/Chez Soi Project." Mental Health Commission of Canada. Accessed June 30, 2020. https://www.mentalhealthcommission.ca/sites/default/files/mhcc_at_home_report_national_cross-site_eng_2_0.pdf.

"National Housing Co-investment Fund." Canada Mortgage and Housing Corporation. Accessed June 30, 2020. https://www.cmhc-schl.gc.ca/en/nhs/co-investment-fund.

"New Pilot Helps Landlords Be Part of the Solution to Homelessness." Enterprise Community. Accessed June 30, 2020. https://www.enterprisecommunity.org/sites/default/files/media-library/where-we-work/new-york/come-home-nyc-2-pager-4-2-15.pdf.

New York City Department of Health and Mental Hygiene. "New York/New York III Supportive Housing Evaluation: Interim Utilization and Cost Analysis." NYC.gov. Accessed June 30, 2020. https://www1.nyc.gov/assets/doh/downloads/pdf/mental/housing-interim-report.pdf.

New York City Office of Civil Justice. "2018 Annual Report." Human Resources Administration. https://www1.nyc.gov/assets/hra/downloads/pdf/final_2018_ojc_report_march_19_2019.pdf.

New York State Senate. "Section 9.58." Accessed June 30, 2020, https://www.nysenate.gov/legislation/laws/MHY/9.58.

NYU Silver Communications Office. "NYU Silver Study Counters Narrative That Street Homeless Are Service Resistant." Silver School of Social Work, New York University. June 4, 2019. https://socialwork.nyu.edu/news/2019/nyu-silver-studycountersnarrativethatstreethomelessareserviceres.html.

"No Safe Place: The Criminalization of Homelessness in U.S. Cities." National Law Center on Homelessness and Poverty. Accessed June 30, 2020. https://nlchp.org/wp-content/uploads/2019/02/No_Safe_Place.pdf.

Office of Governor Gavin Newsom. "Governor Gavin Newsom Signs 18 Bills to Boost Housing Production." News release, October 9, 2019. https://www .gov.ca.gov/2019/10/09/governor-gavin-newsom-signs-18-bills-to-boost-housing-production/.

O'Flaherty, Brendan. "Homelessness Research: A Guide for Economists (and Friends)." *Journal of Housing Economics* (2019).

O'Flaherty, Brendan. "Wrong Person or Wrong Place: For Homelessness, the Conjunction Is What Matters." *Journal of Housing Economics* 13 (2004): 1–15.

O'Flaherty, Brendan, and Ting Wu. "Homeless Shelters for Single Adults: Why Does Their Population Change?" *Social Service Review* 82, no. 3 (2008): 511–50.

Office of Policy Development and Research. "Evaluation of the Rapid Rehousing for Homeless Families Demonstration (RRHD) Program." Washington, DC: US Department of Housing and Urban Development, November 2014.

Office of the Controller. "Homelessness Gross Receipts Tax: Economic Impact Report." Office of the Controller, City and County of San Francisco. November 2018. https://sfcontroller.org/sites/default/files/Documents/Economic% 20Analysis/hgrt_economic_impact_final.pdf.

Olivet, Jeffrey, Ellen Bassuk, Emily Elstad, Rachael Kenney, and Lauren Jassil. "Outreach and Engagement in Homeless Services: A Review of the Literature." *Open Health Services and Policy Journal* 3, no. 1 (2010): 53–70.

"Opening Doors: Federal Strategic Plan to Prevent and End Homelessness." US Interagency Council on Homelessness, updated 2015. Accessed June 23, 2020. https://www.usich.gov/resources/uploads/asset_library/USICH_ OpeningDoors_Amendment2015_FINAL.pdf.

Oreskes, Benjamin. "Homeless People Could Lose the Right to Sleep on the Sidewalks If Western Cities Have Their Way." *Los Angeles Times.* September 25, 2019. https://www.latimes.com/california/story/2019-09-25/boise-homeless-encampment-amicus-brief-supreme-court-appeal-cities.

Organisation for Economic Co-operation and Development. *Working Together for Local Integration of Migrants and Refugees in Paris.* Paris: OECD Publishing, 2018. https://doi.org/10.1787/9789264305861-en

O'Sullivan, Feargus. "Paris Declares War on 'Ghettos for the Rich.'" *Citylab,* May 17, 2016. https://www.citylab.com/equity/2016/05/paris-declares-war-on-ghettoes-for-the-rich/483072/.

Padgett, Deborah K., Benjamin F. Henwood, and Sam J. Tsemberis. *Housing First: Ending Homelessness, Transforming Cities, Changing Lives.* Oxford: Oxford University Press, 2016.

Park, Jung Min, Stephen Metraux, Gabriel Brodbar, and Dennis P. Culhane, "Public Shelter Admission among Young Adults with Child Welfare Histories by Type of Service and Type of Exit." *Social Service Review* 78, no. 2 (2004): 284–303.

"People Experiencing Homelessness and COVID 19 Interim Guidance." US Centers for Disease Control and Prevention. March 22, 2020. https://www .cdc.gov/coronavirus/2019-ncov/community/homeless-shelters/unsheltered-homelessness.html.

"Permanent Supportive Housing: Essential for Ending Homelessness." Homeward Trust Edmonton. Accessed June 30, 2020. http://homewardtrust.ca /wp-content/uploads/2017/06/PSH-Report.pdf.

Piketty, Thomas. "About Capital in the Twenty-first Century." *American Economic Review* 105, no. 5 (2015): 48–53.

Piketty, Thomas. *Capital in the Twenty-First Century.* Translated by Arthur Goldhammer. Cambridge, MA: Harvard University Press, 2014.

Pleace, Nicholas, Dennis Culhane, Riitta Granfelt, and Marcus Knutagård. "The Finnish Homelessness Strategy: An International Review." Helsinki: Ministry of the Environments, 2015. https://helda.helsinki.fi/bitstream /handle/10138/153258/YMra_3en_2015.pdf.

"The Police Response to Homelessness." Police Executive Research Forum. June 2018. https://www.policeforum.org/assets/PoliceResponsetoHomelessness .pdf.

"Poll: The Public Overwhelmingly Believes Housing Affordability Should Be a Top National Priority; Expects Congress and President to Take Major Action." Opportunity Starts at Home. March 28, 2019. https://www .opportunityhome.org/pollpressrelease/.

"Pone en marcha Mancera el primer 'Hogar CDMX.'" Cronica.com.mx. January 31, 2017. http://www.cronica.com.mx/notas/2017/1007813.html.

"Protocolo Interinstitucional de Atención Integral a Personas en Riesgo de Vivir en Calle e Integrantes de Poblaciones Callejeras en la Ciudad de México." *Gaceta Oficial de Ciudad de Mexico* 95 (2016): 5–58. http://www.data .educacion.cdmx.gob.mx/oip/2016b/A121/FI/148_LinmeamientosINFO-MEX2016.pdf.

"Public Safety." Downtown Alliance. Accessed June 30, 2020. https://www .downtownny.com/public-safety.

Rayman, Graham, and Ginger Adams Otis. "NYPD Top Cop Defends Homeless Outreach amid Series of Crimes Related to Shelter Residents." *New York Daily News.* December 21, 2016,

"Rental Assistance: I Am a Landlord or Broker." NYC Human Resource Administration. Accessed June 30, 2020. https://www1.nyc.gov/site/hra /help/landlords.page.

"Report and Recommendations of the Ad Hoc Committee on Black People Experiencing Homelessness." Los Angeles Homeless Services Authority. December 2018. https://www.lahsa.org/item.ashx?id=2823-report-and-recommendations-of-the-ad-hoc-committee-on-black-people-experiencing-homelessness.pdf&dl=true.

"Response to Encampments on Public Land." City of Edmonton. Accessed June 30, 2020. https://www.edmonton.ca/city_government/documents/PDF /EncampmentResponseFlowCharts.pdf.

Rice Kinder Institute for Urban Research. "The 2019 Kinder Houston Area Survey: Tracking Responses to the Economic and Demographic Transformations through 38 Years of Houston Surveys." May 2019. https://kinder.rice.edu /sites/g/files/bxs1676/f/documents/KI%202019%20Houston%20Area%20 Survey%20Report.pdf.

Rocha, Luisa Fernanda Zamudio. "Homelessness Policies in Bogotá, Colombia: Towards Integral Human Development." *Campos Magazine in Social Sciences* 6, no.1 (2018): 48–49.

Rog, Debra. "Permanent Supportive Housing: Assessing the Evidence." *Psychiatric Services* 65, no. 3 (March 2014): 287–94. https://ps.psychiatryonline .org/doi/pdfplus/10.1176/appi.ps.201300261.

Rolston, Howard, Judy Geyer, and Gretchen Locke. *Evaluation of the Homebase Community Prevention Program: Final Report.* Bethesda, MD: Abt Associates, June 2013.

Rosen, Brenda and Jamie Rubin, "How New York Is Ending Homelessness." *Apolitico,* June 25, 2019. https://apolitical.co/solution_article/how-new-york-is-ending-homelessness/.

Rosenblatt, Muzzy. "The Needs of the So-Called 'Service-Resistant.'" BRC (Bowery Residents' Committee). April 1, 2016. https://www.brc.org/needs-so-called-service-resistant.

Rossi, Peter H. *Down and Out in America: The Origins of Homelessness.* Chicago: University of Chicago Press, 1991.

Sadowski, Laura S., Romina A. Kee, and Tyler J. VanderWeele. "Effect of a Housing and Case Management Program on Emergency Department Visits and Hospitalizations Among Chronically Ill Homeless Adults: A Randomized Trial." *Journal of the American Medical Association* 301, no. 17 (May 2009): 1771–78.

San Francisco Department of Homelessness and Supportive Housing. "Navigation Centers Presentation." Accessed October 2, 2020. https://hsh.sfgov.org /wp-content/uploads/2019/03/HSH-Nav-Slideshow-FINAL.pdf.

Sapounakis, Aristides. "Homelessness in a Mediterranean Country: The Case of Greece." *Contributions in Sociology* 135 (2001): 119–34.

"Schizophrenia." National Institute of Mental Health. Updated May 2018. https://www.nimh.nih.gov/health/statistics/schizophrenia.shtml.

Scholl, Diana. "Critics of Homeless Program Fight to Save It." *City Limits,* March 11, 2011. https://citylimits.org/2011/03/11/critics-of-homeless-program-fight-to-save-it/.

Schwartz, Mary, and Ellen Wilson. "Who Can Afford to Live in a Home? A Look at Data from the 2006 American Community Survey." US Census Bureau.

Accessed November 16, 2020. https://www.census.gov/housing/census
/publications/who-can-afford.pdf.

Scott, Janny. "Homeless Given Apartments in Buildings Called Unsafe." *New
York Times,* February 2, 2007. https://www.nytimes.com/2007/02/02
/nyregion/02homeless.html.

Secret, Mosi. "Clock Ticks for a Key Homeless Program." *New York Times,* May
31, 2011. https://www.nytimes.com/2011/06/01/nyregion/new-york-city-
close-to-ending-key-housing-program.html.

"Selected Initial Findings of the 2017 New York City Housing and Vacancy
Survey." NYC. February 9, 2018. https://www1.nyc.gov/assets/hpd
/downloads/pdfs/about/2017-hvs-initial-findings.pdf.

Shinn, Marybeth. "Homelessness, Poverty, and Social Exclusion in the United
States and Europe." *European Journal of Homelessness* 4 (December 2010):
19–44.

Shinn, Marybeth, Andrew Greer, Jay Bainbridge, Jonathan Kwon, and Sara
Zuiderveen. "Efficient Targeting of Homelessness Prevention Services for
Families." *American Journal of Public Health* 103 (December 1, 2013):
S324–S330. https://doi.org/10.2105/AJPH.2013.301468.

Shinn, Marybeth, Jim Baumohl, and Kim Hopper. "The Prevention of Homelessness Revisited." *Analyses of Social Issues and Public Policy* 1, no. 1
(2001): 95–127.

Smedley, Audrey, and Brian Smedley. "Race as Biology Is Fiction, Racism as a
Social Problem Is Real: Anthropological and Historical Perspectives on the
Social Construction of Race." *American Psychologist* 60(1) (January 2005):
16–26.

Smith, Doug. "Desperate to Build More Homeless Housing, L.A. County Seeks
Help from the Private Sector." *Los Angeles Times,* December 6, 2019. https://
www.latimes.com/california/story/2019-12-06/
homeless-housing-county-supervisors-private-sector-help.

Song, Chris. "Mayor Cooper Releases Statement on Metro Emergency Shelters
and Announces New Permanent Supportive Housing Center." Press release,
October 17, 2019. Nashville.gov. https://www.nashville.gov/News-Media
/News-Article/ID/8985/Mayor-Cooper-Releases-Statement-on-Metro-
Emergency-Shelters-and-Announces-New-Permanent-Supportive-Housing-
Center.aspx.

"Spotlight on PATH Practices and Programs: Motivational Interviewing."
SAMHSA (Substance Abuse and Mental Health Services Administration),
US Department of Health and Human Services. Accessed November 1,
2020. https://www.samhsa.gov/sites/default/files/programs_campaigns
/homelessness_programs_resources/path-spotlight-motivational-interview-
ing.pdf.

"State of Texas Plan for Disaster Recovery: Amendment 5, Hurricane Harvey—Round 1." Texas General Land Office Community Development and Revitalization Program. Accessed June 30, 2020. https://recovery.texas.gov/files/hud-requirements-reports/hurricane-harvey/5b-apa5-nonsubstantial.pdf.

Stiff, Kevin, and Joe Polzak. "Law Enforcement Strategies to Address Homelessness." PowerPoint of presentation, CIT International Crisis Intervention Team conference, Kansas City, MO, August 15, 2018. http://www.citinternational.org/resources/Documents/H.O.T.%20Cops%20-%2021st%20Century%20Policing%20of%20the%20Homeless.pdf.

Substance Abuse and Mental Health Services Administration. "A Treatment Improvement Protocol: Behavioral Health Services for People Who Are Homeless." US Health and Human Services. 2013. https://www.ncbi.nlm.nih.gov/books/NBK138725/pdf/Bookshelf_NBK138725.pdf.

Sullivan, Brian. "HUD Marks 20 Years of McKinney-Vento Homeless Assistance Act: Landmark Legislation Credited with Saving Hundreds of Thousands of Lives." News release no. 07-109, July 18, 2007. HUD Archives News Releases https://archives.hud.gov/news/2007/pr07-109.cfm.

"Supportive Housing." US Interagency Council on Homelessness. Updated August 15, 2018. https://www.usich.gov/solutions/housing/supportive-housing/.

"Supportive Housing Funding Sources Now Available for NY City and State." Corporation for Supportive Housing. Updated June 2017. https://www.csh.org/2017/06/supportive-housing-funding-sources-in-now-available-for-ny-city-state/.

Suttor, Gregor. *Still Renovating: A History of Canadian Social Housing Policy.* Montreal: McGill-Queens University Press, 2016.

Teixeira, Ligia, and James Cartwright, eds. *Using Evidence to End Homelessness.* Bristol, UK: Bristol University Press, 2020.

"Tent City, USA: The Growth of America's Homeless Encampments and How Communities Are Responding." National Law Center on Homelessness and Poverty. 2017. https://nlchp.org/wp-content/uploads/2018/10/Tent_City_USA_2017.pdf.

Terrazas, Aaron. "Lower-Income Renters Pay Almost 2/3 of Their Income on Even Modest Apartments." Zillow. September 6, 2018. https://www.zillow.com/research/q2-2018-affordability-21286/.

To, Matthew J., Thomas D. Brothers, and Colin Van Zoost. "Foot Conditions among Homeless Persons: A Systematic Review." *Plos One* 11, no 12 (December 9, 2016): 1–14. https://journals.plos.org/plosone/article?id=10.1371/journal.pone.0167463.

Troisi, Catherine. "Houston, Pasadena, Harris, Fort Bend, and Montgomery Counties 2019 Point-In-Time Homeless Count & Survey Independent

Analysis." Coalition for the Homeless. April 2019. http://www.homelesshou-ston.org/wp-content/uploads/2019/05/2019-PIT-Report-Final.pdf.

Tsai, Jack. "Lifetime and 1-Year Prevalence of Homelessness in the US Population: Results from the National Epidemiologic Survey on Alcohol and Related Conditions–III." *Journal of Public Health* 40, no. 1 (2018): 65–74.

Tsemberis, Sam. "Housing First: The Pathways Model to End Homelessness for People with Mental Illness and Addiction Manual." *European Journal of Homelessness* (2010).

Tsemberis, Sam, Leyla Gulcur, and Maria Nakae. "Housing First, Consumer Choice, and Harm Reduction for Homeless Individuals with Dual Diagnosis." *American Journal of Public Health* 94 (April 2004): 651–56.

Tsemberis, Sam, Linda Moran, Marybeth Shinn, Sara Asmussen, and David Shern. "Consumer Preference Programs for Individuals Who Are Homeless and Have Psychiatric Disabilities: A Drop-In Center and a Supported Housing Program." *American Journal of Community Psychology* 32, nos. 3–4 (2003): 305–17.

Turner, Alina. "Everyone Counts: A Guide to Point-in-Time Counts in Canada." 2nd edition. Employment and Social Development Canada. January 2015.

2018 Progress Report: Edmonton's Plan to Prevent and End Homelessness." Homeward Trust Edmonton. Accessed June 30, 2020, http://homewardtrust.ca/wp-content/uploads/2018/12/2018-Goals-and-Targets.pdf.

"Two-Generation Playbook." Ascend: The Aspen Institute. September 2016. https://ascend.aspeninstitute.org/resources/two-generation-playbook/.

"The Unhealthy State of Homelessness: Health Audit Results, 2014." Homeless Link. 2014. https://www.homeless.org.uk/sites/default/files/site-attachments/The%20unhealthy%20state%20of%20homelessness%20FINAL.pdf.

United Nations Economic Commission for Europe. "Conference of European Statisticians Recommendations of the 2010 Censuses of Population and Housing." 2006.

Urahn, Susan K. "American Families Face a Growing Rent Burden." *Pew Charitable Trusts* (April 2018): 4–20.

US Census Bureau. "Fact Sheet for 1990 Decennial Census Count of Persons in Emergency Shelters for the Homeless and Visible in Street Locations." Press release, April 12, 1991; reprinted in *Joint Hearing on Quality and Limitations of the S-Night Homeless Count* (Y 4.G 74/9:S.hrg.102–296) in May 1991.

US Census Bureau. "QuickFacts: Los Angeles City, California." Census.gov. Accessed on June 23, 2020. https://www.census.gov/quickfacts/fact/table/losangelescitycalifornia/RHI125218.

US Census Bureau. "2018 American Community Survey 1-Year Estimates Population Division—New York City Department of City Planning." NYC. November 2019. https://www1.nyc.gov/assets/planning/download/pdf/planning-level/nyc-population/acs/dem_2018acs1yr_nyc.pdf.

US Department of Health and Human Services. "The Evidence: Permanent Supportive Housing." Substance Abuse and Mental Health Services Administration. 2010. https://store.samhsa.gov/sites/default/files/d7/priv /theevidence-psh.pdf.

US Department of Housing and Urban Development. "A Guide to Counting Unsheltered Homeless People." 2nd revision, January 15, 2008. https://files .hudexchange.info/resources/documents/counting_unsheltered.pdf.

US Department of Housing and Urban Development. "Homeless Prevention and Rapid Re-Housing Program: 1 Year Summary." June 2011.

US Department of Housing and Urban Development. "HUD 2019 Continuum of Care Homeless Assistance Programs Housing Inventory Count Report." Mayor's Office of Homeless Services (Baltimore). Updated October 16, 2019. https://homeless.baltimorecity.gov/sites/default/files/CoC_HIC_State_MD_ 2019.pdf.

US Department of Housing and Urban Development. "HUD 2019 Continuum of Care Homeless Assistance Programs Homeless Populations and Subpopulations." (January 28, 2019).

US Department of Housing and Urban Development. "A Report on the 1988 National Survey of Shelters for the Homeless." March 1989. HUD User. https://www.huduser.gov/portal/publications/other/survey_homeless.html.

Van den Bree, Marianne B. M., Katherine Shelton, Adrian Bonner, Sebastian Moss, Hollie Thomas, and Pamela Taylor. "A Longitudinal Population-Based Study of Factors in Adolescence Predicting Homelessness in Young Adulthood." *Journal of Adolescent Health* 45, no. 6 (December 2009): 571–78. https://www.jahonline.org/article/S1054-139X(09)00144-X/fulltext.

Vitale, Alex S. *City of Disorder: How the Quality of Life Campaign Transformed New York Politics.* New York: New York University Press, 2008.

Von Wachter, Till, Marianne Bertrand, Harold Pollack, Janey Rountree, and Brian Blackwell. "Predicting and Preventing Homelessness in Los Angeles." California Policy Lab and University of Chicago Poverty Lab. September 2019.

Watson, Nicole Elsasser, Barry L. Steffen, Marge Martin, and David A. Vandenbroucke. "Worst Case Housing Needs: 2017 Report to Congress." Washington, DC: Office of Policy Development and Research, US Department of Housing and Urban Development, August 2017.

"We Can End Poverty: Millennium Development Goals and beyond 2015." United Nations. Accessed June 30, 2020. https://www.un.org/millenniumgoals /poverty.shtml.

Wenger, Yvonne. "Baltimore Turns Vacant Public Housing Apartments into Homes for Chronically Homeless Families." *Baltimore Sun*, February 14, 2019.

"What Are the Value-Based Programs?" Centers for Medicare and Medicaid Services. Updated January 6, 2020. https://www.cms.gov/Medicare

/Quality-Initiatives-Patient-Assessment-Instruments/Value-Based-Pro-grams/Value-Based-Programs.

Wood, Michelle, Jennifer Turnham, and Gregory Mills. "Housing Affordability and Family Well-Being: Results from the Housing Voucher Evaluation." *Housing Policy Debate* 19, no. 2 (2008): 367–412.

Wright, James D., and Joel A. Devine. "Counting the Homeless: The Census Bureau's 'S-Night' in Five U.S. Cities." *Evaluation Review* (August 1992). https://doi.org/10.1177/0193841X9201600401.

Young, Bernard C. "Jack." "Mayor Young to Launch Independent Office of Homeless Services." Press release. City of Baltimore, Maryland. June 6, 2019. https://content.govdelivery.com/accounts/MDBALT/bulletins /24946a7.

Zacks, Stephen. "Design for Dignity" *Oculus* (Winter 2018). AIA New York.

Index

Founded in 1893,
UNIVERSITY OF CALIFORNIA PRESS
publishes bold, progressive books and journals
on topics in the arts, humanities, social sciences,
and natural sciences—with a focus on social
justice issues—that inspire thought and action
among readers worldwide.

The UC PRESS FOUNDATION
raises funds to uphold the press's vital role
as an independent, nonprofit publisher, and
receives philanthropic support from a wide
range of individuals and institutions—and from
committed readers like you. To learn more, visit
ucpress.edu/supportus.